RECOVERING FROM
CIVIL CONFLICT

THE CASS SERIES ON PEACEKEEPING
ISSN 1367-9880
General Editor: Michael Pugh

This series examines all aspects of peacekeeping, from the political, operational and legal dimensions to the developmental and humanitarian issues that must be dealt with by all those involved with peacekeeping in the world today.

1. *Beyond the Emergency: Development within UN Missions*
   edited by Jeremy Ginifer

2. *The UN, Peace and Force*
   edited by Michael Pugh

3. *Mediating in Cyprus: The Cypriot Communities and the United Nations*
   by Oliver P. Richmond

4. *Peacekeeping and the UN Specialized Agencies*
   edited by Jim Whitman

5. *Peacekeeping and Public Information: Caught in the Crossfire*
   by Ingrid A. Lehman

6. *US Peacekeeping Policy under Clinton: A Fairweather Friend?*
   by Michael G. MacKinnon

7. *Peacebuilding and Police Reform*
   edited by Tor Tanke Holm and Espen Barth Eide

8. *Peacekeeping and Conflict Resolution*
   edited by Tom Woodhouse and Oliver Ramsbotham

9. *Managing Armed Conflicts in the 21st Century*
   edited by Adekeye Adebajo and Chandra Lekha Sriram

10. *Women and International Peacekeeping*
    edited by Louise Olsson and Torunn L. Tryggestad

RECOVERING FROM CIVIL CONFLICT
Reconciliation, Peace and Development

LONDON AND NEW YORK

First published in 2002 by Frank Cass & Co. Ltd.

This edition published 2013 by Routledge
2 Park Square, Milton Park, Abingdon, Oxon OX14 4RN
711 Third Avenue, New York, NY 10017

*Routledge is an imprint of the Taylor & Francis Group,
an informa business*

British Library Cataloguing in Publication Data

Recovering from civil conflict : reconciliation, peace and development. – (The Cass series on peacekeeping)
1. Reconciliation 2. Civil war 3. Peaceful change (International relations)
I. Newman, Edward, 1970- II. Schnabel, Albrecht
327.1'72
ISBN 07146 5324 1 (cloth)
ISBN 0 7146 8267 5 (paper)
ISSN 1367 9880

Library of Congress Cataloging-in-Publication Data:

Recovering from civil conflict: reconciliation, peace, and development editors, Edward Newman, Albrecht Schnabel.
p. cm. – (The Cass series on peacekeeping, ISSN 1367-9880)
Includes bibliographical references and index.
ISBN 0-7146-5324-1 (cloth) – ISBN 0-7146-8267-5 (paper)
1. Peacekeeping forces. 2. Nationalism. 3. Peace-Economic aspects.
I. Newman, Edward, 1970- II. Schnabel, Albrecht. III. Series.
JZ6374. R43 2002
341.5'84-dc21

2002005256

This group of studies first appeared in a special issue of
International Peacekeeping [ISSN 1353-3312] Vol.9, No.2 (Summer, 2002)
published by Frank Cass and Co. Ltd.

All rights reserved. No part of this publication may be reproduced, stored in or introduced into a retrieval system, or transmitted, in any form or by any means, electronic, mechanical, photocopying, recording or otherwise, without the prior written permission of the publisher of this book.

Contents

Acronyms and Abbreviations		vii
Introduction: Recovering from Civil Conflict	Edward Newman and Albrecht Schnabel	1
Post-Conflict Peacebuilding and Second-Generation Preventive Action	Albrecht Schnabel	7
'Transitional Justice': The Impact of Transnational Norms and the UN	Edward Newman	31
The UN, Peacekeeping and Collective Human Security: From *An Agenda for Peace* to the Brahimi Report	Sorpong Peou	51
On the Challenges and Achievements of Reforming UN Peace Operations	Jean-Marie Guéhenno	69
World Bank, NGOs and the Private Sector in Post-War Reconstruction	Vesna Bojicić-Dzelilović	81
Peace Operations Finance and the Political Economy of a Way Out	Jean Daudelin and Lee J.M. Seymour	99
Post-Conflict Elections: Constraints and Dangers	Benjamin Reilly	118
Current International Civil Administration: The Need for Political Legitimacy	Sally Morphet	140
Refugees and Post-Conflict Reconstruction: A Critical Perspective	B.S. Chimni	163
Demobilization, Reintegration and Peacebuilding in Africa	Kees Kingma	181
Building Peace after Mass Crimes	Béatrice Pouligny	202

Notes on Contributors 222

Abstracts 224

Index 229

Acronyms and Abbreviations

ANC	African National Congress
CBM	Confidence Building Measure
CIS	Commonwealth of Independent States
CIVPOL	Civilian Police
DRC	Democratic Republic of the Congo
DPA	United Nations Department of Political Affairs
DPKO	United Nations Department of Peacekeeping Operations
DRC	Democratic Republic of the Congo
ECOMOG	Economic Community Military Observer Group, Liberia
ECOWAS	Economic Community of West African States
ECPS	Executive Committee on Peace and Security
EISAS	Executive Information and Strategic Analysis Secretariat
EU	European Union
FRETELIN	Revolutionary Front for an Independent East Timor
ICC	International Criminal Court
IDRC	International Development Research Centre (Canada)
IDP	Internally Displaced Persons
INTERFET	International Force for East Timor
KFOR	International Kosovo Force
KLA	Kosovo Liberation Army
MNC	Multinational Corporation
MONUA	United Nations Mission of Observers in Angola
MONUC	United Nations Mission in the Democratic Republic of the Congo
NATO	North Atlantic Treaty Organization
NGO	Non-Governmental Organization
OAS	Organization of American States
OAU	Organization for African Unity
ONUC	United Nations Operation in the Congo
OSCE	Organization for Security and Cooperation in Europe
PKO	Peacekeeping Operation
RUF	Revolutionary United Front (Rwanda)
UNCIVPOL	United Nations Civilian Police

UNDP	United Nations Development Programme
USAID	United States Agency for International Development
USC	United Somali Congress
UNAMIR	United Nations Assistance Mission in Rwanda
UNAMSIL	United Nations Mission in Sierra Leone
UNAVEM	United Nations Verification Mission in Angola
UNFICYP	United Nations Force in Cyprus
UNHCR	United Nations High Commissioner for Refugees
UNITA	National Union for the Total Independence of Angola
UNITAF	Unified Task Force in Somalia
UNMIBH	United Nations Mission in Bosnia and Herzegovina
UNMIK	United Nations Interim Administration Mission in Kosovo
UNOMIL	United Nations Observer Mission to Liberia
UNOSOM	United Nations Mission to Somalia
UNPROFOR	United Nations Protection Force
UNTAC	United Nations Transitional Authority in Cambodia
UNTAES	United Nations Transitional Administration for Eastern Slavonia, Baranja and Western Sirmium
UNTAET	United Nations Transitional Administration in East Timor
UNTAG	United Nations Transitional Assistance Group
UNTSO	United Nations Truce Supervision Organization

Introduction:
Recovering from Civil Conflict

EDWARD NEWMAN and ALBRECHT SCHNABEL

Conflict-torn societies are characterized by the traumatic impoverishment of economic, political and social relations between groups and individuals. Previously existing divisions within society are exacerbated, and new divisions are created. Once violence ceases, it becomes extremely difficult to re-create a sense of identity and belonging among communities that have experienced political, economic and socio-cultural breakdown. While it may be possible to impose a sense of order from outside, the sense of community has to grow from within. The tasks of rebuilding physical infrastructure are no less daunting.

Violently divided societies are cursed by institutional breakdown: weak or non-existent political institutions; weak or non-existent civil society institutions; and limited government legitimacy and authority. Without legitimate government, power vacuums create fierce competition for influence, and for access to territory and economic resources. The appeal of nationalist or religious identities, being the most convenient common denominators and 'trusted' sources of pride and power, can reignite fear and retaliation among ethnic or religious groups in multi-communal states.

Without strong institutions (judicial, political, economic, cultural) states cannot be rebuilt, and outside actors have no legitimate internal partners to collaborate with. Weak societies need strong and legitimate institutions to help rebuild trust, confidence and to invest in a more stable future. However, weak and divided societies cannot produce strong and legitimate governments. International organizations have helped societies in building their own institutions, or by replacing those institutions with a trusteeship until the political environment is safe enough – and domestic civic culture is mature enough – to engage in internal competition for power and government.

Rebuilding institutional structures is a difficult task, particularly in societies torn apart by internal war. Reconciliation and confidence building are important ingredients in creating functioning institutions that represent society at large. Democratization attempts are thus caught in a difficult situation: true democratization cannot occur without a strong, established, well-functioning and broadly supported civil society

– which produces potential leaders and socializes and mobilizes citizens around democratic and civic duties and responsibilities. However, such organizations can only prosper in an environment characterized by order, stability and freedom of expression. That environment, in turn, requires the existence of a functioning democratic process.

If domestic capacities are lacking, external support may be required. External support of transition processes, by non-governmental and intergovernmental organizations, or through bilateral arrangements, ideally creates the foundations for sustainable progress even after such assistance has ceased. However, such sustained efforts will only work if ownership of the process of capacity building has been transferred to local actors during the transition period.

Finally, the remnants of war-time military and security systems pose great risks to internal security: bloated armies with little or no civilian control; irregular and paramilitary forces; overabundance of arms and ammunition in private and government hands; and weak internal security and police forces.

A culture of violence, persistent intergroup tensions, and little or no central control of regular and irregular military forces, as well as an abundance of arms and ammunition among civilians and ex-combatants, create a condition in which conflicts can re-escalate very quickly – sometimes much quicker than during the initial outbreak of violence. Soldiers have to be decommissioned and reintegrated into society, and insurgency troops and civilians have to be disarmed. This is very difficult to accomplish by local institutions that are neither firmly in place nor legitimate in the eyes of former warring parties. External actors have a crucial role to play in this process. The internal security system – both military and police – have to be placed under civilian control and have to regain the trust and confidence of the population. This requires that security and police forces are representative of – or at least sensitive towards – all ethnic and religious groups. A functioning and legitimate government, supported by the entire population, is the basic requirement for putting such a system in place, and for preventing it from renewed deterioration along the fault lines of previous antagonism.

Economic and social breakdown is characterized by economic instability and decline, human resource shortage, refugees and displacement, infrastructural damage, land mines, competing territorial claims, and a weakened social fabric characterized by a culture of violence. The longer an internal conflict lasts, the more devastating are its consequences for both the economic and social fabric of society. War, particularly if fought on one's own territory and – in the cases of civil wars – in every village, town and back street, destabilizes not only the national but especially the local economy. Civil war leads to a breakdown of normal trade and production, driving much of the economy underground. Their facilities destroyed or raided, large companies go out of business, small companies and shops are short of supplies and merchandise. Even basic foods become very expensive and have to be purchased on the black market, often brought into the country by smugglers and organized crime, the flourishing entrepreneurs of war and conflict. Agricultural production, the most basic and enduring of all local industries, is hampered by land mines and unexploded munitions, making cultivation difficult if not impossible even years after the conflict has ended.

War itself disrupts school life and educational opportunities. School and university students are deprived of regular classes for months or years on end. Teachers and professors flee the country, join armed forces, or cannot be paid anymore. Students have no means to travel to school, or have to stay at home and work to secure their families' survival. School buildings are destroyed, there are no supplies, and meaningless certificates are handed out after the end of the school year. This situation improves only slowly after violence has ceased: educational spending is not a priority of struggling governments and economies, and public coffers are empty, with little or no tax revenues raised in an environment of underground trade and widespread tax evasion. This produces a dreadfully undereducated post-war generation – at a time when talent is desperately needed to rebuild the local economy.

In addition, many people have left – voluntarily to escape war, fear and poverty, or they have been forced out. Few return home immediately after the war, and many wait until after conditions have improved before returning home. Economic, political and intellectual elites are often among the first to leave, triggering a brain drain that has devastating consequences for the post-war society. Those who do return have often spent years as refugees in host countries, have enjoyed relative prosperity, safety and education. They are resented by those who stayed behind. On the other hand, internally displaced persons (IDPs) and those refugees who return from other war-ridden or least developed countries place additional pressures on an already fragile economy. Where ethnic cleansing has taken place, returning refugees and IDPs upset new post-war ethnic divisions and balances, adding further difficulty to fragile peace and stabilization efforts. Finally, unresolved land claims (particularly from refugees and IDPs) and destruction of infrastructure require effective political and judicial structures in place to address the reintegration of an uprooted society.

Minority protection and/or increased autonomy arrangements for minority groups (often a cause for civil war) have to be worked out – with the assistance and facilitation of external third parties. The culture of violence that permeates war-torn societies can take years, perhaps decades, to overcome. In some cases, temporary if not permanent territorial partition along ethnic lines may be necessary to avoid the recurrence of inter-group violence and conflict. Peacebuilding efforts have to reintegrate society, with the help of institutional arrangements, grassroots organizations, and the facilitation (and protection) of regional and international organizations.[1]

Successful assistance to fledgling post-conflict societies must aim at building the foundation for long-term, sustainable peace, through institutions and social relations that will prevent the recurrence of violence and war. In Albrecht Schnabel's contribution he observes that whilst conflict prevention finds greater support at the post-conflict stage, this must not distract from the priority of pre-conflict preventive action. After all, in most parts of the world societies in transition from violence will receive no or only limited support from the international community. While prevention is of course cheaper than rebuilding, doing neither is even cheaper. Nevertheless, while post-conflict assistance is a luxury, much of that burden has to be carried by the local societies themselves. Ultimately it is they who make or break peace and development in a society, and who can put in place and maintain long-term preventive measures that will prevent future conflict and devastation. This has to be done speedily, while assistance is still readily available. In the process, and driven by the demand for quick and visible success, questions of justice and accountability are often neglected. Instead, pragmatic and speedy movement towards a sense of order, stability, and (negative) peace is what the international community values above all. Nevertheless, Edward Newman shows that peace and justice do not have to be irreconcilable. However, they easily fall victim to political decisions, made locally and by those international actors who may, or may not, find it convenient or desirable to enforce international norms of justice.

If the international community finds the necessary resolve to act in cases of war and human suffering, it may have to do so with force, and by intervening collectively to stop the violence and re-establish peace and order. Sorpong Peou argues that such actions must be driven by a collective understanding and application of human security. If taken seriously, this approach could serve as a powerful tool in promoting international commitment, perhaps even responsibility, for post-conflict assistance. It could generate greater resolve to engage in early prevention, strengthening the ability of states to provide human security and thus escaping the need for costly interventions in war and post-war recovery efforts. The UN has moved slowly, but consistently, towards supporting the active engagement of collective human security, most prominently with *An Agenda for Peace* and, most recently, with the Brahimi Report. As Jean-Marie Guéhenno shows, UN peacekeeping has reflected the troublesome efforts of the UN to practice what it preaches, and to live up to its primary responsibility to maintain international

INTRODUCTION

peace and security. Peacekeeping operations throughout the years have attempted to live up to greater demands and wildly expanding mandates. Peacekeeping has become more courageous, has taken great risks and as a result has, at times, failed miserably. However, the courage of the Organization and its Secretary-General in engaging in honest, sometimes blunt, self-reflection, has put it on the path to potentially greater success in the future – that is, if member states are willing to offer the minimum in financial resources to equip the UN with the capacity to become more effective in conflict and post-conflict peace operations.

Yet, while military presence is often a crucial prerequisite for effective assistance in the post-conflict phase, other actors play a more critical role in putting a society's war-ravaged economy back on its feet. Vesna Bojicić-Dzelilović explains the crucial roles played by the World Bank, non-governmental organizations and the private sector. Without explicitly addressing the root causes of violence, the results of such assistance will be short-lived. Economic recovery may take place, but it will not be sustainable if it does not, in an integrated fashion, address the many other ills of society. Indeed, there can even be a tension between the liberal economic agenda embraced by international organizations and the social and welfare needs of post-conflict societies that can, if not managed sensitively, seriously obstruct post-conflict peacebuilding.

Sustainable peace can be achieved only if peacebuilders directly manage the reconstruction of local economies, as Jean Daudelin and Lee J.M. Seymour argue. Local resources are often at the root of violence, and post-war competition over their control may easily reignite conflict. However, when the distribution of local resources is in the hands of outsiders, local communities can search, and may find, renewed trust and confidence in each other. Furthermore, control over local resources allows external actors to generate and centrally allocate those resources to maximize their own peacebuilding efforts.

The creation of a legitimate political order, ideally based on democratic, transparent and participatory governance, is central to post-conflict peacebuilding. Elections are an important step in that process and thus occupy much of the attention, energy and resources of peacebuilding missions. However, as Benjamin Reilly warns, ill-timed, badly-designed or poorly-run elections may do more harm than good to democratization and state-building processes in post-war societies. The decision to organize and hold elections has therefore to be based on a thorough understanding of the political choices available, and the associated risks and benefits for political and social stability. However, it is not only political, but also legal and broader normative choices that inform the pace and direction of peace- and statebuilding in societies emerging from conflict. Sally Morphet argues that civil administrations must follow international legal norms and standards if they are to be successful in launching a transition period that will evolve into long-term stability. Commitment to such standards will set an important example for local actors, who look to civil administrations as the models for responsible statehood at the national as well as international levels. Local actors must be integrated into a transition process that reflects best practices according to international standards, not ad hoc mission-specific behaviour that follows current political priorities of the major national or regional troop contributors.

The final three contributions address key challenges in the post-conflict peace- and society-building process: the return of refugees, demobilization and reintegration of ex-combatants, and the psychological wounds of warfare. B.S. Chimni shows that today's approach to repatriation is fundamentally flawed and is counterproductive to rebuilding efforts. Repatriation is often driven by the political and economic interests of states that host refugees, or by those who fear the negative consequences of refugee movements on their own societies. As a result, repatriation of refugees and internally displaced persons is often done on an ad hoc basis, without a clear understanding of, and concern for, the impact of returning populations on post-war society. Without a clearer focus on 'sustainable return', post-conflict states will suffer greatly. Similarly, the reintegration of ex-combatants is a crucial, and equally demanding, component of human development and peace processes. As Kees Kingma argues, without an appreciation of the wider social, economic and political impact of the potential pitfalls of demobilization and reintegration, chances for renewed conflict, especially at the local level, increase greatly. Béatrice Pouligny concludes this collection of essays with an examination of the difficulties of sustained peacebuilding in societies where mass crimes have been committed. In order to create assistance programmes that are sensitive to the psychological, social and political impact of mass crime, the reasons such crimes were committed, as well as the local capacities to deal with the perpetrators and victims of such crimes, must be identified and must form the foundation for constructive peacebuilding.

NOTES

1. The above issues are elaborated upon in greater detail in Albrecht Schnabel, 'Peacebuilding and Democratization', in Amin Saikal and Albrecht Schnabel (eds), *Democratization in the Middle East*, Tokyo: United Nations University Press, forthcoming, 2002. See also Nicole Ball, 'The Challenge of Rebuilding War-Torn Societies', in Chester A. Crocker, Fen Osler Hampson with Pamela Aall (eds), *Managing Global Chaos: Sources of and Responses to International Conflict*, Washington, DC: United States Institute of Peace Press, 1996, pp.615–16.

Post-Conflict Peacebuilding and Second-Generation Preventive Action

ALBRECHT SCHNABEL

Both the jurisdiction and capacity of international organizations, in particular the United Nations, in preventing internal conflicts, are still weak. This seems to be counterintuitive: with greater experience with such conflicts over the past ten years, the international community should be in a better position to address internal conflict – by preventing it in the first place, by successfully managing and ending it once it has broken out, and by preventing its re-emergence through sustainable post-conflict peacebuilding. This essay evolves around three core arguments: first, peacebuilding is only sustainable if it embraces core principles of conflict prevention; second, preventive action is more feasible (yet more complex) in the post-conflict environment; and third, lessons from post-conflict preventive action must encourage and inform pre-conflict prevention – still the most effective stage of preventive action.

In the long run, however, there are limits to the international community's commitment to prevent the emergence and re-emergence of internal violence: after all, intrastate disputes remain the primary responsibility of the state, and external actors have to respect the supremacy of state sovereignty even when they feel morally compelled to act. The inviolability of a state's sovereignty is an important feature of the international legal and political order, protecting the state from unwelcome incursions from outside actors, and limiting powerful states' opportunities to impose their values, will and might on weaker states. Yet, in post-conflict situations the international community (and the agents who carry out the brunt of the peacebuilding tasks) enjoy sweeping authority by controlling and staffing many of the key institutions that are responsible for the political and economic life of a post-conflict society. The UN Interim Administration Mission in Kosovo (UNMIK) and the UN Transitional Administration in East Timor (UNTAET) are examples of international 'protectorates' that, for the time being, assure stability and political, and economic (if not social) healing.

However, once the international community leaves, stabilization of peace, consolidation of justice and prevention of renewed violence becomes again the responsibility of local actors. At that stage it becomes crucially important that the prevention of a re-escalation of violence is addressed more seriously than in the past. Post-conflict preventive efforts are both blessed and cursed: on the one hand postwar societies are keenly aware of the high cost of conflict and may be more willing to seek non-violent solutions in an already ravaged postwar environment; on the other hand, maintaining and strengthening peaceful relations is all the more difficult in post-conflict settings, where war has greatly exacerbated intergroup hostilities and distrust.

The essay begins with an examination of the roots, challenges and consequences of internal conflict. Then it assesses international organizations' efforts in developing and applying mechanisms to prevent the escalation and re-escalation of intercommunal conflicts. The UN and regional organizations' approach to conflict management is still primarily focused on the conflict stage and, increasingly, the post-conflict stage. At these stages troops and materials can be sent to trouble spots where massive humanitarian disasters have aroused the consciousness of the international community, or where the potential for conflict spillover poses a direct threat to neighbouring or nearby nations. The essay then examines specific post-conflict opportunities for preventive action. It concludes with lessons from the post-conflict experience for more effective preventive measures before violence breaks out.

Challenges and Consequences of Internal Conflict

Since the end of the Cold War the world's attention has focused on violent conflicts within states. This created the impression of an explosion of internal conflicts. The growing awareness of internal conflict has also influenced the scholarly community. The United Nations and regional organizations refocused their attention from superpower competition, defence and deterrence to the many non-traditional security threats that now became fashionable topics to study and debate – environmental threats, human security threats, ethnic conflicts or refugee movements. Some organizations, created during and for the Cold War, had to find new tasks to assure their continuing viability. The North Atlantic Treaty Organization (NATO) is a case in point: initially it was created as a defence alliance to counter a Soviet threat. Unlike the Warsaw Pact it survived the end of the Cold War. In 1999 it launched its first military attack against a sovereign non-member state to protect an oppressed ethnic minority (Kosovo 1999).[1] Many regional organizations originally created to facilitate economic and, at most, political cooperation, have added security cooperation to their competencies (including the OAU, OAS, or ASEAN). Others are actively pursuing military capacities to underscore their new security role (such as the EU's Common Security and Defence Policy and plans for rapid reaction military forces).[2]

Many recent domestic conflicts are the direct result of the collapse of the Soviet system. In Eastern and Southeastern Europe and the former Soviet Union, the political and economic transitions experienced by most countries left many or most of them weak and vulnerable to internal and external political and economic pressures. As previous elites began to compete for power with newly emerging elites, many of these countries struggled through their first-ever experience with democracy and free political and economic competition. In addition, many of them were created after the Second World War and during the Soviet reign, their demographic make-up was reshuffled by forced population movements. After 1991, populations throughout the post-communist camp experienced a dramatic drop in wealth, personal security and living standards. A combination of economic collapse, political vacuum and demands for political strongmen caused the eruption of internal conflict and war. The former Yugoslavia, the Southern Caucasus and Central Asia have suffered most from this development.

In the meanwhile, internal conflicts, often with significant involvement from neighbouring states, have continued to rage in Africa, Asia and Latin America. From Somalia to Rwanda, from Cambodia to East Timor, and from El Salvador to Haiti, internal conflicts have continued to destabilize their regions, causing immense human suffering. The most atrocious conflicts take place in Africa. Many African conflicts are rooted in governments' lack of respect for the rights of individuals, corruption, lack of efficient administration, poor infrastructure and weak national coherence – ills that are in turn rooted largely in the colonial legacy of randomly drawn borders, destruction of traditional communities and their governing and conflict management mechanisms, and economic exploitation. Democracy and political stability are still distant goals in many African countries. The combination of weak states and the struggle by elites for natural resources and wealth, the culture of looting, as is particularly obvious in the case of diamond mines in Angola, Congo, Liberia and Sierra Leone, has resulted in a dangerous structural environment that fuels conflict.[3] The patterns of conflict are often very similar: military hostilities between rebel groups and the incumbent government. Characteristic is the use of force to settle disputes and the fact that most conflicts in Africa take the form of 'irregular warfare' in which for strategic reasons civilians – instead of professional soldiers – are targeted.

Finally, almost all conflicts in Africa have been commercialized. Huge amounts of arms have been used to destabilize the continent.[4] While most conflicts are fought for access and control over resources in the absence of responsible governments, many conflicts have a decisive external dimension – neighbouring countries that support either government or rebel groups. At least in theory these conflicts could be resolved or prevented rather easily – certainly easier than supposed primordial and ethnic intergroup conflicts. It is usually quite apparent what caused the conflict, and who the responsible parties are. The OAU and other subregional organizations are trying to prevent and manage conflicts, but they can do little without the necessary resources and lack of interest in regional cooperation among member states, who are either part of the conflict or do not care about its resolution. The North's indifference to inequality, injustice, humanitarian plight and war-lordism in many African countries, along with poorly designed development strategies over many decades, have done little to prevent violence on the African continent.[5]

Internal, often intergroup conflicts carry a high price tag – for the populations involved in violence and for those willing to offer assistance in settling and resolving it. The example of Mozambique's 16-year civil war is illustrative of the tremendous costs of conflict: 490,000 children died from war-related causes; 200,000 children were orphaned or abandoned by adults; at least 10,000 children served as soldiers during the conflict; over 40 per cent of schools were destroyed or forced to close; over 40 per cent of health centres were destroyed; economic losses totalled US$15 billion, equal to four times the country's 1988 GDP; and damage to industry was so heavy that post-war production equalled only 20–40 per cent of pre-war capacity.[6] Intergroup conflicts affect the whole of society, irrespective of age, occupation and gender. Targeting civilians has become a deliberate strategy of warfare, with the result that an estimated 90 per cent of the casualties of today's civil wars are civilians, mostly women and children. This high rate of civilian casualties characterizes more than anything else today's internal wars, contributing to the deep sense of hatred and hostility that make it a difficult task to rebuild war-torn societies once a settlement has eventually been reached.

SECOND-GENERATION PREVENTIVE ACTION

The international community finds it extremely difficult to assist societies in managing violent conflict and in recovering from its consequences.[7] International actors are limited in their work by the principle of state sovereignty, prohibiting intervention in another state's domestic affairs; by high levels of violence; and by limited political and domestic support for missions that require long-term commitments. Non-state and state actors alike who are active in ongoing or recent war zones face threats to their own security, pressure from their donors or political supporters to produce visible results, and the moral dilemma of assisting those (on all sides of a conflict) who are responsible for violence and who may use external assistance to feed their fighters, to regroup, rearm and continue the violence.[8]

Without a clear exit strategy and hopes for an eventual solution to a conflict and for durable peace, few countries and organizations are willing to bear the risks involved in resolving violent internal conflicts. Thus, the eventual resolution of conflict, and the international community's patience to commit to post-conflict rebuilding projects, depend to a large degree on the commitment of the conflicting parties themselves and their leaders to just peace and good governance.[9] Only in the presence of such commitment to peace will there be sustained support from member states to allow international organizations to participate in – and remain committed to – peace operations.[10] In contrast to pre-conflict prevention action, during the post-conflict phase the international community can draw on direct experience with the cost of degeneration and violent conflict, and they can build on the investment they have already made in securing peace. At this stage, there is much on which to capitalize – but, without the required commitment, there is also much to lose.

It is doubtful that the UN, regional organizations, or alliances of concerned states will intervene in domestic conflicts on a principled basis, whenever and wherever intervention is necessary. The human, economic and political risks are too high to allow systematic military intervention in ongoing conflicts. The best strategy is to prevent those conflicts from escalating to violence in the first place.

The Case for Prevention: Idealist Agenda or Pragmatism?

The management of emerging conflicts, with clearly identifiable entry points for outside intervention (in the form of mediation, negotiation, facilitation, sanctions or even military deployment) is clearly possible. Few would doubt the truism that preventing a conflict is far less costly than addressing its consequences. As Ouellette reports,

[t]he costs of conflict prevention in Bosnia have been assessed at $33.3 billion, compared with an estimated $53.7 billion spent on dealing with the violent phase of the conflict and its aftermath. In the case of Haiti, cost estimates for conflict prevention were established at $2.3 billion, compared to $5 billion in remedial action. Somalia is another case where prevention would have cost far less: $7.3 billion compared with $1.5 billion for prevention. In Macedonia, successful prevention ($300 million) saved the international community a great deal of money ($15 billion if the conflict had reached an intermediate level of intensity).[11]

However, as Ouellette shows, prevention still does cost money, requiring political will and commitment at times when resources are scarce and most non-state and interstate organizations are hard pressed to meet all of their obligations in emergency situations, where violence and disasters have already struck. The challenges of 'reaction' leave little room for effective 'proaction'. Creativity and political skill are required to mainstream preventive action in the work of national, international and non-governmental organizations. But what is 'conflict prevention'? What distinguishes this concept from, say, development assistance or crisis diplomacy? The concept has little utility for policy formulation if it does not have unique explanatory or prescriptive power above and beyond what we already know. Unfortunately, the concept, as debated and applied, is too broad to evade its critics. Numerous definitions have emerged, some more and some less helpful for attempts to describe and prescribe conflict prevention activities of state and non-state actors.[12]

The former UN Secretary-General Boutros Boutros-Ghali described conflict prevention as preventive diplomacy, an 'action to prevent disputes from arising between parties, to prevent existing disputes from escalating into conflicts and to limit the spread of the latter when they occur'.[13] He further argued that

> the most desirable and efficient employment of diplomacy is to ease tensions before they result in conflict – or, if conflict breaks out, to act swiftly to contain it and resolve its underlying causes ... Preventive diplomacy requires measures to create confidence; it needs early warning based on information gathering and informal or formal fact-finding; it may also involve preventive deployment and, in some situations, demilitarized zones.[14]

Boutros-Ghali's understanding of conflict prevention was that of crisis prevention – when problems appear, they can be detected through early warning tools that, in turn, should ideally trigger appropriate response mechanisms. Michael Lund offers a more comprehensive definition:

> [C]onflict prevention entails any structural or interactive means to keep intrastate and interstate tensions and disputes from escalating into significant violence and to strengthen the capabilities to resolve such disputes peacefully as well as alleviating the underlying problems that produce them, including forestalling the spread of hostilities into new places. It comes into play both in places where conflicts have not occurred recently and where recent largely terminated conflicts could recur. Depending on how they are applied, it can include the particular methods and means of any policy sector, whether labelled prevention or not (e.g. sanctions, conditional aid, mediation, structural adjustment, democratic institution building etc.), and they might be carried out by global, regional, national or local levels by any governmental or non-governmental actor.[15]

Applied conflict prevention consists of policies and institutions that are taken deliberately to keep particular states or organized groups within them from threatening or using organized violence, armed force, or related forms of coercion, such as repression, as the means to settle interstate or national political disputes, especially in situations where the existing means cannot peacefully manage the destabilizing effects of economic, social, political and international change.[16]

Most importantly, early recognition of degeneration, and early application of preventive measures are crucial to effective prevention of violence, resembling a 'longer-term approach, aimed at addressing the structural causes of conflict and fostering institutions which will promote the kinds of distributive and procedural justice that have been shown to make violent conflict less likely'.[17] This reflects an agenda for prevention that incorporates development, democracy, human rights and peace, and one that is based on the key principles of the recent debate on human security. Addressing structural causes of conflict and strengthening institutions that can foster democracy, development, human rights and peaceful relations between groups and states, are fundamental components of a long-term, early approach to conflict prevention. This also holds true for successful post-conflict peacebuilding strategies: actual conflict *resolution*, beyond mere settlements, is key to the prevention of renewed violence.

The Challenge of Conflict Prevention

As Carment and Schnabel argue, the international community's track record in preventing the outbreak or recurrence of violent conflict is not strong.[18] Some examples over the last decade demonstrate this point:[19]

- the failure to prevent the relapse of 'successful' consolidation processes (Cambodia, Angola);
- the failure to prevent the slow collapse of states in Central and West Africa – despite clear understanding of when and where such events would occur and the availability of forecasts for predicting and explaining their causes and manifestations (Congo, Guinea);
- the failure to anticipate the moral hazards that are generated by the symptoms of conflict, such as refugee flows, ethnic cleansing and clan warfare (Rwanda, Somalia);
- the failure to understand how biased interventions can accelerate conflict between combatants (Kosovo, Sierra Leone);
- the failure of policy makers to understand how weak responses to warring factions can generate even greater conflict, and increase the likelihood of conflict (Rwanda, Bosnia);
- the failure to understand how values promoting conflict reduction mechanisms such as democracy and human rights can lead to actions that might actually promote the risk of state failure (Bosnia, East Timor/Indonesia).[20]

Nonetheless, throughout the same period conflict prevention has been receiving increasing attention from political leaders (most notably Canada's former foreign minister Lloyd Axworthy), regional organizations and the UN, with Kofi Annan as the strongest promoter of enhancing the organizations' preventive capacity.[21] Many studies and reports have in recent years highlighted the key challenges that need to be resolved before the roots of violent conflict can be effectively addressed and violence can be prevented. These reports include, among many others, the *Carnegie Commission's Report on Preventing Deadly Conflict*, a variety of policy papers produced by Canada's International Development Research Centre (IDRC), the Conflict Prevention Network of the European Union, the Swedish, Dutch, Canadian and British Foreign Ministries and, most recently, the Brahimi Report (which itself is informed by the UN Secretary-General's *Millennium Report*.)[22]

Those key challenges can be summed up as follows. First, successful prevention requires coherence and coordination between relevant actors – including those engaged in development as well as conflict management. Second, not only the better-understood security dimensions, but also the economic dimensions of conflict prevention need to be addressed.[23] Third, abstract academic models and frameworks need to be translated into meaningful and feasible models that are policy-friendly and relevant. As well, methodologies of risk assessment need to be practicable and accessible to policy makers. In light of this concern, several UN agencies, regional organizations and NGOs are developing the means by which they can identify the relevant tools and techniques for useful conflict management and prevention.[24] As a result of these and other efforts the momentum towards mainstreaming conflict prevention is accelerating, combining policy-specific knowledge with conflict prevention expertise, and generating social, economic, political and security instruments. Mainstreaming is thus about establishing an in-house 'culture of prevention'.[25] Fourth, there must be increased support for fact-finding and mediation – areas traditionally associated with the activities of the Secretary-General's Good Offices in preventive diplomacy. Coherence, integration and coordination among all actors need to be carried out at both the analytical stage (information gathering, risk assessments, evaluation and impact assessment) and at the implementation stage (engaging local, regional and international actors). By now, these suggestions have become accepted at most levels of national, intergovernmental and non-governmental levels. Mainstreaming conflict prevention has undoubtedly made huge strides in recent years.[26]

Unfortunately, rhetoric, policy and commitment are often three different notions when it comes to conflict prevention.[27] There is much talk by many governments, international organizations and scholars about the utility of, and necessity for, conflict prevention. However, little is in fact done to give this concept a leading role in foreign policy and to generate the commitment necessary to actual implementation. Resources are limited, political and domestic support for measures that address pending or emerging problems at home or abroad take a backseat to measures that address highly visible emergencies. International organizations are limited in their influence on member states by their very own nature: They have to respond to, and are held accountable by, the needs of their members. The United Nations and regional organizations can only do as much as their member states allow them to do.

International organizations have mostly been created to protect and defend, not to challenge and undermine, state sovereignty. Most states believe that intervention must be an exception to the rule of non-intervention, only to be applied if there is a clear international consensus on the necessity for external involvement in the solution of domestic crises of a member state.[28] The reason could be humanitarian catastrophes (droughts, intergroup warfare or 'ethnic cleansing'), aggression (attack by one state on another), or a threat to international peace and security (state-sponsored terrorism, or development of nuclear arsenals by an authoritarian state without public accountability). However, a loose interpretation and application would offer too much room for abuse – usually by the strong against the weak, the rich against the poor, the organized against the disorganized. So far, no commonly accepted legal definition of humanitarian intervention has emerged and could serve as a guideline to allow intervention in cases where harsh measures are called for, and to prohibit intervention where it is inappropriate and counterproductive to international peace and human security.

There are structures in place through which the international community intervenes in degenerating situations and strengthens or provides the good governance that is necessary to avoid instability, fear and violence. The international community engages in conflict prevention – both long-term and short-term prevention – through the UN and regional organizations, interested states, interested groups of states, non-governmental organizations (both public and private) and prominent individuals. With their various activities, on smaller local or larger national, regional or even global scales, these actors offer social services not provided by the state, provide economic and environmental assistance, or organize inter-group mediation on disputes.

However, few of the existing conflict prevention activities are systematically organized and coordinated. As Kofi Annan rightly notes in the context of the UN, '[t]he challenge before us is how to mobilize the collective potential of the United Nations system with greater coherence and focus for conflict prevention, without necessarily requiring new resources'.[29] The same task applies to coordination between various international actors. Without it many well-intentioned but isolated steps will add up to very little. When non-state, state and inter-state actors pursue their own activities, with little or no coordination and – at worst – competition over the same resources and responsibilities, very little can be gained.

Every attempt by the international community to prevent or manage an internal conflict requires international legitimacy, regional resources and local expertise. Collaboration on conflict prevention should be based on a division of labour in which the UN offers international legitimacy, and where regional organizations and neighbouring states or concerned groups of states contribute both regional and local knowledge as well as the necessary political will to pursue the quick settlement of conflicts that may destabilize an entire region. Local actors – non-governmental organizations from within and outside society – know what can be accomplished at the local level. Despite some efforts, little collaboration and coordination has thus far been accomplished in pre-war preventive action.[30]

If collaboration cannot be forged in more general terms, it needs to be forged in each individual case. The initiative can best be taken by a state or group of states with direct interest in the resolution of an evolving conflict. However, an important question – and potential obstacle – remains: why would states be any more willing now than in the past to support preventive measures, particularly if they require international agreements on the permission to intervene in weak or failing states? Are we condemned to conclude every study of preventive action with a hollow call for more 'political will' that may or may not be forthcoming? In essence, the answer is 'yes'. In an international system without shared sovereignty or supranational institutions, action by international organizations depends on the good will and cooperation of member states. Such cooperation is only forthcoming if national interests are directly affected and thus motivate joint approaches to shared problems, and if enlightened, responsible and charismatic leaders manage to secure the support of their citizens, and of their political friends and foes at home and abroad, for proactive measures.

Post-Conflict Peacebuilding: A Second Chance for Preventive Action

In general, conflicts result from long-term instability and insecurity that are both visible and curable. The warning signals for societies at risk of violent internal conflict are well known and documented. They include:

- demographic pressures: high infant mortality, rapid changes in population, including massive refugee movements, high population density, youth bulge, insufficient food or access to water, ethnic groups sharing land, territory (i.e. groups' attachment to land), environment (i.e. the relationship between ethnic groups and their physical settings).

- a lack of democratic practices: criminalization or delegitimization of the state, or human rights violations;
- regimes of short duration;
- ethnic composition of the ruling elite differing from the population at large;
- deterioration or elimination of public services;
- sharp and severe economic distress: uneven economic development along ethnic lines and a lack of trade openness;
- a legacy of vengeance-seeking group grievance;
- massive, chronic, or sustained human flight.[31]

Therefore, preventing conflict, before or after violence has erupted, requires, among others, the following to be accomplished:

- reduce demographic pressures: lower infant mortality, stabilize, avoid and prevent rapid changes in population, resettle refugee and internally displaced persons, modernize rural regions, offer employment opportunities for the young, improve agricultural techniques and provide access to clean water, facilitate multiethnic land management and environmental protection initiatives;
- support transitions to democracy, popular participation, and thus increase the legitimacy of, and popular faith in, the state; and help reduce state-sponsored human rights abuses;
- assist in the creation of popularly supported and stable regimes;
- ensure that the ethnic composition of the ruling elite reflects divisions within the population at large;
- ensure sufficient and broad provision of public services;
- stabilize the national economy, create a stable, transparent and non-discriminatory environment for private sector development and investment; assure trade liberalization and even economic development along ethnic lines;
- resolve long-standing inter-group grievances and facilitate reconciliation;
- prevent human flight and create an attractive environment for local talent and expertise.

In peaceful societies these basic security needs are met by the state, a responsible government and non-state actors. Societies at risk are unstable societies, divided societies, war-torn societies, with weak

SECOND-GENERATION PREVENTIVE ACTION

political and economic stability and deep-rooted inter-group or class frictions. Societies at risk are marked by the traumatic impoverishment of economic, political and social relations between groups and individual citizens. During times of conflict, already existing divisions within society are compounded, and new divisions are added. Societies who have experienced war and internal conflict, but have not resolved the root causes of their disputes, are prone to erupt in more armed violence in the future.

Rebuilding political, economic, social and security systems in the aftermath of civil war is a daunting task. It presents us with a dilemma: without legitimate and trusted institutions, rebuilding in other areas will be impossible. In turn, without a clear sense of community, hope for economic recovery and internal security, political institutions will be highly unstable. The key factors are endurance and commitment; the willingness of all actors to prepare for long-term rebuilding and reconciliation efforts, along with sustained investment in the prevention of renewed outbreak of violence.

Key Issues of the Post-Conflict Agenda

A brief look at recent post-conflict peacebuilding missions highlights the rehabilitative as well as preventive characteristics of those missions: UNMIK was established in June 1999 to assist the people of Kosovo in their transition to progressively expanded autonomy and possibly eventual self-rule. The mission's main tasks are to perform basic civilian administrative functions; promote the establishment of substantial autonomy and self-government in Kosovo; facilitate a political process to determine Kosovo's future status; coordinate humanitarian and disaster relief of all international agencies involved on the ground; support the reconstruction of key infrastructure; maintain civil law and order; promote human rights; and ensure the safe and unimpeded return of all refugees and displaced persons to their homes in Kosovo.[32] UNTAET, established in October of the same year to administer East Timor during its transition to independence, is empowered to exercise all legislative, executive and judicial authority. Its main tasks are to provide security and maintain law and order throughout the territory of East Timor; to establish an effective administration; to assist in the development of civil and social services; to ensure the coordination and delivery of humanitarian rehabilitation and development assistance; to support capacity-building for self-government; and to assist in the establishment of conditions for sustainable development.[33] Both mission mandates combine immediate, operational reconstruction with longer-term, structural prevention.

Long-term, structural prevention of threats to individuals and communities is the main prerequisite of stability and peace at national, regional and international levels. Preventing violence, through efforts from inside or outside a society at risk, must focus on the stabilization, maintenance and enhancement of peace, stability and justice – through the promotion and protection of human security. As the office of the Special Co-ordinator of the Stability Pact for South-Eastern Europe notes, '[c]onflict prevention and peace building can be successful only if they start in parallel in three key sectors: the creation of a secure environment, the promotion of sustainable democratic systems, and the promotion of economic and social well-being. Only if there is progress in all three sectors can a self-sustaining process of peace get underway'.[34] It is the pursuit of both prevention and stabilization that holds the key to success in post-conflict missions.

What Will Work at the Post-Conflict Stage that Did Not Work Before?

This essay has so far highlighted a number of key obstacles to effective preventive action. Among them are:

- attention to pending or emerging problems is side-tracked by highly visible emergencies;
- state sovereignty limits external involvement in the prevention or resolution of internal problems, particularly at pre-conflict stages;
- no commonly accepted legal definition of intervention in a pre-conflict situation (when, how, why and who) has so far emerged;
- limited availability of resources for potential crises;
- lack of meaningful and feasible models that are policy-friendly and relevant;
- limited access to intelligence and fact-finding, and thus inadequate early warning and analysis of risk assessment;
- weak record of addressing the economic dimensions of conflict and conflict prevention;
- lack of coherence and coordination between and within relevant non-state, state and inter-state actors;
- even if limited cooperation takes place, it does so in the context of poor understanding of, and coordination based on, the comparative advantage of cooperating actors;
- difficulties in cooperating with, and assisting, local civil society.

The above-listed obstacles to preventive action do not exist, or are less significant, in the post-conflict environment, in that:

- Post-conflict operations are responses to highly visible emergencies. They receive particularly close attention if international presence has aided in ending violence, mediating settlements, and safeguarding ceasefires. This attention is a crucial asset in mobilizing government and public support for ongoing peacebuilding and preventive efforts.
- In post-conflict situations, particularly when external presence has come at the invitation of conflicting parties, the UN Security Council has mandated participating organizations in peace operations with wide-ranging political, economic, legal and military authority. Particularly in the case of international protectorates, peacebuilders have strong influence over present and future structural and policy arrangements that resolve existing conflicts and prevent potential ones.
- Humanitarian military intervention at pre-war stages remains illegal under international law. However, the international scholarly and policy community is considering the possibility where intervention may be warranted at pre-war stages when states fail to provide security to part or all of their population. Leaving aside the operational and legal challenges of preventive intervention in peacetime, such a concept has not yet evolved.[35] Nevertheless, military intervention can be authorized by the Security Council in cases of threats to international peace and security by evoking Chapter VII of the UN Charter. Once such interventions have taken place, or peace operations have been conducted with the consent of the parties in conflict, particularly the military presence can be utilized to provide the security necessary for political, economic and social transition in post-conflict environments. IFOR and SFOR in Bosnia, or KFOR in Kosovo, provide the security necessary to keep potential peace spoilers at bay and allow political, social and economic rebuilding to take place at minimum threat.
- While financial means for post-conflict rebuilding tasks are never at an ideal level, particularly when sustainable support is so crucial to the long-term prevention of conflict recurrence, international actors do commit significant resources to preventive action once a conflict has broken out, and once it has been settled and peacebuilding efforts are under way. The European Union's Stability Pact for Southeastern Europe or World Bank spending in post-conflict zones illustrate the willingness to invest in peace once war has been stopped.[36]

- In post-conflict societies key problems and needs are abundantly transparent. Nevertheless, in the face of multiple challenges, and yet limited resources, priority tasks need to be established. Pre-mission training and in-mission training prepare individual participants in post-conflict peace operations for their tasks, while international aid agencies and other external donors collaborate in identifying key initiatives for immediate response.[37]
- Fact-finding is far less an obstacle in post-conflict activities. Presence on the ground, freedom to collect available data, and opportunities for access to, and collaboration with, local civil society actors greatly facilitate the collection of reliable data.
- The ability to both understand and address the economic dimensions of conflict and peace are greatly enhanced. Moreover, regional and global financial institutions have become increasingly sensitive to the economic underpinnings of instability and conflict. The World Bank's post-reconstruction work is but an example for multilateral financial institutions' growing awareness of their impact on peace and security in their countries of operation.[38]
- A number of recent post-conflict missions have shown that collaboration between the UN and regional organizations can be very fruitful. In Kosovo the UN developed an integrated cooperative approach between the OSCE, the EU, UN agencies and NATO.[39] In Bosnia NATO works closely with the OSCE, the UN and the EU. In both cases collaboration with NGOs is sought and coordinated. Albeit not without difficulties, post-conflict missions have proved to be fruitful testing grounds for inter-organizational cooperation.
- Mission mandates can be written around participating organization's capacities and resources. Both the General Framework Agreement, guiding post-Dayton transition of Bosnia, and UNMIK's mandate in Kosovo, draw on institutional strengths and comparative advantages to coordinate inter-organizational divisions of labour.
- In the post-conflict mission theatre, collaboration with local actors, including civil society organizations, is key to eventual transition to local ownership and control. This is still a challenge when international actors fear that cooperation and shared responsibility for the execution of peacebuilding tasks may undermine mission success. However, eventually mission success depends on the ability of local actors to carry on the work of external peacebuilders. Although they may be in need of long-term external assistance, local actors are eventually responsible for the sustainability of peacebuilding initiatives. Possibilities for collaboration and partnership between external and local actors are limitless, compared

to the difficulties of cooperation experienced in pre-war preventive efforts.[40]

The opportunities that exist for more effective and targeted preventive efforts in post-conflict situations must in turn inform the pre-conflict preventive agenda. This is all the more important as the opportunities for second-generation prevention raise significant moral and ethical problems: is effective intervention and reconstruction only possible in the aftermath of war? First, if a society has to go to war to produce the humanitarian catastrophe or threat of conflict spillover that is required to draw international attention to a people's plight, the costs of attention and subsequent response are tremendous. Second, post-conflict peace initiatives apply only to post-conflict societies where external actors have facilitated or enforced an end to violence – for reasons that have so far been shown to be a combination between national or regional self-interest and security and humanitarian concerns (the former clearly the dominating factor).

In cases where the direct interests of potential external actors are not affected, or where regional groupings may be affected but do not possess the necessary human and financial resources to launch peacemaking and peacebuilding missions, little will be done to stop violence, and even less will be done to prevent its recurrence. In those situations (in particular, conflicts in Africa) war will continue without external intervention. If wars are resolved by the conflicting parties themselves, no external organization is tempted to shore up its investment with post-conflict assistance. If there is no external stake in either peace or war, rebuilding will be primarily in the hands of local actors. This means that wars in the North (or close to northern interests) will possibly be contained and resolved by the 'international' community of states and their various regional organizations, while wars in the South will with frequent regularity continue unabated. Only long-term assistance for regional and subregional organizations in the South will help alleviate this double-standard and the resulting tragedy for war-ravaged societies.

Moreover, at a minimum, long-term assistance during times of peace and in the aftermath of conflict has to follow the principle of 'do no harm', advocated by Mary Anderson: no action by external actors should worsen the existing situation. This requires all external actors to scrutinize their programmes, initiatives and other business in conflict-prone countries for negative consequences that may exacerbate frictions, inequalities and grievances that may already exist.[41] While this seems to be a self-evident proposition, much external action in societies at risk aid the escalation of troubles – evaluation of one's activities in this light is key in mainstreaming conflict prevention in the cabinets and boardrooms of governments and businesses.

Conclusion: The Perverse Nature of Prevention, or the Failure to Get it Right in the First Place

The perverse nature of prevention can be illustrated with the following medical analogy: although most people know of the potential dangers of a hazardous or unhealthy life style, they rarely take preventive measures until after they have for the first time experienced the negative consequences of their actions. We are prone to fall into the same trap over and over again: first, until verified by personal experience, we refuse to let lessons learned by others determine our own behaviour, and second, we are unwilling to invest resources and personal inconvenience to prevent potential disasters that may or may not happen. This we do even when all indicators point to the eventual certainty of disaster, and where naive faith in everlasting safety and security is nothing but a coping strategy that permits ignorance of the unavoidable crisis. This strategy might even make sense: one cannot possibly prepare for all eventualities, crises and disasters that may strike, and thus opt to simply address only those problems that actually emerge. The risk associated with this 'wait-and-see' approach is obvious: once disaster strikes for the first time, the damage done may be irreparable, and subsequent preventive strategies may only – and at best – limit the negative consequences of that damage.

A similar scenario applies to conflict prevention: the necessary resolve to invest in preventive measures, particularly if they require additional resources and activities, only materializes once blood has been spilled, once the consequences of violence are deemed unbearable. The post-conflict environment is highly conducive to wide-ranging external involvement in bringing about rapid and drastic change. Third-party investment in brokering peace settlements more often than not leads to requests for third-party assistance, indeed implementation, of peace agreements. The lapse – or void – of indigenous institutions that have the legitimacy to govern creates an open door for external transitional organizations that are tasked with rebuilding the new state from the ground up. As experienced in UNMIK and UNTAET, international organizations (both the UN and regional organizations) enjoy wide-ranging authority over the political, social and economic life of their host country. If committed to effective cooperation with local actors, and transition to local ownership within a reasonable period of time, such protectorates build the foundation of post-conflict state and society, in direct response to the threats and fears that have led to instability and conflict escalation in the first place. Mastering the thin line between effectiveness and collaboration with local actors is a challenge, as is the maintenance of post-conflict financial and human resource commitment by intervening states and organizations.[42]

Given the tendency to become proactive only after disaster strikes, is there a way forward? To begin with, while all efforts have to be gathered to mainstream prevention in official foreign and overseas development assistance programmes and the activities of international organizations, we have to recognize that first-generation prevention will remain rare, and its successes will be mostly invisible. On the other hand, in order to launch effective preventive programmes, violence and destabilization may have to take place in order to create opportunities and support for second-generation prevention. As problematic as this proposition may be, the results may prove its merit – but only if, once conflict breaks out, efforts toward a settlement are quick, expose the dangers of further destabilization, and create a venue for sustainable second-generation preventive action.[43]

This is, however, a risky strategy: the extent of damage and human suffering 'required' to draw international attention and produce settlements may be so great that the damage will be irreparable. Moreover, while for instance in Europe, regional organizations and the UN are quick to react to war within and outside its fringes, in regions with a very high threshold of international concern (such as Africa) the response time – if there is a response at all – will be very slow. The case for second-generation preventive action may be pragmatically sound, but it is morally and ethically deeply flawed. Nevertheless, commitment to post-conflict prevention – more difficult, more costly, longer term – will likely continue to be more pronounced than efforts geared at proactive conflict prevention. Nevertheless, we must not lose sight of the clear priority for pre-conflict preventive action, in particular because many wars will not be settled and reconstruction will not be supported by external actors. To enhance the chances for more effective early prevention, lessons must be learned from the post-conflict experience for proactive initiatives. These include the following:

- First, prevention will continue to require long-term, visionary commitment, beyond the point where the momentum for post-conflict attention fades away.

- Second, second-generation prevention deals with much deeper social, political and economic wounds than those that need to be healed to prevent the outbreak of violence in the first instance. By this logic, pre-conflict prevention is always less costly in the short term (no eruption of violence) than in the long term, as grievances have not yet been exacerbated and compounded by the experience of violent conflict.
- Third, the costs (in both human and economic terms) incurred by the outbreak of violence and the eventually necessary external involvement to stop it are in addition to the costs of post-conflict reconstruction and preventive action. Thus, overall requirements for both cost and commitment are much higher than proactive measures.
- Fourth, the effectiveness of post-war conflict prevention owes much to the level of authority granted to external agents of peacebuilding; protectorates build and run countries, with far-reaching freedom and local consent. A similar scenario at the pre-conflict stages is currently not foreseeable, unless an international consensus can be reached on failed states, the abrogation of state sovereignty, and authorization of and support for regional or global institutions to intervene early, including through the establishment of protectorates, if needed.

Addressing the key dilemma of prevention (the perverse preference for reactive prevention) must be a central responsibility for academics, policy analysts and policy makers alike: we have to develop methods that allow the international community to act not only in response to, but increasingly in anticipation of violence. Conditions that make effective second-generation prevention possible must be emulated at the pre-conflict phase. These include universally supported rules for early intervention and the international community's ability to revoke a state's right to sovereign rule when it refuses to provide basic security for its population. They also include the availability of both effective mandates and sufficient resources; effective tools and application of early warning and risk assessment; and coordination and division of responsibility among actors that possess the will and capacity to join preventive initiatives. Finally, the gap between interest-based and needs-based responses to emerging crises must be narrowed and the United Nations must be embraced as the key facilitator in creating the legitimate framework for international campaigns to improve preventive and remedial action to violent conflict.

NOTES

1. For an extensive examination of the Kosovo conflict, see Albrecht Schnabel and Ramesh Thakur (eds), *Kosovo and the Challenge of Humanitarian Intervention: Selective Indignation, Collective Action, and International Citizenship*, Tokyo: United Nations University Press, 2000.
2. 'Communication from the Commission on Conflict Prevention', COM (2001) 211 final, Brussels: European Commission, 11 April 2001.
3. Teferra Shiawl, 'OAU and Conflict Prevention in Africa', presentation delivered at a workshop, From Rhetoric to Policy: Towards Working Conflict Prevention at the Regional and Global Level, organized by the United Nations University, Tokyo, Japan and held at INSTRAW, Santo Domingo, Dominican Republic, 14–16 Dec. 1999. See also Ian Smillie, Lansana Gberie and Ralph Hazleton, *The Heart of the Matter: Sierra Leone, Diamonds and Human Security*, Ottawa: Partnership Africa Canada, 2000.
4. Abdul-Rasheed Draman, 'Conflict Prevention in Africa: Establishing Conditions and Institutions for Durable Peace', presentation delivered at From Rhetoric to Policy workshop (n.3 above).
5. 'Preventing Wars within States: What can Intergovernmental Organizations do in Africa?', in Elizabeth Sidiropoulos (ed.), *A Continent Apart: Kosovo, Africa and Humanitarian Intervention*, Johannesburg: The South African Institute of International Affairs, 2001, pp.13–36.
6. See Carnegie Commission on Preventing Deadly Conflict, *Preventing Deadly Conflict*, Final Report, New York: Carnegie Corporation of New York, 1997, p.20. For detailed accounts and analyses of casualties, injuries, economic, social, developmental and environmental damage of seven major conflicts in the 1990s (the Gulf War, Indonesia's invasion of East Timor, the civil wars in Mozambique and Sudan, the guerilla war in Peru, the independence struggle in Kashmir, and the war in the former Yugoslavia), see Michael Cranna (ed.), *The True Cost of Conflict: Seven Recent Wars and Their Effects on Society*, New York: New Press, 1995.
7. Albrecht Schnabel, 'International Organizations and the Prevention of Ethnic Conflicts: Searching for an Effective Formula', in Symeon Giannakos (ed.), *Ethnic Conflict: Religion, Identity and Politics*, Athens: Ohio University Press, 2001.
8. For a discussion of the high price tag of the international community's response to war-ravaged societies, see Carnegie Commission on Preventing Deadly Conflict (n.6 above), pp.20–21; and Cranna (n.6 above).
9. This point has recently been reiterated by UN Secretary-General Kofi Annan as one of the most crucial requirements for success of UN peace operations. See *Implementation of the Recommendations of the Special Committee on Peacekeeping Operations and the Panel on United Nations Peace Operations*, A/55/977, 1 June 2001.
10. Ibid.; *Report of the Panel on United Nations Peace Operation*, A/55/305-S/2000/809, 21 Aug. 2000.
11. See Michael E. Brown and Richard N. Rosecrance (eds), *The Costs of Conflict: Prevention and Cure in the Global Arena*, Lanham, MD: Rowman & Littlefield, 1999, p.225.
12. For further conceptual analyses of conflict prevention, see, among others, Bruce

Jentleson (ed.), *Opportunities Missed, Opportunities Seized: Preventive Diplomacy in the Post-Cold War World*, Lanham, MD: Rowman & Littlefield, 1999; Janie Leatherman, William DeMars, Patrick Gaffey and Raimo Vayrynen, *Breaking Cycles of Violence: Conflict Prevention in Intrastate Crises*, Bloomfield, CT: Kumarian Press, 1999; Michael Lund, *Preventing Violent Conflicts*, Washington, DC: United States Institute of Peace Press, 1996; and Connie Peck, *Sustainable Peace: The Role of the UN and Regional Organizations in Preventing* Conflict, Lanham, MD: Rowman & Littlefield, 1998.
13. Boutros Boutros-Ghali, *An Agenda for Peace*, New York: United Nations, 1992, para. 20.
14. Ibid., para. 23.
15. Michael Lund, 'Improving Conflict Prevention by Learning from Experience: Context, Issues, Approaches and Findings', paper presented at the Conflict Prevention Network Annual Conference, Berlin, 31 Oct. 1999.
16. Michael Lund, 'Early Warning and Preventive Diplomacy', in Chester A. Crocker, Fen Osler Hampson, with Pamela Aall (eds), *Managing Global Chaos*, Washington, DC: USIP Press, 1996, p.379.
17. Connie Peck, Discussion Paper, *Seminar on Strengthening Co-operative Approaches to Conflict Prevention: The Role of Regional Organizations and the United Nations*, International Development Research Centre, Ottawa, Canada, 11–13 March 1998, p.3.
18. See David Carment and Albrecht Schnabel, *Building Conflict Prevention Capacity: Methods, Experiences, Needs*, IDRC Working Paper No. 5, Ottawa: The International Development Research Centre, June 2001, p.6.
19. For these and other examples, see Michael Lund, 'Creeping Institutionalization of the Culture of Prevention?', in *Preventing Violent Conflict: The Search for Political Will, Strategies and Effective Tools*, The Report of the Krusenberg Seminar, 19–20 June 2000, p.23.
20. Robert H. Dorff, 'Democratization and Failed States: The Challenge of Ungovernability', *Parameters*, Summer 1996, pp.17–31.
21. See *Prevention of Armed Conflict*, Report of the Secretary-General, A/55/985-S/2001/574, 7 June 2001.
22. Although the Brahimi Report is largely concerned with UN-led peace support operations and post-conflict peacebuilding, it does provide some insights on broader conceptions of conflict prevention especially in light of the desire to render the UN a more effective and forward-looking organization through enhanced intelligence gathering and preventive diplomacy (n.10 above).
23. See, for instance, Mats Berdal and David Malone (eds), *Greed and Grievance: Economic Agendas in Civil Wars*, Boulder: Lynne Rienner, 2000.
24. These include the UN's Departments of Peacekeeping Operations (DPKO) and Political Affairs (DPA), the UN Development Programme (UNDP), the European Union (EU), the Organization for Security and Cooperation in Europe (OSCE), the Organization of African Unity (OAU), and the Forum for Early Warning and Early Response (FEWER).
25. 'Mainstreaming' is about providing appropriate means and procedures to effectively follow a *mainstream* policy, in this case conflict prevention. As opposed to a *sidelined* subject, the mainstreamed issue is systematically incorporated in and becomes an integral and equal part of all essential areas of engagement. This definition was provided by Martina Huber of the Conflict Prevention Network,

SECOND-GENERATION PREVENTIVE ACTION

Berlin, 10 Jan. 2001. The author thanks David Carment for sharing this information.
26. The above three paragraphs summarize findings reported in Carment and Schnabel (n.18 above), pp.4–6.
27. See 'Chapter 3: The Responsibility to Prevent,' in International Commission on Intervention and State Sovereignty, *The Responsibility to Protect*, Ottawa: IDRC for the International Commission on Intervention and State Sovereignty, 2001, para. 3.1. See also Gareth Evans and Mohamed Sahnoun, 'Intervention and State Sovereignty: Breaking New Ground', *Global Governance*, Vol.7, No.2, Apr.–June 2001, pp.119–25.
28. Ibid., para. 3.34.
29. *Prevention of Armed Conflict* (n.21 above), para. 15.
30. See Kofi Annan's comments at the 1998 high-level meeting between the UN and regional organizations on the theme of Cooperation for Conflict Prevention. Kofi Annan, '"Structural" and "operational" cooperation for conflict prevention', Press Release, SG/SM/6658, New York, 29 July 1998.
31. Carnegie Commission on Preventing Deadly Conflict (n.6 above), p.44. See also the sources on which the Carnegie Commission's findings were based: Daniel C. Esty, Jack A. Goldstone, Ted Robert Gurr, Pamela T. Surko, and Alan N. Unger, *Working Paper: State Failure Task Force Report*, 30 Nov. 1995; Pauline H. Baker and John A. Ausink, 'State Collapse and Ethnic Violence: Toward a Predictive Model', *Parameters*, Vol.26, No.1, spring 1996, pp.19–36. See also Nicole Ball, 'The Challenge of Rebuilding War-Torn Societies', in Crocker, Hampson, with Aall (n.16 above), pp.608–12.
32. Security Council Resolution 1244, 10 June 1999.
33. Security Council Resolution 1272, 25 Oct. 1999.
34. Special Co-ordinator of the Stability Pact for South-Eastern Europe, 'About the Stability Pact', Brussels, June 2001; available at www.stabilitypact.org/stability pactcgi /catalog/cat_descr.cgi?prod_id=1806.
35. See International Commission on Intervention and State Sovereignty, *The Responsibility to Protect: Report of the Commission* (see n.27 above).
36. See Hans-Georg Ehrhart, 'A Good Idea, but a Rocky Road Ahead: The EU and the Stability Pact for South Eastern Europe', in Carment and Schnabel (n.18 above); Carnegie Commission on Preventing Deadly Conflict (n.6 above), p.21; World Bank, *The Road to Stability and Prosperity in South Eastern Europe*, Washington, DC: World Bank, March 2000.
37. For instance, in preparation of their South East European regional strategy paper (ibid.), the World Bank collaborated with the European Commission, the European Bank for Reconstruction and Development, the European Investment Bank, the Organization for Economic Cooperation and Development, the Council of Europe, and the Council's Development Bank. For information on the UN Department of Peacekeeping's mission training activities, see the webpage of UNDPKO's Training and Evaluation Service.
38. See World Bank (n.36 above).
39. See Albrecht Schnabel, 'Political Cooperation in Retrospect: Contact Group, EU, OSCE, NATO, G-8 and UN Working toward a Kosovo Settlement', in Kurt R. Spillmann and Joachim Krause (eds), *Kosovo: Lessons Learned for International Cooperative Security*, Bern and Frankfurt: Peter Lang, 2000, pp.21–44.
40. The experience of the Open Society Foundation particularly in countries throughout

Eastern Europe and the former Soviet Union is instructive for the work of international NGOs in both pre- and post-conflict preventive action and long-term development. See www.soros.org/osi.html.
41. See Mary Anderson, *Do No Harm: How Aid Can Support Peace – Or War*, Boulder: Lynne Rienner, 1999.
42. For a critical reflection on the UN's failure to find this balance, see Jarat Chopra, 'The UN's Kingdom of East Timor', *Survival*, Vol.42, No.3, autumn 2000, pp.27–39.
43. Implementation of the recent Brahimi Report on reforming UN peace operations would be crucial for prompt response to violence (n.10 above). See also Albrecht Schnabel and Ramesh Thakur, 'From *An Agenda for Peace* to the Brahimi Report: Towards a New Era of UN Peace Operations?', in Ramesh Thakur and Albrecht Schnabel (eds), *United Nations Peacekeeping Operations: Ad Hoc Missions, Permanent Engagement*, Tokyo: United Nations University Press, 2001, pp.238–55.

'Transitional Justice': The Impact of Transnational Norms and the UN

EDWARD NEWMAN

A perennial challenge in post-conflict societies is how to balance claims for justice, truth and accountability with the need for peace and stability. The manner in which (sometimes volatile) transitional societies have dealt with a history of widespread human rights abuse and dictatorship is a major theme of the literature on post-conflict and democratic transition.[1] It has led to the concept of 'transitional justice' in post-conflict and post-authoritarian situations, a process that is conditioned by political compromises and practical constraints not present in 'normal' societal situations. Accordingly, the modalities of dealing with a past of human rights abuse and achieving justice and accountability are conditioned by the terms of peace settlements and political transitions within a society. Justice is invariably a key issue in post-conflict situations, but it is one often neglected in the interests of peace and stability. However, increasingly in recent years, international norms are impinging upon this process and there is a growing consensus that some form of justice and accountability is integral to – rather than in tension with – peace and stability.

Kritz has argued that there has been a 'paradigm shift' in attitudes: it is increasingly accepted that accountability and justice are an essential part of peace in post-conflict societies.[2] This attitude is reflected in the presence of international institutions, norms and laws, which are today important factors in the perennial dilemmas and tensions of 'transitional justice'. In turn, the role of the United Nations in post-conflict societies has gone beyond peacekeeping, as a natural extension of the UN becoming more involved in societal structures, moving away from the idea of impartiality/neutrality, and recognizing that there is an ethical dimension to peace. The UN is now a conduit for the application of international norms and standards of accountability in countries such as Guatemala, El Salvador, Rwanda, former Yugoslavia, Sierra Leone, and Cambodia. However, is international justice really viable in such circumstances? Or will pragmatism and the need for stability (rather than justice) win through as always?

This contribution will explore the modalities of dealing with past abuses of human rights, and consider whether the growing prominence of transnational forces – international law, international tribunals and courts – is changing the balance of transition in favour of accountability and justice. It will consider whether the internationalization of justice is challenging the pragmatism and impunity that traditionally appear to be the price of democratic transition and stability.[3] The classical formula of 'balancing ethical imperatives and political constraints'[4] and 'settl[ing] a past account without upsetting the present transition'[5] may be evolving in the context of international norms and laws that impose expectations of accountability. However, the essay concludes that dealing with past abuses of human rights is as much about politics and trade-offs as it is about justice and accountability, especially in post-conflict and transitional situations. The internationalization of justice is not altering this reality – although it is introducing new variables into the equation. While the input of international norms and institutions may increase the prospects of justice in countries such as Sierra Leone and Cambodia, transitional societies must embrace other values – such as peace, stability, development – that are not necessarily co-terminal. Moreover, the process will inevitably be conditioned by the predilections of powerful political actors outside the societies in question.

Dealing with the Past: The Perennial Challenges

After serious civil conflict or widespread human rights abuse, an important issue in the success of transition is the management of past human rights abuses and crimes against humanity. A sense of justice and accountability for the past is integral to peacebuilding and to installing a sense of confidence and trust into public life. Moreover, this is often not just a 'historical' issue of the 'past': the appearance of impunity for past crimes undermines confidence in new democratic structures and casts doubt upon commitments to human rights, which are integral to successful consolidation.

Simultaneously, however, the search for truth and accountability can be destabilizing and can prolong, even obstruct, the transition to and consolidation of democracy and peace in the short term. In many cases peace settlements and the transition from authoritarian rule depend upon the cooperation of actors and individuals directly involved in human rights abuses in the past. This often involves a delicate balance. The victim's demands for justice must surely be addressed, but the participation and support of all major actors –

including the perpetrators of crimes and their supporters – in the post-conflict system is sometimes essential for its short-term survival. There is a paradox to be solved: some sense of justice is necessary to move forward; it is integral to the peace and democratization process. But stability and the inclusion and support of all actors make the search for truth and justice difficult.

Managing the Past: Options and Constraints

The orthodox 'political science' formula suggests that the nature and pace of a transition has, in most cases, defined the parameters, opportunities, and constraints within which successor governments have been able to seek truth, accountability and justice. Where peace processes or processes of democratization are transitional and negotiated, powerful actors dictate the pace and nature of change in post-conflict societies. This has characterized Latin America, for example, where policy options for accountability for past crimes are limited because the actors implicated in these crimes defined the terms of transition. In contrast, revolution, upheaval or foreign occupation (including UN administrations) tend to offer greater opportunities for seeking accountability and redress, but these are less common models of political change.

These different paths have had a strong bearing upon the issue of accountability and justice in post-conflict and post-authoritarian societies. The outcomes have been a condition of a number of variables: the political, institutional and legal framework left over after violent conflict or after transition from authoritarianism; the position and power of former combatants after transition; the decision-making and leadership of the successor government; the level of public consciousness and mobilization; and the input of international actors. To deal effectively with past abuses of human rights requires that certain abstract principles or values – which can be complementary or in tension – be achieved to the level 'expected' in the context of the process. These values are accountability, truth, justice, compensation, restitution and deterrence. In a transitional society, these values must be achieved alongside other values: stability and peace, economic development, (re)building national institutions, and democracy, among others. A number of so-called policy 'options' exist for transitional societies in coming to terms with past abuse of human rights, and this has been a favourite subject for political scientists, sociologists and comparativists for many years.[6] A common point is that dealing with the past is essential to *building* a healthy democratic society, but in the immediate post-authoritarian context dealing with the past can *threaten* the building of a democratic society. There can clearly be a tension between these values.

Within this frequently observed conundrum, a number of abstract policy options exist, depending on the nature of the transition. These are often identified as: prosecution of all perpetrators of serious human rights; prosecution of the perpetrators of the most horrendous human rights abuses; partial or complete amnesty; concentrating on truth and reconciliation as an alternative to accountability; forgetting; and compensation to victims. Perhaps the major division of opinion is between (1) seeking accountability and justice, including criminal prosecutions, and (2) a more pragmatic approach, often involving amnesties, forgiveness and emphasizing the need to move forward, or for more practical reasons, being flexible in the interests of stability and democratic consolidation. In philosophical terms, one could make a distinction between the search for *absolute justice*, as an abstract ideal irrespective of political, practical and legal conditions; and *societal justice*, that is, approaching reconciliation within the limits and opportunities presented within a particular context, in the interests of society. This is in turn often presented as a dichotomy or a tension between justice and pragmatism, or justice and stability, especially in volatile or post-authoritarian situations.

The reality is quite different to the theory, of course. The issue of whether to 'punish or pardon' is assumed, especially by observers outside the societies in question, to be a dilemma, a conscious decision, and a clear choice between two opposites. The challenge is often presented as striking a balance between a 'whitewash' and a 'witch hunt'.[7] It is in fact rarely the case that such policy options are laid out as a simple choice with equal feasibility; the options are a condition of a number of constraints and political balances. Thus, to ask the question of whether to punish or pardon, or how to deal with a legacy of human rights abuses, is quite meaningless in an abstract sense; policy options cannot be considered out of context, and each context is different.

Justice and Accountability above Pragmatism

In post-conflict and post-authoritarian societies the instinct may be to support a process of legal accountability and justice for past crimes that may involve prosecution. There are a number of abstract arguments in favour of pursuing justice and accountability to the full. A thorough accounting with the past is necessary in order to draw a line under the past, to make a fresh beginning, to give social institutions confidence and credibility. Moreover, a policy of justice and accountability is surely more likely to ensure against future repression; conversely, a climate of impunity is not conducive for the foundation of a democratic society or regime.

Given that many transitional societies aspire to democracy, this also brings with it certain requirements. Democracy involves many norms and values; above all, the security of the individual against arbitrary arrest, torture, and extra-judicial execution are fundamental. For a democracy to have meaning, these principles must have meaning.[8] The rule of law is integral to democracy and, thus, within the framework of the law, accountability is essential for the justice that is owed to victims and the families of the victims, and also so that society and the institutions of democracy can be purged of repressive elements. In this context, justice and accountability involve the reform of institutions (such as the police, judiciary and armed forces). While impunity survives and where the perpetrators of injustice remain prominent in public or private society, democracy has little meaning. If impunity remains, the social divisions remain open and volatile; if the state has not granted a public acknowledgement of the wrongs of the past, these wrongs constitute a continuing affront to society. This is not just an intangible issue of ethics. In the absence of justice and accountability repressive institutions are unreformed, and while there may be democratic regime change, human rights abuse can continue, albeit under a different ideological guise.

A rigorous accounting of the past is also important for the formal restoration of the dignity of victims and an acknowledgement of wrongdoing. Just as important, accounting for the past is obviously important from a perspective of excluding certain elements from positions in public institutions in post-conflict societies, such as the police. The continuing presence of unreformed or recalcitrant individuals and institutions in public life can be damaging in the intangible sense of souring democracy but also in a more substantive manner. Again, the pursuit of justice and accountability is not only an issue of the past. It is indivisible from human rights standards in the present.

From a philosophical point of view, while forgiveness is better than punishment for reconciliation, forgiveness is a positive action – yet amnesties preclude forgiveness. As Hannah Arendt observed, 'men are unable to forgive what they cannot punish'.[9] Forgiveness is a 'transaction' between the forgiver and the forgiven, a shared acknowledgement of past wrongdoing, an acknowledgement of appropriate punishment, and a demonstration that contrition and repentance have been met by mercy.[10] Contrition must be supported by positive restorative steps by the forgiven: reparations, community service, compensation. And in its pure form, forgiveness is a voluntary act by an individual – not an imposed policy for a whole society, or a 'legislated forgetting' imposed for political reasons, irrespective of the wishes or needs of those touched by suffering.[11] The restorative meaning of forgiveness – a concept of reconciliation based upon repairing relations – is undermined when it is faced with recalcitrance, lack of information, and disputes about wrongdoing.

A further angle is that justice and accountability in transitional societies may be necessary under international law covering human rights, and particularly crimes against humanity, genocide and torture. There are therefore limits to the discretion of individual states in terms of punishment and clemency.[12] The Universal Declaration of Human Rights of 1948, and subsequently the International Covenant on Civil and Political Rights in 1966, codified the internationalization of human rights and placed certain rights within a transnational, rather than merely domestic, context. This movement has strengthened in recent decades, placing significant limitations upon the ability of governments to grant amnesties and clemency, and sometimes overriding national statutes of limitation. Articles V and VI of the Convention on the Prevention and Punishment of the Crime of Genocide hold that perpetrators of genocide shall be punished irrespective of position or office, and that international mechanisms for pursuing justice shall be used if necessary. The Convention on the Non-Applicability of Statutory Limitations to War Crimes and Crimes Against Humanity and the Convention Against Torture and Other Cruel, Inhuman or Degrading Treatment or Punishment support this principle.

In the regional context transnational human rights regimes have also had an effect, and Latin America is rich with insights on this. For example, in 1992 the Inter-American Commission on Human Rights determined that Uruguay's 1986 Law Nullifying the State's Claim to Punish Certain Crimes (*Ley de Caducidad*), which effectively removed the possibility of prosecution relating to human rights abuses in that country for all military personnel, violated Uruguay's obligations under the American Convention on Human Rights. Considering the array of legal instruments in effect across Latin America and the amnesties that have been passed, one observer has suggested that 'arguably, none of these amnesties is valid under international law'.[13] The Inter-American Commission on Human Rights has consistently held that many such amnesties violate states' obligations under the American Convention on Human Rights.[14] The criticism by the Inter-American Commission on Human Rights in December 1999 of the amnesty law that allowed the killers of six priests in El Salvador – in addition to many other known killers – to go free is a further example of pressure against impunity. In the wider context of international legal and political norms and the strengthening of international humanitarian law, transnational forces are steadily intruding into 'national' forms of dealing with the past. The option of a country coming to terms with its past, and making whatever trade-off and balances it feels necessary and legitimate within its own political, social and legal context, is being slowly eroded by transitional forces and norms. The impact of these forces and norms upon the achievement of reconciliation is a crucial and relatively new perspective to this debate.

The Pattern of Pragmatism and Impunity

There are a host of arguments that challenge the primacy of accountability and justice. These usually reject the concept of abstract, absolute justice as idealist and infeasible, and invariably argue that there is no universal model with which transitional societies can deal with past human rights abuse. This argument offers a utilitarian alternative as a moral and practical option: the route of absolute justice may not only be practically infeasible, it may also not be in the interests of democratic consolidation and reconciliation. Consequently, accountability and justice are bound to reflect a political process.

It may not be feasible or physically possible to confront human rights abuses in a just manner if it jeopardizes peace and transition. Thus, while not dealing with the past may sour peace and democracy; to deal with it may *threaten* peace. Therefore, the principal obstacle, in a transitional situation, may be that the actors upon whom democratic transition depends for its success – often the military or rebel combatants – are the same actors responsible for human rights abuse in the past. A negotiated transition will invariably involve compromises on past human rights abuses, and in many cases outright amnesties or immunities. The corollary is that a rigorous treatment of past human rights abuse may prolong war or provoke instability, a coup, or authoritarian regression. For example, the peace process in Guatemala was characterized by political compromises and balances, and these were reflected in the institutional and legal arrangements that were created for the 'democratic' successor government. The military had a strong bearing upon the terms of transition and obviously resisted a thorough accounting for past abuses of human rights. In 1996 the 'Law of National Reconciliation' created a partial amnesty but stated that 'crimes of genocide, torture, and forced disappearance' are not covered. Yet the UN Historical Clarification Commission agreed not to publish names. A general who was in power during the most oppressive period, in the early 1980s, Efrain Rios Montt, remains a prominent politician. Society continues to be polarized, and in some way traumatized; the military remains recalcitrant and unrepentant; and the government seems unwilling or unable to take serious steps towards accountability on the basis of the Commission's recommendations. Many human rights organizations were unhappy with the basis of the official Historical Clarification Commission, seeing it as a compromise tied into the peace negotiations. In 1995 the Guatemalan Catholic Church began its own project for the Recovery of Historical Memory, and presented its report in 1998.

Similarly, the international nature of the peace agreement in El Salvador did not appear to have significantly increased openings for accounting for past abuses. To attempt a rigorous pursuit of the military during the negotiations to end the civil war would have prolonged the conflict; to have attempted criminal proceedings after a peace agreement would have seriously risked regression. Even if there had not been a coup, former offenders could resist and elude punishment/prosecution. As a general point, this can be damaging to the credibility of a new government and possibly be even worse than not doing anything at all. One of the members of the UN truth commission in El Salvador, Thomas Buergenthal, recalled that even in trying to uncover the truth – rather than punish – 'it was obvious to us that the military had built a defensive wall to protect itself. As we interviewed more officers, this wall appeared to be becoming more formidable... All of them, moreover, seemed to have great faith in the ability of the system to cover up, to protect them, and to punish those who talked'.[15]

The case of the former Yugoslavia appears to suggest that a major international (including military) presence and a high level of international political support can result in a 'culture of accountability', however tenuous that notion is. There was once a common criticism that the international criminal tribunal for the former Yugoslavia would not have jurisdiction over the most senior offenders because to do so would jeopardize the peace process in Bosnia. This is the sort of trade-off that Kofi Annan criticized when he wrote that 'justice, not expediency' should be the guiding light of international criminal tribunals.[16] The former Chief Prosecutor of the International Criminal Tribunal for the former Yugoslavia and Rwanda bemoaned the 'shameful apathy' of the international community in failing to uphold the mandates of the tribunals.[17] Yet the former President of Yugoslavia, Slobodan Milosović, now stands before the court, and despite the terribly slow legal process in The Hague, prosecutions are being made and indictees are even turning themselves over to the court's jurisdiction. Nevertheless, there is a persuasive argument that senior NATO officers – and no doubt political leaders also – prioritized the maintenance of peace and stability and the safety of their own forces above the arrest of suspected war criminals during the early stages of the court when the security situation in Bosnia was still particularly volatile.

In addition to the obvious physical challenge posed by recalcitrant armed groups there is also the argument that a thorough accounting for the past can prolong the return to 'normality' by maintaining enmity in public life and not allowing the wounds of the past to heal. This has a familiar ring to it: we cannot change the past, we cannot even be sure of the facts of the past, so move forward, concentrate on the future.

There are also practical problems to prosecution: it is rarely possible to prosecute everyone responsible for human rights abuses. Thus, the decision on how/who to prosecute cannot be fair, if pursued on an 'absolute justice' basis. In most transitional societies efforts are arguably best channelled into national recovery and development. The expense and length of time taken for criminal proceedings are also a practical challenge. Moreover, prosecution can hinder or indeed conflict with the search for truth, which is arguably just as crucial for society. People – particularly perpetrators – are less likely to disclose information if it would implicate them legally. It may be worth compromising on justice in order to achieve truth – a trade-off at work with the Truth and Reconciliation Commission for South Africa. And while it might be argued that a legal truth is the most irrefutable truth, it takes much longer to establish. If one considers the time allowed under the Chilean Truth and Reconciliation Commission's terms of reference – less than a year – then legal procedures would have been impossible. In that and other cases, the speed with which a report could be issued was very important.

Finally, people who counsel against a rigorous accounting with the past sometimes put events into a historical context: they see the past as a struggle where 'all sides did bad things'. There is also often the militating moral and legal argument that combatants followed orders and should therefore not be held accountable for illegal orders, especially when to resist such orders would put their own life in peril.[18] The general political argument in favour of 'looking forward instead of backwards' argues that mistakes were made on all sides and that complete justice and accountability is elusive – and perhaps illusory –

and therefore the energies and resources of society would be best put to progress and development, rather than mired in the past or in witch hunts. Moreover, a rigorous pursuit of accountability could be in danger of appearing as 'victor's justice'.

The conventional wisdom of political scientists is that the policy options – what is politically feasible – are determined by the dynamics of transition within a delineated political community. Transition is a condition of power political dynamics. Justice and morality are normative issues and inhabit a quite different sphere of discourse. Samuel Huntington presents such an analysis: arguments for and against punishment/prosecution may well be moral/legal, but the practice has been largely conditioned by political factors and the distribution of power before and during transition.[19] This will always result in compromise and trade-off, and the cases in Latin America appear to support this.[20] The conventional wisdom of political and comparative scientists is that justice – as well as accountability and truth telling – will necessarily be secondary to pragmatism and political balances of achieving a transition. Is the conventional wisdom being challenged by the emergence of transnational norms?

Transnational Forces

An important and relatively new dimension to this debate concerns the internationalization of norms of transition and political morality, which have increasingly impinged upon 'national' or 'communitarian' attempts to come to terms with the past. In this context there have been rapid and fundamentally important developments in individual criminal responsibility at the international level, and in particular for grave breaches of humanitarian law.[21] In a landmark 1993 decision, the UN Security Council determined that violations of international humanitarian law in the former Yugoslavia constituted a threat to international peace and security. The International Criminal Tribunal for Rwanda was also created, in 1994, under Chapter VII of the UN Charter – invoking enforcement powers in the context of threats to international peace and security. UN members are thus committed to upholding the mandates of these tribunals, which clearly internationalize jurisdiction of humanitarian and criminal law in these cases, although not without difficulties.[22] The statute of the International Criminal Court is also a landmark in both the ethos and the process of internationalization of humanitarian law.[23] The cumulative effect is that the modalities of dealing with the past – the constraints and possibilities and indeed responsibilities – and the balance between justice and pragmatism that characterizes every such society, are no longer solely a condition of the dynamics of transition within a particular society.

The internationalization of the justice and reconciliation issue has had a number of effects. Clearly, international laws, norms, and institutions have conditioned the modalities of dealing with the past in transitional societies. One could argue that justice and morality are likely to be more prominent (at least in theory) rather than if the transition is governed by local political dynamics and compromises. International laws and norms can theoretically be more impartial than purely local solutions, which are more likely to be conditioned by local power balances rather than concerns of justice. Moreover, in polarized transitional societies, local approaches can inevitably be accused of bias. Transnational standards or expectations of behaviour constitute a minimum level of behaviour that transcends the tendency for transitional societies to fudge the issue of justice in the interests of political trade-off. For example, it is possible that without a UN presence in Guatemala, the indigenous peoples who represented the vast majority of the massacre victims would not have received the recognition that they did, given the social and ethnic dimensions of the conflict. In El Salvador, it was thought that no-one from the society could win the confidence of the populace in establishing truth; none of the commissioners on the truth commission were therefore citizens of the country.

A number of countervailing arguments are also persuasive. From what can be described as a communitarian perspective, social values and norms can never be universal or abstract. These values are unique to a particular society. Solutions cannot be imposed from outside. The tools employed to deal with challenges of transitional justice, if they are to be sustainable, must be an extension of these values. The opportunities and constraints of transition are a product of the circumstances of a particular society, and if this means that accountability is constrained by expediency and the need for compromises, then so be it. Ultimately, external actors cannot change the destiny of a community; this change, if it is to be sustainable, must come from within. The fundamental dynamics of transition – in particular, the distribution of power – and the social complexion of a society, cannot be readily altered. But more than that, the communitarian argument holds that the people – their attitudes and perceptions – upon whom the chances of reconciliation finally rest, cannot be fundamentally changed by outside intervention.

How have these issues been played out in the two latest developments of international justice: Sierra Leone and Cambodia?

Sierra Leone: Independent Special Court

Sierra Leone's civil war began in 1991. The main protagonists were the government forces, the opposition Revolutionary United Front (RUF) and other rebel groups such as the Armed Forces Revolutionary Council. The conflict was characterized by atrocities against civilians – the defining image being the amputation of limbs – and the RUF has generally been seen as the worst perpetrator of such atrocities.[24] The Lomé Peace Agreement of July 1999 brought a temporary end to the conflict, involving a ceasefire, amnesty and representation in the government for the rebels. The agreement also called for the establishment of a Truth and Reconciliation Commission. However, the ceasefire did not hold, and the government approached the UN for assistance. On 14 August 2000 the UN Security Council passed a resolution by 15–0 vote to establish the 'independent special court'. It noted the 'prevailing situation of impunity' and the importance of individual accountability for war crimes in the interests of 'national reconciliation and...the restoration and maintenance of peace'. It stressed that earlier amnesty provisions attached to the Lomé agreement did not apply to crimes of genocide, crimes against humanity, and war crimes. While the Resolution was not explicitly passed under Chapter VII enforcement provisions – unlike in the case of Rwanda and the former Yugoslavia – the text did reiterate that the situation in Sierra Leone constituted a threat to international peace and security in the region, thus making an indirect allusion to Chapter VII. The tribunal in Sierra Leone is to try 'crimes against humanity, war crimes and other serious violations of international humanitarian law, as well as crimes under relevant Sierra Leone law committed within the territory of Sierra Leone'.[25] Coming just one month after the Security Council voted to ban diamond sales from the country under a Chapter VII mandatory embargo (resolution 1306 of 5 July 2000), the court appears to be a part of a belated but serious effort towards the reconstruction of Sierra Leone's basic security.

The Security Council Resolution relating to the special court left many things open, and a subsequent report by the Secretary-General filled in the details.[26] The special court will have three organs, similar to the International Tribunal for the former Yugoslavia: the chambers (two trial chambers and an appeals chamber); the prosecutor's office; and the registry. The trial and appeal chambers will each have five judges and be of mixed composition – some appointed by the government of Sierra Leone, and some by the UN Secretary-General in consultation with ECOWAS and the Commonwealth. The prosecutor will be appointed by the Secretary-General, with a local deputy appointed by the government. The registrar will be accountable to the Secretary-General. By making this a 'mixed court' it is hoped that it will learn from and avoid the experience of Rwanda and the former Yugoslavia, whose tribunals have been extremely slow in processing cases and extremely expensive. But more importantly, mixed courts combine international laws of accountability with local norms of justice, thus aiming to utilize and remain sensitive to 'communitarian' sources of legitimacy but also embrace international legal requirements. In the case of Rwanda – where a national court also addresses the same charges – the international tribunal has not won the confidence of the government, largely because of this slow process. The draft statute of the Sierra Leone court takes its authority from customary and convention law relating to crimes against humanity, violations of the Geneva Conventions and Protocol II relating to war crimes, and 'other serious violations of international humanitarian law'. It also explicitly incorporates Sierra Leoneon law, and explicitly waives any amnesty (Article 10). It is a sad reflection of the conflict that there is a section on 'juvenile offenders' and specific references to the crime of enlisting child soldiers and attacks on peacekeepers. The articles on child soldiers were among the most difficult upon which to reach agreement: where to apply responsibility and how to balance punishment with rehabilitation? Article 7 extends jurisdiction to persons over the age of 15; children between 15 and 18 ('juvenile offenders') will stand before a Juvenile Chamber to take their age and the need for rehabilitation into account.

There are a number of controversies, the solution of which will – or will not – have a strong bearing upon the credibility of the court if and when it is esbtablished. In terms of personal jurisdiction, Article 1 of the draft statute echoes the words of the Security Council Resolution in limiting the focus to 'persons most responsible for serious violations' since 30 November 1996. This flexible, but obviously pragmatic, terminology is bound to create controversy: how to legally define persons 'most responsible'? There are few, if any, legal precedents to such an approach, although the language appears to reflect the practice of previous tribunals, such as Rwanda and Yugoslavia. The temporal jurisdiction obviously means that the court will not hold anyone accountable for crimes committed since the start of the war in 1991 and 1996. This has caused consternation among activists in Sierra Leone due to the obvious window for impunity that this leaves open. There are also concerns about the relationship between the Court and the Truth and Reconciliation Commission. Clearly, if the Truth and Reconciliation

Commission seeks to establish an authoritative truth, individuals involved in human rights abuses would be wary of disclosing evidence that might be used against them in the special court. In addition, there remain doubts about the geographical remit of the court. The conflict in Sierra Leone must be seen in the context of regional conflict, and in particular that of Liberia. Many people hold Liberian President Charles Taylor partly, or largely, responsible for the conflict. A court that did not place responsibility at the real or underlying source of conflict would be a superficial exercise for many people.

Perhaps the biggest challenge concerns the inevitably political nature of the court in the context of the local situation. Part of the reason why the government has asked for international help and has been so supportive is because the most prominent prisoner to face the tribunal will be Foday Sankoh, leader of the rebel Revolutionary United Front, who undermined the 1999 peace settlement. Local observers even believe that the President of Sierra Leone has proposed the court as a means of trying RUF members and thus for his personal political aggrandizement. But Sankoh is not the only person responsible for atrocities, and human rights groups such as Amnesty International have called for the trial of other leaders, some of which are allied to the government in the context of the peace process, and even members of the government's armed forces: 'No single individual or party to the conflict should be singled out for prosecution to the exclusion of others. There should be a non-selective, balanced and independent prosecution policy. Trials should focus on those most responsible for the grave abuses of human rights committed since the conflict began in 1991, whether they are members of the Revolutionary United Front, the Armed Forces Revolutionary Council, the Sierra Leone Army, or the Civil Defence Forces, and regardless of their current political position or allegiance'.[27]

Certainly, such an even-handed approach would dispense with the taint of 'victor's justice', which will be the impression if the court is seen as something that works in the interest of the government and against the opposition, despite the fact that atrocities may have been perpetrated on both sides (albeit mainly by the RUF). A particularly sensitive issue here concerns the leaders of the Armed Forces Revolutionary Council under Johnny Paul Koroma, a former ally of the RUF, and associated with atrocities – but now in support of the government. In the event of a wide remit for the court, these commanders are unlikely to embrace the political peace process if they fear arrest and trial. If the court might try individuals associated with the government, would the government's support of the court remain, or would the court degenerate into a political sideshow? Activists campaigned successfully for an independent foreign prosecutor in the hope of ensuring impartiality. But there is scepticism among local human rights activists whether government allies will be scrutinized, and whether the appearance of 'victor's justice' can be avoided – which could re-ignite violence in the country and taint the credibility of the UN and international norms of justice.

As always, the pragmatic questions arise. Where to draw the line – is the general interest, which in Sierra Leone can mean peace, served by pursuing the worst abusers of human rights and accepting that others will evade justice? Transitional justice, especially when pursued simultaneously to a peace process, is inevitably a highly political process. Whether deliberate or not, the Security Council resolution relating to Sierra Leone has an inbuilt element of pragmatism to it, focusing upon 'persons who bear the greatest responsibility'. In the case of Sierra Leone, this is not an abstract philosophical concept: many people fear that the perception of wide trials may obstruct the process of disarmament, which means the continuance of weapons on the streets and the constant threat of violence.

The case of Sierra Leone is particularly sensitive because an earlier agreement basically imposed by the international community – in 1999 – included a fairly wide amnesty in the interests of the peace process. It obviously did not have a positive impact: the worst atrocities against civilians continued unabated after that agreement. That earlier approach – in effect giving Sankoh the diamond mines, a place in the government and an amnesty – was a failure, achieving neither peace nor justice. The UN subsequently backed away from the amnesty, and with the establishment of a joint national/international court under Security Council authorization, much will be at stake: it must meet a certain standard of thoroughness or risk the appearance of continuing impunity for political reasons. Yet few actors would risk a return to major violent conflict by apprehending suspects. Thus, as in the classical formula, does this mean that the balance of forces on the ground will determine the scope of justice and accountability?

Cambodia: International Justice in Doubt

Similar variables present themselves in the case of Cambodia. In the 1970s up to 1.7 million people died of mistreatment or starvation in Pol Pot's murderous social revolution. The various peace settlements that have taken place since the landmark 1991 Paris Accord have privileged peace and stability over justice. However in August 2001

King Norodom Sihanouk signed the Law on the Establishment of the Extraordinary Chambers in the Courts of Cambodia for the Prosecution of Crimes Committed During the Period of Democratic Kampuchea. This followed legislation passed in January 2001 to create such a tribunal, a resolution in the UN Human Rights Commission in April 2001 calling for the establishment of a tribunal, and a series of negotiations on the composition and nature of the court. Following the King's assent a memorandum of understanding was supposed to be established between the government and the UN. The Cambodian government is particularly sensitive about sovereignty and the mixed nature of the court, with foreign and Cambodian judges. But this is not just an issue of legal sovereignty: the government's sensitivity about the composition of the court reflects its concern that the process could have a negative impact on the delicate political situation in the country and the political deals struck among former protagonists. To detach the court from local political rivalries – which are in some ways still tied to the country's agenda of peace and reconstruction – would require a high level of independence and impartiality. Doubts remain as to whether the mixed nature of the court can achieve this, or indeed if it will even be established.

The appearance is that justice and accountability are finally being achieved in Cambodia. However, formidable challenges would have to be overcome for this to be the case. Throughout the 1990s peace and stability have been promoted above accountability for past atrocities. For example, in 1996 (then) Second Prime Minister Hun Sen pardoned Ieng Sen, a senior Khmer Rouge leader, in return for his defection. That defection was a serious blow to the remaining Khmer Rouge forces and certainly hastened their defeat and helped bring about a semblance of stability. Other high-profile suspected perpetrators of human rights abuse who are 'reformed' and now allied with the government have been given an amnesty, or are in the position to cause instability if they so desire. The government – including Prime Minister Hun Sen[28] – is not enthusiastic about 'reopening old wounds' and threatening to ignite instability. This is a sentiment widely shared in Cambodian society, after such a long period of instability and conflict. However, transnational pressures and norms are impinging upon the local political scene. The international donor community – upon whom Cambodia is dependent – is calling for the application of international standards of justice and accountability, despite the acquiescence (or complicity, according to some) of many Western members of the 'international community' during and after the Khmer Rouge years.

As with Sierra Leone, the number of indictees would be limited – perhaps 20 or less – but it is the position of such people rather than the overall number that will be the sensitive issue. If this process is seen to be unduly tainted by political factors – and in particular the compromises and pardons that have been awarded to former Khmer Rouge leaders – the credibility of the tribunal may be undermined. If it were over-zealous, it would not be in tune with the feelings of many Cambodians and the government to prioritize development and the consolidation of peace and democracy.[29] Local activists understand that, given the conflict of interests of the various parties involved (both Cambodian and international), it would be difficult to have a tribunal based on purely legal and moral grounds. But for the minimum of credibility and justice, the jurisdiction must be open; according to some, pardons should not be recognized, and jurisdiction should be a legal decision of the court. Indeed, there may be a tension between peace and justice, but this is not necessarily inflamed by focusing on the top echelon of the former Khmer Rouge leadership.[30]

Conclusion

Transnational (both regional and global) norms, laws and standards of human rights are playing an increasing role in transitional and post-conflict societies. The emergence of international regimes, tribunals and mixed courts is clearly having a significant impact upon transitional peace building. This appears to conform to the growing political consensus that some form of justice and accountability are integral *to* – and not necessarily in tension *with* – sustainable peace and stability. However, the question of when and where international norms of accountability and justice are applied is still a function of essentially political – rather than legal or moral – factors. The presence of international processes and standards in transitional peacebuilding processes is not altering a well-established fact of social life: in terms of dealing with past human rights abuse, the question of who is held accountable remains largely a political issue. Justice is a variable among a balance of values that a particular society must come to terms with.

International norms and institutions can only contribute to this process, in terms of the number of cases to which international institutions can be applied, and in terms of the dilemmas faced in those particular cases. Thus, international assistance cannot bring the solution; it can only assist local forces and actors, albeit in introducing more forcefully the presence of international standards of human rights and accountability. But this will not mean that international standards of accountability and human rights will apply in transitional societies: it will mean that these standards will be one among a number of factors that are balanced but which are not necessarily complementary. Transitional justice will continue to be as much a political as a legal and moral process. Not to realize this will result in unrealistically high expectations and undermine the credibility of international norms of justice and accountability. At the same time, 'mixed courts' – combining international laws of accountability with local norms of justice, thus aiming to utilize and remain sensitive to 'communitarian' sources of legitimacy but also embrace international legal requirements – offer real hope for promoting a sense of accountability at the international level, but also justice that is rooted in the reality and predilections of a particular society. But this will always be a sensitive balance, as Sierra Leone and Cambodia show.[31]

There are real limitations – for political, financial and practical reasons – upon the number of cases in which special courts or tribunals can be established, or that the International Criminal Court would be able to deliver judgment upon. This immediately raises a question of consistency: if international norms and standards are invoked in one case, then why not another? It is thus not a global norm, but a selective one. There are hundreds of situations in which grave human rights abuses, crimes against humanity, war crimes and torture have been or are being committed. Substantial international involvement cannot take place in every such case. Therefore, despite the interest in international tribunals and the International Criminal Court, resources must also be directed towards developing indigenous capacity in transitional situations because these dilemmas and challenges will most often have to be addressed locally. Kritz wrote that 'the ghosts of the past, if not exorcised to the fullest extent possible, will continue to haunt the nation tomorrow'.[32] This may well be true, but in volatile post-conflict societies justice must sometimes be weighed against other more immediate needs. And exorcising the ghosts of the past must be an issue for the communities involved as much as for international actors.

ACKNOWLEDGEMENTS

The author would like to acknowledge with thanks the feedback of Kao Kim Hourn, Executive Director and Senior Research Fellow of the Cambodian Institute for Cooperation and Peace in Phnom Penh, and Abdul Omoranike Babatunde Tejan-Cole, a barrister and solicitor in Freetown, Sierra Leone.

NOTES

1. A number of excellent volumes have been written or compiled in this area of 'transitional justice'. See, for example, the definitive three-volume collection by Neil J. Kritz (ed.), *Transitional Justice: How Emerging Democracies Reckon with Former Regimes*, Washington, DC: United States Institute of Peace Press, 1995; A. James McAdams (ed.), *Transitional Justice and the Rule of Law in New Democracies*, Notre Dame: University of Notre Dame Press, 1997; Naomi Roht-Arriaza (ed.), *Impunity and Human Rights in International Law and Practice*, New York: Oxford University Press, 1995. The journal *Ethics and International Affairs*, Vol.13, 1999, has a number of interesting contributions to the debate: David Crocker, 'Reckoning with Past Wrongs: A Normative Framework'; David Little, 'A Different Kind of Justice: Dealing with Human Rights Violations in Transitional Societies'; Susan Dwyer, 'Reconciliation for Realists'; and Margaret Popkin and Nehal Bhuta, 'Latin American Amnesties in Comparative Perspective: Can the Past Be Buried?', *Ethics and International Affairs*, Vol.13, 1999.
2. Neil J. Kritz, 'War Crimes Tribunals and Truth Commissions: Some Thoughts on Accountability Mechanisms for Mass Violations of Human Rights', paper presented at the USAID Conference Promoting Democracy, Human Rights, and Reintegration in Post-conflict Societies, 30–31 Oct. 1997, p.1.
3. Guillermo O'Donnell and Philippe Schmitter, *Transitions From Authoritarian Rule: Tentative Conclusions about Uncertain Democracies*, wrote of 'coaxing the military out of power and inducing them to tolerate a transition toward democracy', cited in Kritz (ed.), *Transitional Justice* (n.1 above), Vol.1, p.64.
4. José Zalaquett, 'Balancing Ethical Imperatives and Political Constraints: The Dilemmas of New Democracies Confronting Past Human Rights Violations', in Kritz (ed.), *Transitional Justice* (n.1 above), Vol.1.
5. Luc Huyse, 'Justice after Transitions: On the Choices Successor Élites Make in Dealing with the Past', in Kritz (ed.), (n.1 above), Vol.1, p.114.
6. See Kritz (ed.), *Transitional Justice* (n.1 above).
7. Neil J. Kritz, in introduction, Kritz (ed.), (n.1 above), Vol.1, p.xx.
8. Amnesty International's 'Policy Statement on Impunity' argues that 'Impunity negates the values of truth and justice and leads to the occurrence of further violations', in Kritz (ed.), (n.1 above), Vol.1, p.220; Human Rights Watch, 'Policy Statement on Accountability for Past Abuses', holds a similar position in rejecting the pragmatist argument of transitional circumstances, calling for the rejection of amnesties, even when applied to rebels or anti-government forces, and argues that popular disinclination to hold abuse accountable does not negate the duty of governments: 'it is not the prerogative of the many to forgive the commission of the crimes against the few', in ibid., p.220.
9. Hannah Arendt, *The Human Condition*, 2nd edition, Chicago: Chicago University Press, 1998, p.241.
10. Little (n.1 above), p.71.
11. Popkin and Bhuta (n.1 above), p.108.
12. See, for example, José Zalaquett, 'Confronting Human rights Violations Committed by former Governments: Principles Applicable and Political Constraints', in Kritz (ed.), (n.1 above), Vol.1, pp.14–17. Also Diane F. Orentlicher, 'Settling Accounts: The Duty to Prosecute Human Rights Violations of a Prior Regime': 'The threat of instability is minimized when prosecutions are backed by unambiguous international law whose requirements are confined within principled limits', in Kritz (ed.), *Transitional Justice*, Vol.1, p.412. See also the response to this: Carlos S. Nino, 'Response: The Duty to Punish Past Abuses of Human Rights Put into Context: The Case of Argentina', in Kritz (ed.), Vol.1.
13. Aryeh Neier, 'What Should be Done about the Guilty', in Kritz (ed.), (n.1 above), Vol.1, p.178.

14. See Popkin and Bhuta (n.1 above).
15. Thomas Buergenthal, 'The United Nations Truth Commission for El Salvador', in Kritz (ed.), (n.1 above), p.303.
16. *Financial Times*, 16 June 1998.
17. Richard Goldstone, 'War Crimes: A Question of Will', *The World Today*, April 1997, p.106. See also Theodor Meron, 'Answering for War Crimes: Lessons from the Balkans', *Foreign Affairs*, Jan.–Feb. 1997.
18. Jeanne L. Bakker, 'The Defence of Obedience to Superior Orders: the *Mens Rea* Requirement', in Kritz (ed.), (n.1 above), Vol.1, discusses the moral and legal difficulties of the due obedience argument.
19. Samuel P. Huntington, *The Third Wave. Democratization in the Late Twentieth Century*, Norman, OK, and London: University of Oklahoma Press, 1991, pp.114–17.
20. See, for example, Guillermo O'Donnell and Philippe Schmitter, 'Transitions from Authoritarian Rule: Tentative Conclusions about Uncertain Democracies', in Kritz (ed.), *Transitional Justice* (n.1 above), Vol.1, p.61.
21. See, for example, Theodor Meron, 'War Crimes Law Comes of Age', *American Journal of International Law*, July 1998.
22. See, for example, Goldstone (n.17 above).
23. Geoffrey Hawthorn describes this as 'new international law' and 'new international politics', in 'Pinochet: The politics', *International Affairs*, Vol.75, No.2, 1999.
24. For example, 'Sierra Leone: Sowing Terror Atrocities against Civilians in Sierra Leone', *Human Rights Watch*, July 1998, Vol.10, No.3; 'Sierra Leone: Getting Away with Murder, Mutilation and Rape', *Human Rights Watch*, A/1103, July 1999.
25. Security Council Resolution 1315, 14 Aug. 2000, para. 2. See also See Boris Kondach and Rita Sileck, 'Special Court for Sierra Leone', *Conflict Trends*, No.1, 2001. The African Centre for the Constructive Resolution of Disputes, South Africa, No.1, 2001.
26. Report of the Secretary-General on the establishment of a Special Court for Sierra Leone, S/2000/915, 4 Oct. 2000.
27. 'Sierra Leone: Ending impunity – an opportunity not to be missed', Amnesty International, AI-index: AFR 51/061/2000, 26 July 2000, internet document.
28. *South China Morning Post*, 7 Aug. 2001.
29. Correspondence to the author by two Cambodian analysts.
30. Kim Hourn, correspondence to author, 12 Sept. 2001.
31. In February 2002 the UN announced that it would no longer negotiate on preparations for the court with the Cambodian authorities. The announcement stated that as currently envisaged, the Cambodian court would not guarantee independence, impartiality and objectivity. Unless negotiations are reopened, the Cambodian government will now have the option of proceeding with its plan for a tribunal without the endorsement of the international community. The decision was not a surprise to those who felt that the government of Cambodia was not serious about the court – or not serious about genuinely upholding international standards. It is too early to conclude whether the idea is truly dead or whether the mixed court can be revived. But it *is* possible to suggest that the inevitably political nature of justice and accountability in Cambodia – as in many other societies – does not always mix well with an emerging norm of transnational legal accountability.
32. José Zalaquett, 'Balancing Ethical Imperatives Against Political Constraints: The Dilemma of New Democracies Confronting Past Human Rights Violations', in Kritz (ed.), (n.1 above), Vol.1, p.205.

The UN, Peacekeeping and Collective Human Security: From *An Agenda for Peace* to the Brahimi Report

SORPONG PEOU

The study of peace operations has grown substantially, in large part due to the increasing number of UN missions to conflict-ridden states since the end of the Cold War in the 1990s. Much of what has been written tends to focus on the rising policy-making demand for peacemaking, peacekeeping, peacebuilding and humanitarian intervention. Policy makers in national governments and international agencies alike have had to deal with intra-state conflicts and their humanitarian effects by concentrating on the planning, design, and implementation of peace missions. Overall, the literature on peace operations is said to suffer from what Roland Paris calls a 'cult of policy relevance' to the neglect of meta-theoretical insights found in the political science literature.[1] To a large extent, this is a fair assessment. Between March and December 2000 alone, the UN put out several major reports with over 300 recommendations on how to enhance UN capacities in undertaking peace operations.[2]

UN peace operations should, however, be seen as part of a broader theoretical framework based on the novel concept of 'collective human security'. The concept became an integral part of positive peace and gave new direction for the peace movements from the 1980s. *An Agenda for Peace*, first published in 1992 by Boutros Boutros-Ghali has further given rise to new thinking about human security. The Brahimi Report (2000) then expands on this vision for world peace and remains part of the idealist faith in the potential for human emancipation. The concept of collective human security embedded in recent UN thinking differs from that of national security: the former focuses on the individual, as opposed to the latter whose emphasis is placed on the state, as the referent point for security. At the same time, the UN vision for human security should be viewed in collective terms: it not only stresses the need to meet basic human needs and to promote distributive justice and political participation but also points out that human security can be achieved through collective intervention action.

The new UN vision for world peace, therefore, challenges the traditional value of order, which rejects interventionism, and expands universal values that acknowledge the unity of humanity, such as social justice, democracy, human rights and humanitarian intervention.

This essay argues that 'collective human security' has challenged the traditional concept of national security, but the UN will need to think more seriously about how to overcome the existing hurdles, also acknowledged in the Brahimi Report.

Why the Brahimi Report? Some Background

The Brahimi Report was a byproduct of the UN leadership's dimming vision to build world peace inspired by *An Agenda for Peace*, which lays the conceptual foundation of collective human security, and resulted from the UN failure to turn that vision into reality. A brief discussion of *An Agenda for Peace* helps shed light on this point. In the aftermath of the Cold War, this landmark report took a bold step in defiance of the realist conception of national security rooted in selfish human nature and international anarchy. It took into account the persisting problems of social injustice and violent culture as independent variables explaining war and violence. It envisaged a system of security that de-emphasized the need to serve the interests of powerful states (a realist understanding of international politics)[3] and considered viable institutional constraints on war-prone state behaviour (a neo-liberal promise for peace).[4] Furthermore, *An Agenda for Peace* presents a genuine challenge to the internationalist, legalistic concept of state sovereignty-based collective security (rooted in the Wilsonian logic of balancing aggression against member states).

The state is no longer seen as the absolute referent point for security. Although Boutros-Ghali took a cautious approach by reaffirming that 'in...situations of internal crisis, the United Nations will need to respect the sovereignty of states',[5] he points out that '[the] time of absolute and exclusive sovereignty...has passed. Its theory was never matched by reality.' He added: 'It is the task of leaders of states today to understand this and to find a balance between the needs of good internal governance and the requirements of an ever more interdependent world.'[6] The UN vision for world peace is built upon the growing realization that inter-state conflict is on the wane and that intra-state conflict has grown more prevalent. The concept of peace in *An Agenda for Peace* was not simply the absence of war between member states. It favours the concept of 'human security',[7] closely related to the radical concept of positive peace associated with social justice and democracy, rather than the traditional concept of national security. Human security is, in broad terms, 'freedom from want' and 'freedom from fear' with reference to individual human beings, not states, as the referent object for security. When it comes to the question of what is being secured against, however, human security is also subject to interpretation.[8]

Particularly noteworthy in *An Agenda for Peace* is the UN's renewed commitment to the protection of human rights with special sensitivity to those of ethnic, religious, social and linguistic minorities. This implies that individuals' rights as human beings are legitimate and cannot be made subservient to states' rights under the tradition of international law based on state sovereignty. Human rights law, although still unenforceable, poses a new challenge to the traditional conception of international society and gives rise to the idea of global community based on the rule of law.

As to the question of what is being secured against, *An Agenda for Peace* provides a comprehensive perspective. Human insecurity includes deprivation of basic human needs rooted in ecological damage, disruption of family and community life, unchecked population growth, crushing debt burdens, barriers to trade, and the growing disparity between rich and poor.[9] Human security also looks beyond the fierce new assertions of nationalism and sovereignty to include brutal ethnic, religious, social, cultural or linguistic strife, seen as threatening the cohesion of states. The threats to 'social peace' include actions against human welfare: greater intrusion into the lives and rights of individuals, new assertions of discrimination and exclusion, and lack of democratic participation. Unconventional sources of insecurity are also acknowledged; they include drug trafficking and acts of terrorism seeking to undermine evolution and change through democratic means. In the broadest possible sense, 'the deepest causes of conflict include economic despair, social injustice, and political oppression'.[10]

On the question of who provides for security, *An Agenda for Peace* advocates collective action broader than conventional state-centric collective security. The organization is now seen as more than a community of independent states led by the Security Council entrusted with the primary responsibility for the maintenance of international peace and security. The UN represents a global community where the General Assembly and all the functional elements of the UN system share this collective responsibility and where regional and non-governmental organizations also play a role in an integrated approach to human security.[11]

On the question of what methods are to be undertaken to provide for security, *An Agenda for Peace* partly rests on an optimistic assessment that global trends favour liberal ideas. That is, 'authoritarian regimes have given way to more democratic forces and responsive Governments'.[12] Democracy is also possible within a community of nations: 'Democracy at all levels is essential to attain peace for a new era of prosperity and justice'.[13] *An Agenda for Peace* thus calls for collective action to achieve this end.

An Agenda for Peace's strategy for peace becomes more intrusive: it ranges from preventive diplomacy to peacemaking to peacekeeping to peacebuilding to humanitarian intervention – all of which aim to build human security. Logically, *An Agenda for Peace* advocates the need for military enforcement of humanitarian aid delivery and its proactive support of forceful humanitarian interventionism. The idea of law enforcement is implicit in *An Agenda for Peace*, whose 1992 version makes scant reference to humanitarian assistance to civilians during continuing warfare and in designated areas; however, the 1995 version gives more serious thought to this operation.[14] The UN under the leadership of Boutros-Ghali also sought better ways to enhance UN peace operations by proposing a 'rapid deployment force', which might comprise battalion-sized units from a number of countries.[15] It makes sense to conceptualize the UN strategy for peace as collective human security.

How close has UN idealism come to reality? UN peace operations have multiplied. Since the late 1980s, the UN has also sought to transform political systems in war-torn countries by getting warring parties to reach a democratic agreement, by organizing free and fair elections, by helping to create democratic institutions, and by assisting in the process of reforming domestic economies. The UN has made efforts to enforce humanitarian and human rights law. In 1993, the UN Security Council established the International Criminal Tribunal for the Former Yugoslavia, where the former president of Serbia, Slobodan Milosevic, now stands trial. In 1994, it also created the International Criminal Court for Rwanda. The UN can apply humanitarian law and hold violators of human rights accountable for their actions. The UN has also put considerable pressure on Cambodia to bring to justice Khmer Rouge leaders who committed crimes against humanity during their 1975–78 reign of terror. Kofi Anann observed that in the worst cases of human rights abuse, state sovereignty may have to give way to higher, humanitarian precepts.

To date, however, not all has gone to plan. *An Agenda for Peace* has had a limited impact on global peace in general. By 1995, Boutros-Ghali had become less upbeat about his agenda for peace in his acknowledgement that neither the Security Council nor the Secretary-

General had the capacity to take enforcement action 'except perhaps on a very limited scale'. He then added that 'the financial foundations of the Organization daily grew weaker, debilitating its political will and practical capacity to undertake new and essential activities',[16] and that 'the Organization is resource-starved and hard pressed to handle the less demanding peacemaking and peacekeeping responsibilities'.[17] At the end of the twentieth century, the UN had failed to deliver on its promises.

The Brahimi Report begins with a reminder of the UN Charter's original objective – 'to save succeeding generations from the scourge of war' – but acknowledges that the organization 'has repeatedly failed to meet the challenge'. In its admirably frank assessment of the UN's existing capabilities, the Report admits that it 'can do no better today'.[18] Unsurprisingly, the Report offers more recommendations to enhance its capacities.

The Brahimi Report's Renewed Vision for Collective Human Security

The report was the byproduct of a series of brainstorming sessions among prominent practitioners, aimed at finding better ways to improve future UN peace operations.[19] The ultimate goal of this report is to enable the UN to promote global peace and security based the novel concept of collective human security.

The report seriously questions the traditional argument that the state is the only legitimate provider of security. Its overall conceptual framework fits more comfortably with the logic of collective human security; while it does not totally reject the traditional role of member states in international peace and security, the report refers to the UN as 'the universal organization', not simply as an international organization. The UN is urged to take the initiative 'to reach out to the institutions of civil society and to strengthen relations with non-governmental organizations, academic institutions, and the media, who can be useful partners in the promotion of peace and security for all'. In its words: 'People everywhere are fully entitled to consider that it is their organization, and as such to pass judgment on its activities and the people who serve in it'.[20]

The report's approach to security builds on three basic methods that can also be found in *An Agenda for Peace*: conflict prevention and peacemaking, peacebuilding and peacekeeping, all of which can be integrated to make peace operations more effective. Conflict prevention and peacemaking are conventional methods of conflict resolution but receive little attention in the report. Conflict prevention is based on diplomatic efforts aimed at addressing structural sources of conflict in order to build a solid foundation for peace. Peacemaking depends on diplomacy and mediation as tools employed by individuals or groups in an attempt to bring to a halt conflicts in progress. Although the concept of collective human security is not explicit in the report, what the Panel has in mind is not simply a peace process leading to the end of inter-state or intra-state violence and war. In its vision to promote human security through collective action, particularly peacekeeping and peacebuilding, the report views peace operations as multidimensional and urges the UN to give more attention to the need for developing inseparable partnership between peacekeepers and peacebuilders.

As a method for promoting human security, peacebuilding includes, but is not limited to, meeting basic human needs, such as education and a demonstrable improvement in the quality of life for people in peace mission areas. More notably, this method is social, legal and political in its orientation: reintegrating former combatants into civil society, strengthening the rule of law, improving respect for human rights and providing technical assistance for democratic development. The report sees the need to include sufficient numbers of international judicial experts, penal experts and human-rights specialists to help strengthen domestic rule-of-law institutions.[21] The Report also makes it clear that 'Free and fair' elections should be held with a view to strengthening governance institutions and that they 'need the support of a broader process of democratization and civil society building that includes effective civilian governance and a culture of respect for basic human rights'. Elections should not 'merely ratify a tyranny of the majority or be overturned by force after a peace operation leaves'.[22] Furthermore, peacebuilding includes actions dealing with unconventional security issues, such as landmines and health.

The report also devotes considerable attention to the role of peacekeeping in promoting human security. The UN must have capacities to deploy its peace operations rapidly and effectively. According to the report, the first six to twelve weeks following a ceasefire or peace accord is often the most critical period for establishing both a stable peace and the credibility of the peacekeepers.[23] Although it recognizes variations in timelines for rapid and effective deployment, the Panel proposes that traditional peacekeeping operations be fully deployed within 30 days of the adoption of a Security Council resolution, and complex peace operations and their mission headquarters within 90 and 15 days, respectively. The report recommends that a revolving 'on-call' list' of about 100 military officers and 100 police officers be created in the Standby Arrangements System (UNSAS) to be available on seven days' notice.

When asked, the report insists, the universal organization must have its international forces 'prepared to confront the lingering forces of war and violence, with the ability and determination to defeat them'. The UN should thus be able to deploy 5,000 troops 'as a brigade formation, not as a collection of battalions that are unfamiliar with one another's doctrine, leadership and operational practices'. They should come from a group of countries that have been working together and could 'develop common training, equipment standards, common doctrine, and common arrangements for the operational control of the force'.[24] The report thus makes it clear that the UN should not be asked to undertake international peace operations in too many places. Moreover, the report stresses the need to ensure compatibility between clear, credible and achievable mandates on the one hand and capabilities on the other. Clear, credible and achievable mandates should contain several components. They should meet such threshold conditions as consistency with international human-rights standards and practicability of specified tasks and timelines. The UN Security Council's draft resolutions should authorize missions with sizeable troop levels. The requirements of peacekeeping operations in potentially dangerous situations should meet such needs as a clear chain of command and unity of effort. When formulating or changing mission mandates, the Secretariat must tell the Security Council what it needs to know, not what it wants to hear.[25]

Perhaps the most significant aspect in the report is the section on 'implications for peacekeeping doctrine and strategy'. On the one hand, the report recognizes that the UN 'does not wage war'[26] and reaffirms the doctrine of peacekeeping, where the consent of adversaries, and peacekeepers' impartiality and their right to self-defence 'should remain the bedrock principles'.[27] It does not endorse enforcement, for such action 'has consistently been entrusted to coalitions of willing States, with the authorization of the Security Council, acting under Chapter VII of the Charter'.[28]

On the other hand, the report seeks to modify the doctrine by moving in the direction of collective peace enforcement, echoing Secretary-General Kofi Anann's earlier calls for the use of force against evil. Inconspicuously worded, one of the panel's recommendations envisages UN peacekeepers balancing against aggression. The principles of consent and impartiality can no longer be taken for granted. Peacekeepers must not only adopt the principle of extended deterrence by defending themselves, other mission components and their mandates, but they must also be equipped and empowered to fight aggressors. Peacekeepers may reject 'a policy of appeasement' by not adhering to the principle of impartiality – that is, the UN should not be equal in the way it 'treat[s] all parties in all cases for all times'.[29] The report makes a clear distinction between 'obvious aggressors' and 'victims' defined in moral terms: it is based on the understanding that 'local parties' are not always 'moral equals'.[30] This distinction is compatible with the concept of collective security defined in terms of balancing against aggression,[31] and justifies the collective use of force on both operational and moral grounds. The report relies on the Security Council's Resolution 1296 (2000), which states that 'the targeting of civilians in armed conflict and the denial of humanitarian access to civilian populations afflicted by war may themselves constitute threats to international peace and security'. The UN's peace strategy then 'must not apply best-case planning assumptions to situations where the local actors have historically exhibited worst-case behavior', and its 'mandates should specify an operation's authority to use force'.[32] The report also makes it clear that 'United Nations forces for complex operations should be sized and configured so as to leave no doubt in the minds of would-be spoilers as to which of the two approaches the Organization has adopted'. Also, '[such] forces should be afforded the field intelligence and other capabilities needed to mount a defense against violent challenges'[33] and should thus be able to 'oppose obvious evil', such as that which took place in Rwanda.[34]

The report further recommends that the UN headquarters be better equipped to deal with violence and war around the world. To prevent conflict, according to the report, the UN will need an Executive Committee on Peace and Security (ECPS) Information and Strategic Analysis Secretariat (EISAS) to be involved in intelligence-gathering or fact-finding aimed at accumulating knowledge about conflict situations. The ECPS is also asked to present a plan to strengthen the permanent capacity of the UN to develop peace-building strategies and to implement programmes in support of those strategies. More financial resources for headquarters support offices (whose total costs do not exceed $50 million per year and represent 2 per cent of the peacekeeping costs) are needed. The report also makes clear that a larger staff is necessary. At present, the UN headquarters employs only 32 officers who provide military planning and guidance to 27,000 troops in the field, 9 civilian police who provide guidance for up to 8,600 police, and 15 political desk officers for 14 current operations and 2 new ones.[35]

The method of selecting effective mission leaders should be systematic, beginning with the compilation of a comprehensive list of responsible individuals, who should be assembled as early as possible and who should receive strategic guidance and plans for anticipating and overcoming challenges to mandate implementation.

The report also calls for further steps to be taken to ensure effective action and better coordination among the UN Secretariat's key implementing departments in peace and security, including the establishment of Integrated Mission Task Forces (IMTFs). Staff seconded to them should come from throughout the UN system; they should plan new missions and help them reach full deployment. The panelists also see the need to make structural adjustments within and without the Department of Peacekeeping Operations (DPKO) and outside the UN Secretariat. Within the DPKO, the Military and Civilian Division should be reorganized into two separate divisions; the Field Administration and Logistics Division should also be divided into two. The existing Lessons Learned Unit should be strengthened and put in the DPKO Office of Operations. The number of Assistant Secretaries-General in the DPKO should be increased from two to three. Outside the DPKO, there should be a unit for operational planning and support of public information in peace operations. Public information planning and support at headquarters and elements of the Department of Political Affairs (DPA), particularly the electoral unit, should also be strengthened. The ability of the UN High Commissioner for Human Rights to plan and support the human-rights components of peace operations would need to be further reinforced.[36]

In short, the Brahimi Report's vision fits nicely with the concept of collective human security, as its authors endeavour to bring the UN vision outlined in *An Agenda for Peace* closer to reality by offering more concrete steps towards building world peace. The panel's vision rests on the faith that the UN as a universal organization should be capable of playing a deeper role in the defence of universal moral standards embedded in the concept of positive peace associated with human security. The question is whether the report will achieve what *An Agenda for Peace* has not.

Overall, the Brahimi Report is moving in the right direction. The Report has now received a comprehensive review offering more modest, more cautious recommendations for implementation. In his report dated 28 May 2001, Kofi Anann expresses his support for most of the recommendations made by the Brahimi-led team but cautioned and recommended against others. Among them are the Brahimi Report's proposal that procurement and budgeting authority be delegated from the Department of Management to the Department of Peacekeeping Operations and his proposal that a small new multidisciplinary policy and analysis unit be a more modest alternative to EISAS. Although the Secretary-General proposes three options that would enable the UN to deploy peacekeeping operations effectively within 30–90-day timeframes, he warns that none of them would achieve this objective. He further states that 'this can only be achieved by the provision of fully self-sustaining and completely self-sufficient troops provided by Member States with the means to do so'.[37]

Ultimately, both the Brahimi-led team and Kofi Annan agree on two major challenges: for the UN to perform its tasks as recommended, it would need the full support of both the Security Council and the member states; it would also depend on the parties to conflict themselves. The Secretariat can only do its part. The question then is whether member states will be willing to do all that is required to ensure that peace operations succeed and whether parties to conflict will cooperate with the UN. We have no way of predicting what states and other global actors would do in the future, but the UN vision for world peace raises several difficult questions to be discussed next.

The Challenge for Collective Human Security

History, theoretical insights, and existing evidence still show that states in today's world are unlikely to take rapid collective action to provide security as a global public good. It is unclear whether the UN's recommendations on structural adjustments within the UN system, even if fully implemented, would make peace operations truly effective. The UN would still be in no position to carry out a NATO-type operation in war zones. For the UN to be able to act rapidly, as recommended by the report, it must be equipped with the capacity to coordinate airlift operations. But this key aspect of effective peace operations receives no attention in the report. Ultimately the UN would have to rely on powerful states' cooperation. The fact that collective action among UN members in a multipolar world – a world that is now emerging in realists' eyes[38] – makes it harder for states to overcome the problem of free riding.[39] Yet a multipolar world will make it harder for the UN to mobilize and coordinate troops from different UN members on an ad hoc, collective basis.[40] The UN has now grown to 189 members, which has already complicated its ability to coordinate their activities. If more numerous non-state actors get actively involved in the planning and implementing process, there is no guarantee for effective coordination among peacebuilders. If a multipolar world is also based on multiculturalism,[41] the challenge for human emancipation defined in universal terms becomes even greater. Still another serious challenge to collective action lies in the fact that sources of insecurity have fast multiplied, ranging from conventional to unconventional threats to human welfare.

There is also ample scepticism about states' willingness to take collective action at their own expense to provide security to the citizens of other states. State sovereignty may have now become less absolute, as Boutros-Ghali indicates, but it has not been 'wholly subverted'.[42] Whether states will become more idealistic in their commitment to the UN vision for world peace remains to be seen.[43] The Brahimi Report also recognizes the limits of states' willingness to make sacrifices. In its words: 'Reluctance to accept [the risks of casualties] has grown since the difficult missions of the mid-1990s, partly because Member States are not clear about how to define their national interests in taking such risks and partly because they may be unclear about the risks themselves'.[44]

If we compare the levels of willingness and commitment by four different types of UN member states – poor/developing, wealthy/ developed, powerful and democratic – it becomes clear that none of them is likely to be of greater assistance to the UN in peace operations, and this immediately calls into question the viability of a multilateral system of peace and security on a grand scale. Poor states are unable to do much. On financial grounds, poor states are simply incapable of making any meaningful contributions. Developing countries have done more than developed countries in terms of troop contributions (77 per cent of the troops deployed in UN operations, as of the end of June 2000, came from developing countries),[45] but they depend heavily on the latter's financial support.

Evidence also shows that wealthy states have become less politically and financially responsible since the Cold War ended, despite their tendencies to dominate the UN system. According to the Brahimi Report, 'no developed country currently contributes troops to the most difficult United Nations-led peacekeeping operations from a security perspective, namely the United Nations Mission in Sierra Leone (UNAMSIL) and the United Nations Organization Mission in the Democratic Republic of the Congo (MONUC)'.[46] To be fair, developed states have paid most of the bills for UN peace operations, which amount to about $100 billion in the 1990s. But they have since done less. The United States remains among the most financially delinquent UN members. It is also unclear whether Japan will continue to contribute as much as it has; it has complained about making more financial contributions to the UN than four of the five permanent members of the Security Council (China, France, Russia and the United Kingdom), although it is itself not a permanent member. Most worrisome, developed countries' foreign aid has declined noticeably in recent years: they have done less, not more, to help alleviate socioeconomic conditions in poor countries, despite their pledges in 1997 to relieve the latter's debt burdens.[47]

More powerful states – the third type – are even less willing to contribute their troops to UN peace operations. In the recent past, they viewed the security of small states as a non-issue in international relations.[48] The permanent members of the Security Council have contributed few troops to peace operations. They often fail to agree on peacekeeping requirements. The Council failed to act quickly in Rwanda, even when reliably informed that violence was already under way. Rather than adding more troops to the existing 2,500-strong peacekeeping force, as requested in 1994, the Council cut the number to a tenth. The same can be said about the Council's actions on the Bosnian war: when Boutros-Ghali asked for 34,000 troops, the Council gave him only 7,400. The Council also hesitated to send troops to deter widespread violence in East Timor. Whenever they make substantial contributions, they do so within their regional strategic alliances. Three of the permanent members (France, Britain and the US), for instance, have contributed sizeable forces to the NATO-led forces in the Balkans.

Liberal democracies – the fourth type – have not been entirely reliable, either. In theory, they should be willing to act in defence of human freedom.[49] When they put clear emphasis on the promotion of democracy, liberal states can help achieve this objective.[50] But when one examines the level of sacrifice by liberal democracies, evidence remains far from conclusive. Liberal democracies may be slow in taking action because of the difficulties they have 'in convincing their national legislatures and public that they should support the deployment of their troops to United Nations-led operations'.[51]

Evidently, the military involvement of democratic states still largely depends on whether or not their interests are at stake. The Brahimi Report takes note of this problem, as developed and democratic countries 'tend not to see their strategic interests at stake'. They have devoted most of their well-trained, well-equipped national military forces to keeping the peace in the Balkans and neglected much-needed peace operations in other regions.[52] Africa, where nearly two-thirds of the 100,000 people killed in worldwide conflicts during the period of January–August 2000, has received the least attention from democratic states. The report bemoans the reality of this situation: 'NATO military planners would not have agreed to deploy to Sierra Leone with only the 6,000 troops initially authorized...the likelihood of a KFOR-type operation being deployed in Africa in the near future seems remote given the current trends'.[53]

It remains unclear how the new UN vision can offer an effective strategy even for negative peace (an end to armed conflict), not to mention positive peace. The doctrinal shift from traditional peacekeeping to peace enforcement in the form of coercive humanitarian intervention remains conceptually problematic.

If the UN is unable to deploy its troops promptly, it is unlikely to prevent massive political violence, which 'can be inflicted faster than the West can learn of and deploy intervention forces to stop it'. Even 'if the West relies mainly on military intervention to prevent genocide and ethnic cleansing, it is doomed to failure', and to 'stop such violence, the West must concentrate on averting its outbreak in the first place'.[54] Unfortunately, less powerful, poor or war-torn states often find any form of political or military interventionism threatening. Connie Peck complains about the lack of progress after *An Agenda for Peace*. She asserts that the clash between UN hawks (sceptics of 'preventive diplomacy') and UN doves (those who think that the concept would permit great power domination and intervention encouraging 'the thin end of another neo-colonial wedge') has stood in the way of real change.[55] During a series of dialogues in Africa, Asia, Latin America and Europe held in February and March 2001, representatives from the non-European regions expressed scepticism about what the UN can do. Representatives from Latin America, especially those from larger and wealthier states, expressed a degree of distrust of UN conflict prevention and humanitarian intervention. Latin American states are committed to the principle of non-interference in domestic affairs by outside powers. Participants from Africa questioned the commitment of the UN and the great powers to helping Africa and called for the strengthening of Africa's own capacity for conflict management and peace operations.[56] In Asia, the role of regional organizations in managing intra-state conflicts, such as those in Aceh of Indonesia and Sri Lanka, received more attention than that of the UN. The ten-member Association of Southeast Asian Nations (ASEAN) remains committed to non-interference in the domestic affairs of states by outside powers. The proposed EISAS has already been sidelined, as the Secretary-General preferred to wait for 'further study' – an indication that some member states found it alarming.[57]

Military intervention may even perpetuate struggles for power among adversaries and most likely leads to failure. Connie Peck makes an excellent point: 'coercion is often met with counter-coercion and "reactance". Counter-coercion simply means that the side uses power tactics in return, setting off a power struggle'.[58] When used to compel one party or another to submit, power is seen as counter-productive. Victory through military submission and defeat within war-torn states does not even guarantee negative peace. Between 1989 and 1993, such victory was achieved in only 17 of 41 cases of conflict termination and it remains precarious, but 'victory in a large number of cases turns out to be elusive and more difficult than expected'.[59]

Caught in a security dilemma, armed adversaries are more concerned about the immediate threat to their survival and security than about what the UN might do to them in the future. According to Robert Paper, punishment 'is likely to succeed only when the [target actors'] resolve is low'.[60] Denial, which should be part of the strategy of compellance, works better than punishment.[61] When compulsion is necessary, the objective is not to punish, but to prevent target actors from achieving their goals by ruining target actors' capabilities 'in ways that undermine [their] expectations of military successes', including supply lines and communication networks.[62] Unless the UN is sufficiently equipped to wage a large-scale war (as the North Atlantic Treaty Organization was in Kosovo in 1999), military operations involve enormous risks:[63] such forceful intervention tends to create its own dynamic of escalating violence.[64]

Moreover, it remains unclear that forceful intervention can effectively build positive peace in the short or immediate term. Most, if not all, adversaries in violent conflict have violated human rights in varying degrees. If applied consistently, the human-rights perspective that seeks to promote positive peace retributively may work against negative peace. The paradox in the logic of democratic/human rights and that of peacekeeping poses a question of how the two can be reconciled. Will human-rights violators mired in violent conflict be willing to welcome UN peace operations?

Even if the UN succeeds in balancing aggression, it remains unclear how human security can be promoted collectively. John Ruggie, for instance, argues that the 'balance of forces' in Cambodia 'created enough space for the UN operation to pursue its non-military objectives, including the repatriation of refugees and conducting a nation-wide election to constitute a legitimate government'.[65] Cambodia has now become more stable under the dominant leadership of Hun Sen, who came to power in 1979, but the UN intervention in the early 1990s did not end the war, which continued until 1998. Since early 1991, the donor community has spent close to US$5 billion on

Cambodia, but its nascent democracy remains precarious and the violation of human rights continues. The country has also become Southeast Asia's most attractive place for transnational crime. As another example, in Kosovo, whether the KLA will be willing and able to promote democratic and human rights after NATO leaves one day remains a big question mark.

One problem that often stands in the way of reaching democratic compromise is the persistence of asymmetrical power relations among adversaries. Both proponents of democratic peace and realists can agree on some democratic realism: a certain balance of power may be a key prerequisite for peace and democratic emergence. There are liberal thinkers, such as Bruce Russett, who remain convinced that liberal norms – democratic norms of conflict resolution, such as respect for minority rights – may be more powerful than structural and institutional constraints.[66] At the same time, Russett concedes that norms 'may be violated and break down'.[67] Just as institutional constraints – a structure of powers, checks and balances – could make it more difficult for democratic leaders to initiate war, they could also make it harder for political leaders to resort to repressive violence against their own citizens.[68] In war-torn and authoritarian states, institutional checks and balances do not exist; only warring factions do. If the logic of institutional checks and balances applies, a certain balance of factional force may be a precondition for democratic emergence. Lake and Rothchild make a good observation: 'When the balance of ethnic power remains stable ... well-crafted contracts enable ethnic groups to avoid conflict despite their differing policy preferences'.[69]

Unfortunately, military action against aggression often works against the logic of democratic balancing. By seeking to punish peace 'spoilers' for their uncooperative behaviour, the UN may not necessarily succeed in building and nurturing democracy. In transnational conflict, it is often difficult to determine the aggressor in the first place.[70] Even if the aggressor can be clearly identified, it remains unclear if military action against it will lead to democracy. Both Lake and Rothchild imply in effect that aggressive spoilers may simply be those most vulnerable in the process of peace-contract making. A less powerful group, they point out, is much more reluctant than a more powerful group when it comes to striking a peace deal and sticking to it.[71]

Conclusion

The Brahimi Report can be seen in the context of recent UN thinking on human security. Humanitarian interventionism as part and parcel of collective human security still raises a number of difficult questions associated with the UN's ability to make good on its promises to regions where its assistance is needed. The main theoretical challenge to the UN's grand idealist vision is to demonstrate not only that individual human beings matter more than states, but also that states are now losing control and becoming less relevant and less capable of performing their traditional task in providing security for their citizens. Unfortunately, evidence still invites caution. States are not about to be relegated to the dustbin of history, nor are they becoming much more willing or able to act against their own interests or at their expense. If states were indeed losing control and relevance, then the UN would face an even greater challenge: their questionable ability to take collective action. The trouble with the unwillingness and inability of developing countries to cooperate with one another is strongly correlated with their structural weaknesses perpetuating internal turbulence that often spreads beyond borders and destabilizes their regions. If states were fully incapacitated, the next question would be whether non-state actors could replace them in providing for security. The free-rider problem would pose an even greater challenge to collective action, especially in a world experiencing an increasing number of states, a proliferation of non-state actors, and growing sources of insecurity. Evidence has also shown that military intervention alone cannot effectively prevent massive political violence or promote human security.

We need to ask more serious questions: who exactly can provide for security and how can collective action be taken? We should never stop thinking about promoting human security collectively but will need to find a recipe more powerful than making countless policy recommendations for change and then conveniently saying that all depends on the political will of UN member states and that of parties to conflict.

NOTES

1. Roland Paris, 'Broadening the Study of Peace Operations', *International Studies Review*, Vol.2, No.3, fall 2000, pp.27 and 44.
2. The report of the Special Committee on Peacekeeping Operations, UN Doc., A/54/839, 20 March 2000; the Report of the Panel on United Nations Peace Operations, UN Doc., A/55/305-S/2000/809, 21 Aug. 2000; the UN Secretary-General's report on the implementation of the Panel's report, A/55/502, 20 Oct. 2000; the Special Committee's response to the Panel's report, UN Doc., A/C.4/55/6, 4 Dec. 2000.
3. This is a rejection of realism, which tends to see peace operations as mere reflections of major powers' strategic interests in international politics. John Mearsheimer, 'The False Promise of International Institutions', in Michael Brown et al. (eds), *Theories of War and Peace*, Cambridge, MA: MIT Press, 1998; Joseph Grieco, *Cooperation Among Nations*, Ithaca, NY: Cornell University Press, 1990; Kenneth Waltz, *Theory of International Politics*, Reading, MA: Addison-Wesley, 1979.
4. Robert Keohane, *International Institutions and State Power*, Boulder, CO: Westview Press, 1989.

THE UN, PEACEKEEPING AND COLLECTIVE HUMAN SECURITY 67

5. Boutros Boutros-Ghali, *An Agenda for Peace*, 1992, p.9; for the 1995 version (n.44 below), see p.44.
6. Ibid., p.9; for the 1995 version, see p.44.
7. Ibid., p.8.
8. Edward Newman, 'Human Security and Constructivism', *International Studies Perspectives*, Vol.2, No.3, 2001, pp.239–51.
9. Boutros Boutros-Ghali, *An Agenda for Peace*, pp.6–7.
10. Ibid., p.8.
11. Ibid.
12. Ibid., p.5.
13. Ibid., p.47.
14. Boutros Boutros-Ghali, *An Agenda for Peace*, 2nd edn, New York: United Nations, 1995, pp.10, 11, 15, 20, 26, 27, 33, 34, 50.
15. Ibid., p.12.
16. Ibid., p.68.
17. Ibid., p.28.
18. *Report of the Panel on United Nations Peace Operations*, UN Doc., A/55/305, S/2000/809, 17 Aug. 2000, p.viii. The Report is the byproduct of investigations by a panel of eminent personalities from around the world: Lakhdar Brahimi former Foreign Minister of Algeria as Chairman, J. Brian Atwood, Ambassador Colin Granderson, Dame Ann Hercus, Richard Monk, General Klaus Naumann, Hisako Shimura, Ambassador Vladimir Shustov, General Philip Sibanda, and Cornelio Sommaruga. The panel was convened on 7 March 2000, on the initiative of UN Secretary-General Kofi Annan.
19. I am thankful to Hisako Shimura, President of Tsuda College, Tokyo, and a member of the Brahimi Panel, for raising this point. Interview, 6 July 2001, Tokyo.
20. *Report of the Panel on United Nations Peace Operations*, p.45 Italics original.
21. Ibid., pp.15–16, 17–28.
22. Ibid., p.7.
23. Ibid., p.9.
24. Ibid., p.19.
25. Ibid., p.12.
26. Ibid., p.10.
27. Ibid., p.9.
28. Ibid., p.10.
29. Ibid., p.9.
30. Ibid.
31. Charles A. Kupchan and Clifford A. Kupchan, 'The Promise of Collective Security', in Brown et al. (eds) (n.3 above), pp.397–406.
32. *Report of the Panel on United Nations Peace Operations*, p.9.
33. Ibid.
34. Ibid.
35. Ibid., pp.29–34.
36. Ibid., pp.34–41.
37. Implementation of the recommendations of the Special Committee on Peacekeeping Operations and the Panel on United Nations Peace Operations, UN Doc., A/55/, 28 May 2001, p.2.
38. Even the arch-realist Kenneth Waltz now recognizes that '[m]ultipolarity is developing before our eyes'. K. Waltz, 'Structural Realism after the Cold War', *International Security*, Vol. 25, No.1, summer 2000, p.37
39. Mancur Olson, *The Logic of Collective Action*, Cambridge, MA: Harvard University Press, 1971.
40. It is worth recalling that the League of Nations' failure to prevent the Second World War from breaking out occurred at a time when the international system was multipolar.
41. Hisako Shimura raised some reservation about the Report because of her belief in multiculturalism. Interview, 6 July 2001.

42. David Held et al., *Global Transformations: Politics, Economics and Culture*, Stanford, CA: Stanford University Press, 1999, p.81.
43. States' behaviour still seems to fit a realist account. See Laura Neack, 'UN Peacekeeping. In the interest of community or self?', *Journal of Peace Research*, Vol.32, No.2, May 195, pp.181–96.
44. Ibid., p.9.
45. *Report of the Panel on United Nations Peace Operations*, p.17.
46. Ibid., p.9.
47. *Washington Post*, 29 April 1999; *The Japan Times*, 1 May 1999.
48. M.S. Rajan, 'The United Nations and the Security of Small States', *International Studies*, Vol.31, No.3, July–Sept. 1994, pp.287–304. The US, for instance, has little enthusiasm for involvement in domestic conflicts. Simon Duke, 'The United Nations and Intra-State Conflict', *International Peacekeeping*, Vol.1, No.4, winter 1994, pp.375–98.
49. For more on this, see Michael Doyle, *Ways of War and Peace: Realism, Liberalism, and Socialism*, New York and London: W.W. Norton & Company, 1997.
50. James Meernik, 'United States Military Intervention and the Promotion of Democracy', *Journal of Peace Research*, Vol.33, No.4, 1996, pp.391–402.
51. *Report of the Panel on United Nations Peace Operations*, p.18.
52. Ibid., p.17.
53. Ibid., p.18.
54. Alan J. Kuperman, *The Limits of Humanitarian Intervention: Genocide in Rwanda*, Washington, DC: Brookings Institution Press, 2001, p.viii.
55. Connie Peck, 'UN Preventive Action', in Muthiah Alagappa and Takashi Inoguchi (eds), *International Security Management and the United Nations*, Tokyo: United Nations University Press, 1999.
56. International Peace Academy and Center for International Cooperation, *Refashioning the Dialogue: Regional Perspectives on the Brahimi Report on UN Peace Operations*, pp.7–10, 13.
57. Ibid., p.16.
58. Connie Peck, *The United Nations as a Dispute Settlement System: Improving Mechanisms for the Prevention and Resolution of Conflict*, The Hague, London and Boston: Kluwer Law International, p.25.
59. Cited in ibid., p.36.
60. Robert Pape, 'Coercion and Military Strategy: Why Denial Works and Punishment Doesn't Work', *Journal of Strategic Studies*, Vol.15, No.4, 1992, p.437.
61. Ibid., pp.423–75.
62. Ibid., p.464.
63. The extent to which the NATO actions in Kosovo can be considered a success remains debatable. See Michael Mandelbaum, 'A Perfect Failure', *Foreign Affairs*, Sept./Oct. 1999, pp.2–8; James B. Steinberg, 'A Perfect Polemic', *Foreign Affairs*, Nov./Dec. 1999, pp.128–133; Ivo Daalder and Michael Froman, 'Dayton's Incomplete Peace', *Foreign Affairs*, Nov./Dec. 1999, pp.106–13.
64. John M. Sanderson, 'Global Flux and the Dilemmas for United Nations Peacekeeping', *Strategic Analysis*, Vol.18, No.3, June 1995, pp.349–74. Shimura also acknowledges that the use of force was part of the problem in Somalia. Interview, 6 July 2001.
65. John G. Ruggie, *Constructing World Polity*, New York: Rouledge, 1998, p.245.
66. Bruce Russett, 'Why Democratic Peace?', in *Debating the Democratic Peace*, pp.106, 92.
67. Ibid., p.113.
68. Ibid., pp.100–101.
69. David Lake and Donald Rothchild, 'Containing Fear: The Origins and Management of Ethnic Conflict', in Michael Brown et al. (eds) (n.3 above), p.301.
70. See William V. O'Brien, 'The Rule of Law in Small States', *Annals of the American Academy of Political and Social Science*, Vol. 541, Sept. 1995, pp.36–46.
71. Lake and Rothchild (n.69 above), p.301.

On the Challenges and Achievements of Reforming UN Peace Operations

JEAN-MARIE GUÉHENNO

Peacekeeping is a complex undertaking. There is no mention in the United Nations Charter of 'peacekeeping operations'. There is no definition for what it entails, no criteria for when operations are to be established, and no guidelines for how to plan and deploy them. The instrument of peacekeeping emerged out of the foresight and ingenuity of the Organization's first leaders, as a creative interpretation of the Charter to respond to the immediate challenges facing the world at that time. The first few operations were developed to avert a collapse of the fragile and possibly explosive post-Second World War international order. What was required, and what seemed to work well for missions such as UNTSO in the Middle East and UNFICYP in Cyprus, was a symbolic presence, consisting of lightly armed or unarmed military personnel from around the world, deployed to 'internationalize' an interstate conflict and raise the political costs of the resumption of war once a ceasefire had been reached.

After the end of the Cold War, the UN was tasked to confront and meet the unique challenges of the post-Cold War era, namely the brutality, destruction and human suffering of internal, often intergroup, conflicts. The same countries that had previously played competing roles in sustaining certain conflicts now saw a common need to bring them to conclusion. Multidimensional peacekeeping operations deployed in the early 1990s to Namibia, El Salvador, Cambodia and Mozambique demonstrated that UN peacekeepers could do far more than merely establish a symbolic presence. These greatly expanded tasks included disarmament, demobilization and reintegration of former combatants into civilian life; assistance in returning refugees and displaced persons to their pre-war homes of origin; supervision, and/or conduct of elections in territories that had until then become well accustomed to the bullet, but had never before seen the ballot; monitoring of local police forces to uphold the rule of law in an impartial and democratic manner, and in accordance with universally recognized human rights instruments; and, as in the case of

Cambodia, assumption of transitional authority for a country, to pave the way to the conclusion of a representative constitutional process and formation of a legitimate and sovereign government. The UN seemed to be the panacea for resolving the scourge of internal conflict that had afflicted the post-Cold War era.

The Sobering Realities of the Mid-1990s

However, the UN's experiences in Somalia, Rwanda, Bosnia and Herzegovina and Angola in the mid-1990s brought with them a strong dose of reality.

- They demonstrated that each conflict is unique. It is one thing to help put a country back on the path to peace when the protagonists' will to fight has been exhausted and their means to wage war have been eliminated. It is quite another to deploy 'Blue Helmets' amidst an ongoing war, leaving them outnumbered by warring factions whose sole objective is to capture as much control of territory and power as possible, even if this means running over the peacekeeping force along the way.

- They demonstrated that, with the emergence of globalization in the post-Cold War era, non-state actors would not necessarily care about international opinion, or feel obliged to respect international conventions and norms. Faced with such an attitude, our traditional instruments of political leverage proved to be woefully inadequate.

- They taught us that it is one thing to deploy a peacekeeping operation with the full support of all the permanent members of the Security Council, as was the case for the missions of the early 1990s, and quite another when those same members have diametrically opposing views on a conflict and varying degrees of commitment to bring it to an end.

- They reminded us that the United Nations, which does not have a standing army, cannot count on its members to provide the tools required to do the job, at all times and whenever and wherever needed. If there is any doubt about that, one merely needs to reflect on the case of Rwanda.

- Finally, they highlighted the dangers of seeing UN involvement in a conflict through the prism of moral equivalency, when the distinction between the aggressor and the aggrieved is often all too apparent.

Retrenchment and Move Towards 'Regionalization'

After the fall of Srebrenica in 1995, the future of UN peacekeeping operations seemed bleak. From 1996 to 1998, the international community looked towards regional organizations to take on peacekeeping tasks, predominantly in their own backyards. The North Atlantic Treaty Organization (NATO) shouldered the peacekeeping tasks in Bosnia and Herzegovina, the Economic Organization of West African States (ECOWAS) in West Africa, and the Commonwealth of Independent States (CIS) in the Caucasus.

The UN presence comprised over 70,000 peacekeeping personnel deployed around the world in 1993, with total expenditures of US$ 3–4 billion per year. This dropped to approximately 10,000 personnel in 1998, with total expenditures barely exceeding US$800 million. Despite the conduct of a very successful operation by the United Nations in Eastern Slavonia in 1996–97, the conventional wisdom was that UN peacekeeping had run its course.

Exponential Resurgence in 1999–2000

Why then did the UN have to establish fully-fledged transitional administrations in Kovoso and East Timor in 1999, followed by the deployment of an expanded mission in Lebanon and the creation of new major operations in Sierra Leone, the Democratic Republic of the Congo and Eritrea/Ethiopia?

There are several reasons for this upsurge in UN peace operations. First, we learned during the 1996–98 period of retrenchment that regional and subregional initiatives were confronted with the same challenges that had previously stymied UN peacekeeping operations. It matters little which organization is leading the operation if the parties on the ground simply are not committed to peace. Second, we learned that, in certain circumstances, regional or subregional organizations are not appropriate to take on the task, because one or more of their members may actually be parties to the conflict. Third, we were reminded of the importance of the universal legitimacy that only the UN can offer, and which some parties to a conflict will consider as the only acceptable form of international involvement. And, fourth, we had to come to terms with the fact that few regional or subregional arrangements have the necessary capacity to do the job. NATO certainly has means that far exceed even those of the UN. But, how many NATOs are there in Africa, or in Asia?

A Vision for the Future of UN Peacekeeping Emerges

Against this backdrop, in 1999 Secretary-General Kofi Annan initiated a serious initiative to reform UN peacekeeping capacities. He sought to reverse the historical trend of treating UN peacekeeping as a temporary aberration, and to articulate the capacities required to meet likely future challenges.

Reconciling with the Past before Looking to the Future

The first step of this reform effort was to come to terms with the failures and tragedies of the past; for, as long as the clouds of Rwanda and Srebrenica remained overhead, it would be difficult to get Member States to invest in rebuilding the Organization's peacekeeping foundations. So, in November 1999, Kofi Annan produced one of the most candid and self-critical documents ever to come out of the United Nations on its role in the war in Bosnia and Herzegovina and the fall of the 'Safe Area' of Srebrenica. Some 7,000 men and boys were captured from Srebrenica and taken to slaughter, despite the presence of UN peacekeepers on the ground and NATO air-power overhead. One month later, in December 1999, the Secretary-General made public an equally critical and hard-hitting report, which he had commissioned from an external panel led by Ingvar Carlsson, the former Prime Minister of Sweden. That report laid bare the anatomy of the genocide in Rwanda.

Both the Srebrenica and Rwanda reports made clear to all that the United Nations is not a monolith. Its constituent parts in the realm of peacekeeping, namely the Security Council, the member states that provide the human, financial and material resources, the Secretariat, and the peacekeepers on the ground, all have responsibilities for which they should be held accountable. Both reports enumerated, with meticulous detail, how each of those constituent parts had failed to do their job properly at critical junctures in those conflicts.

The Brahimi Report

Having exposed the failings of the past, the Secretary-General then quickly initiated a process to present a prescription for the future. The Millennium Summit scheduled for September 2000, which was the largest gathering of Heads of State and Government the world had ever seen, provided an ideal forum to launch a new vision for the future of United Nations peacekeeping. With this in mind, he commissioned a major report from an external panel of experts, to make far-reaching and ambitious, yet realistic, recommendations for the future. Chaired by Lakhdar Brahimi, the former Foreign Minister of Algeria, the panel included nine other eminent personalities from around the world. The panel's report was submitted to the Secretary-General in August 2000. The Secretary-General accepted the panel's findings and transmitted its report and findings for consideration by member states, beginning at the Millennium Summit.

The Brahimi Report concluded that United Nations peacekeeping operations had for too long been used by member states as a means to be seen as 'doing something' in the face of public outcry, especially when the will to do the right thing had been lacking, or consensus about what the right thing to do had been elusive.

The Brahimi Report stressed that doing the right thing sometimes means not deploying an operation at all, when the conditions for success simply do not exist. In other cases, it means deploying far better resourced and supported operations, in direct relation to the magnitude of the task and the inherent risks. In essence, the Brahimi Report called for an end to half-measures, where wishful thinking substituted for a clear and well-supported plan of action.

The report contains some 57 explicit recommendations, and over 100 implicit recommendations. Most of the recommendations address strengthening each of the building blocks required to plan, deploy, manage and sustain a successful operation as follows:

- The creation of enhanced analytical capacities to better understand the conflicts to which the UN is asked to respond, which requires a pooling of knowledge from throughout the UN system.

- Authorization from the Security Council to start conducting contingency planning earlier on, in order to understand the magnitude of the task and canvass member states to see if they are ready to commit the necessary human, materiel, and financial resources before an operation is established. As the Secretary-General often observes, most armies in the world first determine their capabilities before declaring war. In the UN, the Security Council figuratively declares war, and only then asks the Secretary-General to build the required capabilities from scratch.

- Clearer mandates from the Security Council, which seek to resolve disagreements among its members before an operation is established, rather than saddle a mission with ambiguities on the ground.

- The institution of a more systematic and integrated approach to mission planning, which better reflects upon experiences of the past.

- Closer consultation between the member states that contribute resources to an operation and the members of the Security Council, to ensure that all concerns are taken into account before an operation goes forward.

- The enhancement of rapid deployment capacities, to enable a mission to be on the ground and fully functional within 30 to 90 days of the adoption of a resolution that creates it, so that it can establish a centre of gravity well before one or more of the parties to the conflict have time to rethink their commitment to the peace process. This entails:

    (1) a renewed commitment by member states to pre-identify and pre-train the appropriate numbers of military, civilian police, and civilian personnel, and place them on standby, for deployment to an operation on very short notice;

    (2) a better and more effective civilian recruitment system to ensure that the Secretariat can deploy the best staff to the field;

    (3) once in the field, staff need to have the support required to do their jobs;

    (4) the provision of a substantial amount of additional funding for DPKO to stockpile the required equipment at its Logistics Base in Brindisi, Italy, as well as to enter into more robust contractual arrangements with commercial service providers; and

    (5) equally important, it requires greater attention on the part of member states and the Secretariat to provide missions with high quality leadership, whether as Civilian Heads of Mission, Force Commanders, or Civilian Police Commissioners.

- The promulgation of more flexible administrative rules and regulations, which enable greater delegation of authority to the field, so that mission personnel are able to adjust more quickly to changing circumstances on the ground.

- Increased attention to, and more reliable funding for, key aspects of peacekeeping operations, such as for public information, security of personnel, as well as for the key peacebuilding tasks that go hand in hand with multidimensional peacekeeping. These include demobilization and reintegration of former combatants; governance, democratization and institution-building; human rights; gender perspectives; and the delivery of 'quick impact' projects to help demonstrate the dividends of peace as early as possible.

- The provision of sufficient staff for the Secretariat, and the Department of Peacekeeping Operations in particular, to manage this entire enterprise. In this respect, the Brahimi Report mentioned that, for the year 2000, the total expenditure for peacekeeping operations was over US$2.5 billion, whereas the total cost for headquarters support to those operations was less than US$50 million per year. This represents about 2 per cent overhead, which is probably less than the minimum overhead requirements by any organization anywhere, either private or public. In 2000, the staff of the Department of Peacekeeping Operations numbered roughly 400 in total, of which only about 250 occupied professional positions. At the same time, UNDPKO had over 30,000 military personnel in the field, but only 32 military officers at headquarters. Over 8,000 civilian police officers were deployed in the field, but less than 10 at headquarters. Only one or two political officers were available at any given time to provide full-time support to operations, such as those in Kosovo, East Timor, Sierra Leone and the Democratic Republic of the Congo; each of which was costing some US$500 million a year. Contrary to public perception, the Department of Peacekeeping Operations was, and still is, far from overstaffed.
- And, last, the institution of a more effective and progressive management culture at headquarters, to ensure that any additional resources are put to their best use possible.

How is the Reform Effort Progressing?

On the political level, the response to the Brahimi Report has been generally very positive, both in the General Assembly and the Security Council. The member states have endorsed it, by and large, as a blueprint that should be followed in strengthening United Nations' peacekeeping capacities for the foreseeable future.

As a result of the Brahimi Report, member states have set a process in motion to increase the staff of DPKO by 50 per cent, from roughly 400 to 600 staff. The additional staff members are now starting to come on board, and will continue to do so throughout 2002. Before authorizing these additional resources, member states insisted that the budgetary requests be based on objective management criteria. DPKO has followed that request and has concluded an exhaustive external management review of every aspect of the department's work. The implementation of the findings produced by an external management consultant will be part of DPKO's work programme for the coming year.

Current discussions focus on major additional expenditure for enhancing rapid deployment capacities and strengthening of the Logistics Base at Brindisi, Italy, which will enable the UN to have a strategic deployment reserve of equipment. Following a thorough exchange of ideas on the logistics concept with member states, especially the major financial contributors, the related budget will be presented. The implementation of the Brahimi Report's further recommendations remains to be seen. It will in large part depend on the decisions of the Security Council and the political will of member states to provide the required resources. We have not yet had to launch a new operation since the release of the Brahimi Report in August 2000. The real test has therefore yet to come.

Latest Achievements and Challenges

In the meantime, a number of ongoing missions presented the UN with some formidable challenges, but also noteworthy accomplishments.

Sierra Leone

In May/June 2000, the peace process in Sierra Leone had crumbled, and UN peacekeepers were taken hostage by the Revolutionary United Front (RUF). Two of the major troop contributing countries announced their intention to withdraw their personnel from the mission, threatening its complete collapse. They argued, not without some merit, that they had not signed up to engage in an enforcement operation and, moreover, that it was untenable that they would have to pay in blood while members of the Security Council and western nations were only willing to pay in dollars at best, or through lip-service at worst. At that time, as remains the case today, some 75 per cent of the troops came from the developing world.

Against that backdrop, the country seemed poised to descend into full-blown war, with the credibility of the UN irreparably damaged once again, as had happened in the mid-1990s. Once again, the warnings had not been heeded: one cannot deploy an ill-equipped and outnumbered force into a hostile terrain, in which the parties to the peace agreement (in this case the Lomé Peace Agreement) were simply not willing to honour their commitments.

However, today the country is not at war, due to a combination of factors: the intervention of UK forces in the immediate aftermath of the crisis was critical, as was the Secretary-General's Special Representative's skilful negotiation of the Abuja ceasefire agreement in November 2000. Together with increased pressure on Liberia through the imposition of sanctions, the Council's authorization of an expanded force size to over 16,000, and the commitment of troops by Bangladesh and Pakistan, this helped to keep the peace process alive and restore the credibility of the peacekeeping operation.

In May 2001, the disarmament, demobilization and reintegration programme started in earnest. The UN Mission in Sierra Leone (UNAMSIL) has managed to deploy throughout the country, including in the sensitive rebel-held diamond producing regions in the eastern part of the country. Voter registration is intended to start in early 2002, followed by elections later in the spring.

It would be imprudent to say that the mission's success is assured, or to say that Sierra Leone's successful transition to peace is guaranteed. Too many uncertain variables remain and the situation is still very fragile. However, one can say that a massive crisis that could have done irreparable damage to the reputation of the United Nations has been averted.

East Timor

During the same period, the United Nations Transitional Administration in East Timor (UNTAET) managed to establish the initial semblances of a governing authority from amidst the ashes of what was essentially a territory that had been systematically razed to the ground. Physical infrastructure, residences, civil structures, archives, etc., were left in ruins. Skilled indigenous management capacities were virtually non-existent, and the United Nations was only just learning – both in Kosovo and East Timor – how to undertake transitional administrations.

Today, throughout East Timor children are back in school. Hospitals are running. Potable water is flowing. Government services are being delivered. Revenues for the future government of East Timor have been assured through the unprecedented negotiation by the UN of new and far more favourable treaty conditions for drilling rights in the Timor Gap.

But, perhaps most importantly, an all-Timorese cabinet is running the Executive Branch, and an all-Timorese Constituent Assembly is debating the constitutional arrangements that will transform this nation into a state. Where fear had reigned for the past 25 years, it is now absent. The Timorese are free to criticize their leaders, to criticize the UN, to criticize whatever or whomever they like, without fear of being tortured, imprisoned, or summarily executed. Few peoples in the post-Second World War era have ever been given such an opportunity to determine their destiny in relative freedom and security, and with the luxury of an unprecedented amount of international assistance and good will.

Despite the criticisms that not enough attention was paid to creating sustainable, participatory systems with sufficient inclusion of the Timorese, or conversely, that the UN did not do enough to give East Timor a better material 'head start', the mission has achieved some remarkable accomplishments to date, thanks to the dedicated efforts of the Secretary-General's Special Representative, the mission's staff, the patience and support of donor countries, the clarity of guidance provided by the Security Council and, most importantly, the efforts of the East Timorese people. There is still a very delicate path to be trod between now and East Timorese independence in May 2002, as well as to ensure the right balance of support for the post-independence phase. But we are on the right track.

The Democratic Republic of the Congo

UN peacekeeping made its way back to the Democratic Republic of the Congo in December 1999 with the establishment of the UN Mission in the Democratic Republic of the Congo (MONUC). Over 35 years ago, the UN faced considerable setbacks, including the tragic loss of its Secretary-General, Dag Hammarskjold, in a plane crash while visiting the region. People were quick to say that the future of UN peacekeeping was bleak. Never again, they said, would – or should – the UN be taking on such missions.

Nevertheless, the UN is back in the DRC and it is taking on missions around the globe that are far more complicated than ever imagined. MONUC is perhaps the best illustration of the realities that we face today. On one level, some argue that it was a terrible mistake to deploy a mission to a country the size of Western Europe, with few, if any, roads or physical infrastructure to speak of. The will of all the Congolese factions to bring the peace process to a successful conclusion is uncertain, as is the commitment to this goal by some of the neighbouring countries. The recommended force size of over 6,000 troops is far too small to present a credible military deterrent, if challenged, while it is perhaps too large to be perceived as a symbolic presence. The risks are tremendous.

We are taking a gamble, partly because the potential rewards are so great. The crisis in this country has cost innumerable lives and has involved not one but several neighbouring countries. However, peace on the African continent cannot become a reality until there is peace in the DRC.

The Future of UN Peacekeeping Operations

Against this backdrop, what is the future of UN peacekeeping operations? It will probably not differ much from the past 53 years, or the present day. There will be times when all conditions exist for the successful conduct of peacekeeping operations, namely: a ceasefire agreement or comprehensive settlement in place (that is, 'a peace to keep'); full commitment and agreement of the neighbouring countries, the members of the Security Council, and donor countries; and all the tools – political, materiel, financial and human resources – required to do the job. Such operations will be launched in response to inter-state conflicts, and well as to internal ones – and they will succeed.

Encouraged by such success, we will also be tempted, once again, to take on far more complex and dangerous operations. The need for them will not disappear. The fact remains that in this current world order too many peoples remain caught between the nexus of true statehood and failed states. Nations need time to develop a solid state, with durable institutions capable of promoting peaceful dissent, rather than crumbling under its weight. However, that time continues to be consumed by the competing demands of the post-Cold War world of globalization. In this world, even the most stable and durable states see their authority challenged by the free movement of peoples, goods, ideas and finances, both in the legal, regulated market as well as through illicit means. Stronger states can find ways of benefiting from the erosion of borders, but the weaker ones cannot always do so. Instead, they face the real risks of this erosion of borders, which promotes the conditions that fuel and finance ethnic, tribal, religious or political rivalries, and results in violence that engulfs not only one country but often spills over across borders to several others.

The transnational conflicts of the globalized world will continue to present us with a dilemma. On the one hand, the failure to respond could be disastrous, allowing initially localized conflicts to spread across a continent. On the other hand, the risk remains that the task might be greater than the Organization's capacity to respond. Hopefully, in the future we will heed the lessons of the past and embrace those most recently articulated in the Brahimi panel's report. Peacekeeping cannot be risk free, but those risks can be better managed if we put in place and strengthen all the necessary building blocks and pursue the deployment of peacekeeping operations in a more judicious and deliberate manner. There are places where peacekeepers should not and must not go, if they are to avert failure. But if and when they do go, they must be given the tools required to complete the mission successfully. The first and most fundamental steps towards preparing for the future are to acknowledge that the need for peacekeeping operations will remain for a long time; that these operations need to be conducted by the United Nations, if at all possible; and that, if given the appropriate means and political support, the UN is both willing and able to succeed in bringing peace to war-torn societies.

ACKNOWLEDGEMENTS

This article is based on the author's keynote presentation given at the 2001 Annual Meeting of the International Association of Peacekeeping Training Centres, United Nations University, Tokyo, 23 October 2001.

World Bank, NGOs and the Private Sector in Post-War Reconstruction

VESNA BOJICIĆ-DZELILOVIĆ

The spread of violent conflicts in the most deprived areas of the world following the end of the Cold War has posed difficult challenges for the theory and practice of development. Pressure to respond to the needs of conflict-affected countries has prompted an increasing number of organizations to add reconstruction to their agendas and has led those already established in the field to adapt some of their practices to take into account the economic and political complexities of new conflicts. Greater complementarity of action is increasingly recognized as crucial for the success of reconstruction programmes. Their engagement, however, continues to be framed by the dominant development approach in which the conceptual tools to address the issue of violent conflict are missing. At the same time, the concern of individual organizations with self-preservation in the light of the changing nature of the international assistance regime affects the modalities of their mutual relations. Thus, in spite of a myriad of institutions and projects aimed at assisting in rebuilding war-torn societies, sustaining peace once donor assistance ends remains an elusive goal for many.

This contribution sets out to explore the role of three of many actors engaged in the reconstruction of war-torn societies: the World Bank, NGOs and the private sector. In particular, it seeks to explore the extent to which their agendas and modes of operations correspond to the needs of conflict-affected countries and contribute to recovery from violent conflict. The point of departure is a discussion of the nature of contemporary warfare and its impact upon the socio-political and economic foundations of affected societies. In the second part, the formal mandates of the World Bank, NGOs and the private sector in reconstruction within the framework of the changing nature of the international assistance regime are analysed. In the third part, we look more closely at how the potential roles of these three actors are played out in practice, focusing in particular on some of the more controversial issues pertaining to the economic aspects of reconstruction. The final section concludes by arguing for a different approach to reconstruction, based on an understanding of socio-political change underlying contemporary conflicts as a precondition for re-defining the roles and rules of engagement of the World Bank, NGOs and the private sector, as well as their mutual relations in the reconstruction of war-torn societies.

The Nature of Post-War Reconstruction

The proliferation of violent conflicts has been one of the distinguishing features of the world's more recent history. Since the Second World War, over 150 conflicts worldwide have been recorded, including 39 major ones in the last decade of the twentieth century alone.[1] A growing body of literature has emerged suggesting that the majority of these conflicts represent a distinct social phenomenon outside the commonly understood notion of wars.[2] A range of terms, including 'new wars' and 'post-modern wars', has been suggested to differentiate them from traditional war and to denote what is essentially the use of violence to meet political ends. The occurrence of these types of conflicts as well as their distinct character, it is argued, have to be interpreted as a corollary of the process of adjustment to the changing nature and dynamics of contemporary development shaped by the process of globalization.[3] They represent an extreme manifestation of the exclusionary mode of development promulgated by key international development players, which is framed around the notion of free markets and liberal democratic politics.[4] While an overview of the relevant literature is beyond the scope of this article, highlighting some of the salient features of the new type of conflicts is necessary to understand the complex nature of economic and societal reconstruction in their aftermath and the roles played by a plethora of actors engaged in this task.

In contrast to earlier periods in history, when wars tended to be inter-state affairs, involving a contest over ideological and geo-strategic interests, contemporary conflicts are predominantly internal, fuelled by competing claims of identity, access to resources and contest over political authority.[5] Although conflict is confined within a territory of one country, its ramifications are felt much further afield in security, economic and political terms, greatly facilitated by the globalization process. It is usually the neighbouring countries or the entire region that take the brunt, which additionally complicates the formulation of an adequate response.

The difference in the motivations that lie behind conflict is reflected in the ways in which wars are fought. Traditional wars deploy armies fighting by and large at and around the front lines; new wars involve disparate armed groups of which formal armies are typically only one segment and that target inhabited areas and key infrastructure. The involvement of external players in new conflicts in the form of diaspora, mercenaries, international organizations, donors, NGOs and various other actors is on a much larger scale and of a different profile, bearing significant implications on the dynamics of conflict. Tapping into various international networks by the local agents engaged in violence plays an important role in the sustenance of conflict. The mode of organizing an economy and society for the war effort is also different. While traditional wars involve a high degree of central planning and concerted mobilization of a country's resources, new conflicts are much more fragmentary and take place against the backdrop of a weakened or collapsing formal economy and societal infrastructure. External funding, the appropriation of humanitarian assistance and illicit activities of combatants are an important source of funding – in contrast to traditional war, in which substantial funds are raised locally from regular economic activity.

The incidence of civilian victims is much higher in contemporary conflicts. Indeed, murder, torture and the displacement of the civilian population tend to figure as one of the main goals of violence, leaving behind deeply traumatized societies. The violence is often directed at the members of opposite ethnic or religious groups within the same nation. Instigating fear and hatred against the ethnic and/or religious 'others' or any other social groups targeted for exclusion from a country's economic and political life is one of the key instruments in perpetuating the conflict. Moreover, the political leadership of warring factions, a range of other actors, both domestic and foreign ('the entrepreneurs of violence'), have a vested interest in continuing violence, which reflects the character of the war economy typical of new conflicts. Violence and predation are instrumental in sustaining an alternative set of economic and social relations that become entrenched in the course of conflict and survive beyond its formal end.[6]

New wars tend to be prolonged while still allowing for pockets of peace amidst violence.[7] Open warfare is usually terminated as a result of weariness and exhaustion of the combatants, with none of the sides able to claim a clear military victory.[8] Peace treaties, engineered under the duress of foreign political pressure, are more often than not compromise documents, which seldom appropriately address the main causes of the conflict.⁹ Thus, the formal cessation of hostilities does not mean an end to a conflict and a shift towards peace. Peace agreements often tend to represent a rough framework within which the task of building lasting peace is yet to be undertaken, as recurrent violence that tends to flare up long into the implementation of the peace agreement seems to suggest. Short of open violence, there is extreme tension between former combatants-made-partners-in-power. Therefore, in reality, reconstruction in a contemporary context often subsumes the peacebuilding agenda.

As with the aftermath of a traditional war, the identification of reconstruction needs following new wars starts by assessing the scale of material damage inflicted upon a country's physical infrastructure, housing stock and economic assets. The rehabilitation of infrastructure and housing are given priority consideration and the largest proportion of funds, particularly in the early stages of the reconstruction effort. New wars leave behind massive physical destruction as well as extensive damage to a country's potential for development. In financial terms, the damage is usually several times greater than the cumulative value of years of a conflict-affected country's output. The drop in output is high, as is the rise in unemployment, the latter easily representing one of the most intractable problems of post-war reconstruction. The productive capacity is drastically reduced due to physical destruction, lack of investment in maintenance as well as the break-up of production, technological and other links due to the fragmentary nature of conflict. The combined effect of these factors renders entire segments of a country's economy useless. The remaining ones are saddled by a lack of funds and, more importantly in the case of new wars, adequate skills and expertise due to massive population shifts as well as the absence of a supportive institutional environment. All kinds of macroeconomic disequilibria are present as a result of decimated production activity and economic mismanagement. The years of warfare and forgone development inevitably alter the country's position in the international division of labour, and reinsertion into the international flows of business and commerce on a competitive footing is difficult if not almost impossible. Consequently, in most cases, dependence on humanitarian and other forms of external assistance persists for years after the conflict is formally brought to an end. The impact is that much harder as new conflicts tend to be concentrated in the economically deprived areas of the world where economic turmoil predates the conflict, contributing to its outbreak and escalation.

The important role of the security 'establishment' as one of the key political and also economic agents, combined with its varied structure, presents another extremely complex aspect of the reconstruction agenda. Rebuilding the formal security sector in the situation of contested governance among the former warring factions is difficult and often subject to obstruction by the parties involved. In many instances, only the sheer presence of international forces prevents the return to warfare. Low security, including a weak rule of law and unprofessional judiciary, therefore remains a distinct feature of the reconstruction environment.

While physical destruction on a scale much larger than in the aftermath of traditional wars remains one of the overwhelming tasks of reconstruction in a contemporary context, the by far more challenging agenda pertains to the rehabilitation of the institutional infrastructure of the societies emerging out of violent conflict. This aspect may include anything from the political reorganization of the country to the election system or to rebuilding administrative, judicial, economic and social institutions of the war-affected country – a task made extremely complex and complicated by the specificities of the new wars. The particular character of the new wars manifested in a profound amalgamation of the new political elite and the criminal elements in the society, accompanied by the displacement of formal processes through networks along the lines of ethnicity and kinship, undermines the governing and economic institutions of a country caught up in a violent conflict. The survival of parallel structures within which economic and political life evolves is based on nurturing divisive identities within society. As argued by Kaldor, this kind of policy is fragmentative, destabilizing and results in pervasive insecurity – in contrast to the inclusive character of policies based on ideas. It results in the economic deprivation of the majority of the population, while concentrating wealth within elite circles. By tearing the social fabric of society apart, it contributes to a protracted frailty of its institutions. No structure – economic, political, social, cultural or civic – is left intact in a country emerging from this type of conflict. In a way, they only formally bear some resemblance to 'normal' institutions, while they are permeated by the negative forms of social relations that are the very essence and product of new wars. It is against this background that the concept of war-torn societies perhaps most accurately depicts the nature of the task at hand.[10] Thus, reconstruction in a contemporary context is essentially about integrating societies by building forms of economic and political existence that are alternatives to those based on exclusion and violence, and which have emerged in the long process of adaptation of these societies to global processes.[11]

The next section looks at the formal mandate, and areas of engagement in post-war reconstruction, of the World Bank, NGOs and the private sector – three of the many social actors in this field.

The World Bank, NGOs and Private Sector: An Expanding Agenda for Action

The frequency and intractability of most of the recent conflicts have prompted an increasing number of institutions to include post-war reconstruction in their field of work.[12] Internationally, the World Bank is the institution that has been established the longest, with a specific mandate to assist post-war reconstruction. It was established as a key agency for channelling aid for the reconstruction of Western Europe following the end of the Second World War. Its original portfolio also included development assistance to its members, which, until the 1980s, accounted for the largest share of funds released by the World Bank. Over the years, the role of the World Bank has grown to become a pillar of the system of international aid to less developed countries. Moreover, membership in the World Bank and the International Monetary Fund has come to be seen (rightly or not) as a catalyst for bilateral aid and private investment.[13] Its involvement with members belonging to the group of industrialized, developed countries has meanwhile diminished – they have become the donors rather than beneficiaries.

The volume of lending to conflict-affected countries has risen sharply since the 1980s, reflecting the increasing incidence of violent conflicts in some of the Bank's poorest members, which are primary beneficiaries of its funds. However, there was hardly any noticeable change in the Bank's standard practices to accommodate for the special needs of these countries. In recognition of this, in 1997 the World Bank's Board of Directors endorsed a policy framework to guide the Bank's activities in post-conflict reconstruction. The organization's Post-Conflict Unit was created as a focal point for enhancing the Bank's operations in this area. New financing tools such as conflict programme grants, IBRD grants, learning and innovation loans have also been introduced.

The World Bank's aid for reconstruction and development covers broad ground. It is aimed at rebuilding the economic and physical infrastructure, strengthening institutional capacity and providing a base for sustainable development. The principles of the World Bank's engagement in post-conflict reconstruction explicitly state that the Bank is not a relief agency and that 'its purpose is defined in terms of assisting its members by financing or facilitating investment for productive purposes and promoting international trade, through loans and guarantees'.[14]

Thus, the thrust of the Bank's assistance is supposed to be on creating the conditions that will allow the private sector and institutions of civil society to resume commercial and production activities. To that end, the Bank focuses on economic policy both in terms of assisting in the design of these policies through a dialogue with local counterparts as well as in facilitating the creation of an environment in which these policies are implemented.

The rebuilding of the physical infrastructure and support for macroeconomic stabilization are recognized by the Bank as its core expertise and an area of comparative advantage with respect to other actors participating in reconstruction.[15] The importance of these two areas in terms of continuing with other aspects of reconstruction make them the highest and the earliest priorities in the Bank's operations in post-conflict situations. Their elevated status reflects the Bank's experience with the post-war reconstruction of Western Europe following the Second World War, in which these two areas played a critical role in its recovery. Since the 1990s the Bank has added new areas of engagement to its core activities: the demobilization of soldiers, demining and the reintegration of the displaced population. It also plays an important role in mobilizing donor funding for reconstruction and more recently in coordinating the overall reconstruction effort in some countries (Democratic Republic of Congo, Bosnia and Hercegovina, West Bank and Gaza).

According to the World Bank's rules of engagement, its main partners are the governments of the borrowing countries. The engagement with NGOs and the private sector plays a subordinate role and, in the case of the former, is largely indirect. The World Bank-financed programmes are designed at a national level and include large-scale projects, extending over a longer period of time. They are aimed at mobilizing whatever local resources and expertise there are through official government structures. The size of individual loans is much higher compared to other sources of reconstruction funds.

The rise to prominence of NGOs as one of the important social actors began in the 1980s and reached its climax in the 1990s, following the end of the Cold War. Their potential role in development had been recognized for a long time, in developed and developing countries alike.

But it was not until the international aid donors' distinct focus on promoting a neo-liberal policy agenda in the 1980s, and the growing recognition of the limitations of the public sector, that NGOs came to be seen as an indispensable player in the theatre of development. Against this background and as a result of theoretical and policy debates following the collapse of communism, their numbers skyrocketed and their deployment in varied roles became a norm in post-conflict situations. Nowadays, NGOs are a major link in the international assistance chain to conflict-affected countries both during the conflict and in its aftermath. They are perceived as potentially efficient providers of social services, channels of aid and facilitators of democratization. These attributes stem from their value orientation, which is allegedly different from that of both the public and private sectors.[16]

Unlike those NGOs that originated in response to relief concerns, and later broadened their mandate to include development issues, the work of many development NGOs in the post-conflict reconstruction framework is not their primary mandate. Rather, it involves an adaptation of their field of expertise situated in different contexts, mostly in countries with no recent experience of violent conflict. At the same time, the availability of funding for post-conflict specific problems, such as psycho-social care, the disabled and displaced people, has resulted in the emergence of a third layer of NGOs with their primary field of engagement in post-conflict countries. Thus, one can identify a range of organizations operating in the area of reconstruction under the collective term of NGO.

The role of NGOs can generally be judged from two angles: as providers of basic services not covered by the state, and as promoters of an alternative form of development based on grassroot initiatives and the empowerment of the local population.[17] As part of the non-profit sector, NGOs are expected to play a role in stimulating development while fostering civic involvement. As such, they are perceived to be the key player in the social transformation of war-affected countries, which is needed to sustain economic and political reforms. Whether they are involved as stand-alone actors or the implementers of donor projects in the first place, NGOs are perceived as low-cost, participatory, flexible, innovative and able to reach the most vulnerable in the aftermath of a violent conflict. They often engage in activities other actors would not. NGOs tend to focus on small-scale, local projects aimed at organizing local self-help efforts.[18] They occupy an intermediate position between the state and the local population. It is the latter, the beneficiaries of their programmes, that figure as the NGOs' main counterparts, at least by the exposition of their mandate. Thus, plurality and mutual influence in a society are perceived as NGOs' key comparative advantage over other social actors.

Unlike both the World Bank and NGOs, there is no specific reconstruction mandate for the private sector. On a general level, the changing nature of the international development assistance, in that private flows now surpass official aid, would suggest a greater role for the private sector in reconstruction. As Nelson observes, its impact as a development actor can be exerted through one of the three main areas of corporate activity: core business operations, social instruments and philanthropic programmes and participation in public policy dialogue, advocacy and institution-building.[19] It is the first of these three areas through which the influence and the role of the private sector is mostly directly felt in the post-war reconstruction framework. This is in line with a common wisdom of development that the private sector plays a key role in generating economic wealth. Recreating development momentum by engaging the private sector is one of the main tasks of reconstruction and it is through this lens that the expected role of the private sector should be judged. Involving the private sector in reconstruction, particularly local enterprises, while providing goods and services to satisfy the needs of the local population and feed into other reconstruction needs, can augment their capacity for job creation.[20] A strong private sector is indispensable for securing public revenues so that the provision of public services is maintained and their outreach and quality upgraded.

When looking at the three actors – the World Bank, NGOs and the private sector – individually, one can identify three distinct areas of engagement based on the logic, mission and social energies they each mobilize in pursuing the reconstruction effort. Prima facie, their roles appear complementary in that, taken together, they address some of the fundamental issues of rebuilding worn-torn societies and presumably, if pursued successfully, can help them make a clear break with past experience. The reality is different, however. The three actors are driven by their own values and particular development paradigms, while at the same time being part of a broader effort of reconstruction, involving a multiplicity of other actors and projects. This raises the issue of the extent to which and of how their work corresponds to the problems of the countries they are dealing with. In the remainder of this essay, we look more closely at how, in reality, the role of the three actors is played out, trying to discern their actual impact, individually and in cooperation with one another, on the rehabilitation of war-torn societies.

The World Bank, NGOs and Private Sector in Reconstruction: Roles and Relevance

The role of these three actors in post-war reconstruction has to be analysed with reference to the changes in international assistance regimes. Despite a tendency to discuss foreign aid in technical terms, the origins of and motivation for international assistance are primarily political. Thus, the dynamics of the international environment and donors' internal agendas are decisive in defining the international assistance regime. Originating in the economic and political concerns of donor countries, the dominant theoretical and political discourse based on the economic doctrine of neo-liberalism captured the domain of the international assistance regime in the 1980s. Neo-liberalism advocated, on efficiency grounds, the primacy of markets and the scaling down of the state, which was perceived as market distorting and prone to inefficiency. Liberalization, privatization, public spending cuts and improvements in labour market efficiency are some of the policies emanating from a development model that advocated export-led growth as the preferred way out of poverty. This was the model promulgated by structural adjustment and stabilization programmes as a framework within which the World Bank and the IMF, respectively, have extended development assistance to eligible countries since the 1980s. The development of an open, market-based economic system became one of the principal goals of assistance. The lending policies of the World Bank as the key multilateral development agency shifted from project to programme-based lending, accompanied by policy conditionality, which gave the Bank more clout over the borrowing countries' domestic policies. The shift reflected new thinking, namely that the policy environment in which development projects were placed was the key to developmental success.

Following the end of the Cold War, the development assistance agenda widened to include concerns of (good) governance, while recognizing that the state too has a role to play in development. This was also in line with the rise of the new orthodoxy on the developmental role of political regimes. For many countries breaking out of communism, political pluralism and the development of liberal democracy were advocated as the natural complement to free markets in the economic realm. The liberal democratic good governance agenda promoted by bilateral and multilateral donors has become known as the 'new policy agenda'. Despite some modifications to address the distributive aspects of the model that the World Bank recognized late into its mandate (the 'poverty focus'), it is essentially the market-driven model that has been implemented through international assistance programmes, including the countries emerging from violent conflict. Moreover, the model reigned supreme in spite of its poor record in many of the countries implementing it and despite evidence that, in some cases, such as the former Yugoslavia, its adverse social effects could be linked to the eruption of conflict.[21]

Before we take a closer look at some specific elements included in reconstruction programmes, we will discuss briefly some of the crucial issues impacting on a programme's success, namely its design, content and ownership. As noted above, it was not until 1997 that the World Bank took concrete action to enable it to deal more closely and specifically with post-war reconstruction. Until then, the World Bank's involvement in countries affected by conflicts had mostly been on an ad hoc basis, as the Bank itself admitted.[22] The role of the Bank in designing the overall programme of reconstruction has varied from country to country. In cases where it has assumed the role of overall coordination, its influence in defining the reconstruction agenda has been preponderant. Although, as with standard Bank-supported programmes, the local government is formally responsible for the programme design and its implementation, we find that, in most instances, it puts forward an agenda overwhelmingly determined by external actors. As such, it does not necessarily reflect the priorities or their ordering as deemed appropriate locally. Often, discussions on the programme involve narrow government circles; in a post-conflict country's complex political setting, this may include participants with contesting political and economic agendas. The Bank has fairly recently adopted the practice of including NGOs and other non-governmental actors in these discussions, but there is little evidence that innovative local initiatives are taken on board by the Bank. The international donor community is increasingly vocal regarding the need for local ownership of the reconstruction programmes. But, given that these programmes are largely externally driven, and that there is a myriad of organizations and institutions involved, local ownership seems a distant goal. And yet, the experience of international aid in different contexts suggests that local ownership is vital for the success of the programme of aid.

The breadth of the reconstruction programmes depends on a country's particular circumstances. In some cases (such as Cambodia, Mozambique, Bosnia and Hercegovina), the issues cover, in one sweep, the transition from war to peace, from one party-system to multi-party democracy and from centrally planned to market economy. What these programmes amount to is an 'overwhelming set of societal transformations'[23] for which war-torn societies simply lack the necessary fundamental preconditions. Indeed, in many respects these have yet to be (re)built. They contain a time-compressed agenda in the sense that a range of reforms and institutional changes, that in the course of normal societal evolution take place over a long time, have to be implemented within a much shorter time span. The World Bank's operational practice, as, indeed, that of NGOs and many other actors involved, is driven by the pressure to disburse funds according to agreed schedules and/or recover the funds, which in reality sets the pace for implementing the programme's agenda. This conflicts with the long-term needs of conflict-affected countries and may backlash politically.

The economic core of reconstruction programmes, the World Bank's main concern, is based on a stabilization–structural adjustment nexus. This is perceived as instrumental in recreating the conditions for the revival of a war-destroyed economy. The central issue within this framework is how to strengthen the private sector. Macroeconomic stabilization, the rebuilding of the infrastructure and institutional and regulatory frameworks are the main lines of the World Bank's engagement towards that end. It reflects the logic that, given the right policy environment, the process will start of its own accord. Rigid adherence to macroeconomic stabilization policies in a post-war setting has, however, proved problematic. While inflation, as an indicator of successful macroeconomic stabilization, is relatively quickly brought under control, sometimes using the most extreme methods (such as the currency board in Bosnia and Hercegovina), it is often accompanied by large budget and foreign account deficits and persistently high unemployment as sustained strong output recovery fails to materialize. These in turn can undermine efforts in other areas of reconstruction, which are essential for peacebuilding, such as improvements in public services and social programmes, and restoring the rule of law, as Hendrickson illustrates using Cambodia as an example.[24] In response to the 'side effects' of macrostabilization, which are considered temporary, budgetary support is extended to recipient governments. This again is not without risk, the most obvious being that it frees up government funds for other purposes not necessarily conducive to consolidating peace and economic recovery. The successful physical rebuilding of infrastructure does not imply its operational sustainability, either. Thus, although roads, railways, water and electricity supply networks are repaired, their functioning may be constrained by lacking funds for recurrent costs, or by the political obstruction of the local parties. Building institutions supportive of economic growth is a complex task in a post-war environment, and the Bank finds its resources spread over an array of activities. It is here that the key weakness of the approach to reconstruction as currently practised is perhaps the most obvious, in that previous structures are difficult to dislodge, which undercuts efforts to strengthen formal economic activity.[25] Obstacles to the recovery of formal economic processes are many, including opaque taxation, which fuels informal activity, thus undercutting public revenues. Instead, a type of speculative business, which often engages in illegitimate activities, is encouraged. Private companies are profit-seeking and that is the guiding principle in deciding on the locality of their operations. Weaknesses pertaining to the business environment and bureaucratic hurdles, which are characteristic of post-war economies exacerbated by political risks, are strong investment deterrents. There is a dearth of productive investment with most new enterprises concentrated in commerce. Thus, one of the key assumptions, which underlies the neo-liberal inspired model of reconstruction that investment both domestic and foreign will pick up, rarely materializes to the extent or within the timeframe envisaged in the World Bank's documents. This puts the entire programme on slippery ground given that, with time, donor assistance tends to wind down and local resources are limited.

The insistence on early and sweeping privatization as one of the cornerstones of reconstruction programmes has recently been questioned by the Bank itself. Rather than removing political influence in economic affairs, it tends to strengthen it as assets are sold at derisory prices to supporters of the political regime. Restructuring privatized enterprises (as the Bank insists on privatization first) is constrained by a lack of funds, skills and weak business infrastructure – an aspect not adequately addressed by the prevalent policies. The same factors, coupled with a poor entrepreneurial culture typical of most post-conflict societies, work against another important element in the applied model, namely the growth of small and medium-sized enterprises. These are expected to compensate for the lack of employment opportunities in the formal sector and, in the longer term, to act as the most dynamic part of the economy as is the case in the developed market economies. In reality, very little sustainable production activity gets off the ground under the schemes often run by the NGOs. Thus the expected contribution of the private sector remains limited and aid dependence becomes protracted.

Before taking up its mandate in Bosnia and Hercegovina, the World Bank did not put social policy at the centre of its reconstruction activities, although, as underlined by P. Stubbs, it represents one of the key pillars of peace, security, good governance and economic regeneration.[26] The state's capacity to provide welfare, already reduced during the conflict, is further undermined by the reconstruction programme's pursuit of structural adjustment policies, so that NGOs frequently step in to fill the vacuum in the provision of services. However, rather than acting as a 'bridge' until the state resumes its obligations to the public, there is a tendency for NGOs to continue providing services normally provided by the state, which results in incomplete coverage, lack of professionalism, and reduced quality of provision.[27]

The role of NGOs, and particularly those concerned with developmental issues, has been controversial due to their dependence on donor funding. Growing competition for funding both by northern as well as southern NGOs has, to a large extent, undermined the capacity of many NGOs to determine their own agenda and consequently their status as an autonomous social actor. Instead, their role is often reduced to that of implementers of donor programmes, which, as we have argued earlier, are often politically motivated and divorced from the needs of local population. In particular, donors tend to stress the service delivery aspect of NGO involvement, and to downplay the social transformation aspects which are so crucial in the context of distorted relations associated with new wars. Moreover, donors often hold substantial leverage over NGOs' operational procedures, staffing and reporting practices, thus weakening NGOs' downward accountability. Besides funding, there are other, more sinister, reasons that drive NGOs closer to donors; these reflect economic realities and the neo-liberal influence described in the first part of this section. As a result, the potential of NGOs to act as a medium for formulating and voicing the needs of the most vulnerable segments of the population is severely constrained, particularly in a post-conflict environment.

Numerous programmes to strengthen local civil society – and NGOs as one of its constitutive parts – are pursued within the reconstruction framework, but the results have, by and large, been disappointing. In most conflict-affected countries, institutions of civil society tend to be underdeveloped. Indeed, the opposite is often true in that 'uncivil,' exclusionary, forms tend to prevail. The approach that a civil society can be created from outside against a blueprint originating in a different cultural context is in itself problematic. It gives rise to organizations that are under pressure to conform to Western models. NGOs attract middle-class local staff in pursuit of better pay but with often little interest in the programme's target groups and their problems, thus maintaining tenuous consultation with local communities. Thus, not only is their political role significantly weakened, but the particular approach to supporting NGOs can also have a lasting impact on the development of civil society. As T. Tvedt observes, 'NGOs have played an important role in bringing Western concepts of development and democracy to new elites in urban centers'.[28] There is also a larger issue of the effectiveness of NGO-supported projects with respect to macro-level policy making, in the sense that the latter can undermine or even annul the results accomplished by small, community-based projects. The population movements that continue for long after the fighting ends complicate the work of the NGOs and diminish its impact.

Cooperation between the World Bank, NGOs and the private sector in implementing reconstruction programmes has expanded. This reflects a growing consensus on the need for partnership in addressing the complex problems facing societies in the aftermath of new wars. The notion of partnership, however, does not capture the true nature of the relationship between these three social actors we have discussed. As far as the World Bank and NGOs are concerned, they do not represent natural partners.[29] Yet it is now common to see them working alongside each other for reasons of improved operational efficiency, and speedier delivery of assistance. Faced with weak and corrupt governments in conflict-affected countries, the World Bank is increasingly turning to NGOs and the private sector to implement its projects as part of a new emphasis on the decentralization in the delivery of international assistance.[30] Nevertheless, their enhanced interaction and the resulting modification in the pattern of cooperation take place in pursuance of a standard capital-driven growth model, so that other concerns and alternative approaches pursued by different development actors play a subordinate role. The model as such does not recognize conflict as anything but a temporary anomaly in an otherwise normal developmental trajectory. Consequently, political and socio-cultural specificities of the local context within which reconstruction programmes take place are not adequately appreciated and the relevance of individual donor projects to the complex problems of war-torn societies is diminished.

Conclusion

The discussion, based on the recent experience of reconstruction, has shown that the dominant model informing the approach followed by the World Bank, NGOs and the private sector has failed to penetrate to the root causes of the conflict, and has, instead, dealt with its symptoms. Thus, despite substantial financial and other forms of international assistance channelled to the countries affected by violent conflicts, they remain caught up in the spiral of insecurity, underdevelopment and deprivation of the large segments of their population. There is a pressing need to improve understanding of the dynamics of contemporary political disputes and violence in order to design reconstruction programmes that are better connected to the realities on the ground. The new approach has to aim at linking economic and political aspects of reconstruction in a more systematic and constructive way. Much greater involvement of local actors is needed, both in the design of projects and their implementation. Ultimately, as argued by Howell and Pearce on the dilemmas of manufacturing civil society from outside, local problems can only be resolved through local political processes.[31] The organizations involved in reconstruction have to adopt the long-term view, focusing on their core activities while strengthening mutual cooperation. This also implies greater flexibility in the way organizations operate so that they can review their strategies and adapt them in light of the developments on the ground.

NOTES

1. N. Ball, 'The Challenge of Rebuilding War-Torn Societies', in C.A. Crocker, F.O. Hampson and P. Aall (eds), *Managing Global Chaos: Sources of and Responses to International Conflict*, Washington, DC: United States Institute of Peace, 1996, pp.607–22; World Bank, Issue Briefs, Sept. 2000.
2. M. Kaldor, *New Wars–Old War: Organized Violence in a Global Era*, Cambridge: Polity Press, 1999; M. Duffield, *Aid Policy and Post-Modern Conflict: A Critical Review*, Occasional Paper No.19, Birmingham: University of Birmingham, 1998.
3. A. Le Sage, 'Engaging the Political Economy of Conflict: Towards a Radical Humanitarianism', *Civil Wars*, Vol.1, No.4, winter 1998, pp.27–55.
4. D. Moore, 'Leveling the Playing Fields and Embedding Illusions: Post-Conflict Discourse and Neo-Liberal Development in War-Torn Africa', *Review of African Political Economy*, Vol.83, No.27, 2000.
5. J. Nelson, *The Business of Peace: The Private Sector as a Partner in Conflict Prevention and Resolution*, London: Prince of Wales Business Forum, 2000; J.L. Rasmussen, 'Peacemaking in the Twenty-First Century', in J.L. Rasmussen and W. Zartman (eds), *Peacemaking in International Conflict: Methods and Techniques*, pp.23–48.
6. V. Bojicić-Dzelilović, 'From Humanitarianism to Reconstruction: Towards an Alternative Approach to Social and Economic Recovery from War', in M. Kaldor (ed.),

Global Insecurity – Restructuring the Global Military Sector, Volume III, London and New York: Pinter, 2000, pp.95–120.
7. The protracted character of new wars makes the notion of 'post-conflict' reconstruction somewhat problematic.
8. Although the incidence of the new type of conflicts is numerically highest in the less developed marginalized areas of the world, their outreach is by far greater. Some facets of this type of violence can, to a varying degree, be found in what are regarded as otherwise developed countries with stable political systems.
9. S. Willet, *Insecurity, Conflict and the New Global Disorder*, IDS Bulletin, Vol.32, Apr. 2001.
10. R. Luckham et al., 'The Politics of Institutional Design: a Concept Paper on Strengthening Democratic Governance in Conflict-Torn Societies', IDS Working Paper, 2000.
11. Moore (n.4 above); A. Le Sage (n.3 above).
12. R. Trivedy, 'Conflict Prevention, Resolution and Management: Improving Coordination for More Effective Action', *IDS Bulletin*, Vol.32, No.2, Apr. 2001 pp.79–89.
13. For a discussion on this issue, see G. Bird, A. Mori and D. Rowlands, 'Do the Multilaterals Catalyze Other Capital Flows? A Case Study Analysis', *Third World Quarterly*, Vol.21, No.3, 2000.
14. World Bank, 'Post-Conflict Reconstruction: The Role of the World Bank', Washington: The World Bank, 1998, p.23.
15. World Bank, 'The World Bank's Experience with Post-Conflict Reconstruction, Washington: The World Bank, 1998.
16. J. Howell and J. Pearce, *Civil Society and Development: A Critical Exploration*, London: Lynne Rienner, 2001.
17. M. Wyts et al., *Development Policy and Public Action*, Oxford: OUP, 1992.
18. P. Nelson, *The World Bank and the NGOs: The Limits of Apolitical Development*, Basingstoke: Macmillan, 1995, p.7.
19. Nelson (n.5 above) p.10.
20. Ball (n.1 above).
21. Illustrative of the model's hegemony is the fact that the same policies that contributed to the break-up of war in Bosnia and Herzegovina were incorporated in its internationally sponsored reconstruction strategy.
22. World Bank, 'The World Bank's Experience with Post-Conflict Reconstruction' (n.15 above).
23. M. Naim, 'Fads and Fashion in Economic Reform: Washington Consensus or Washington Confusion?', *Third World Quarterly*, Vol.21, No.3, June 2000.
24. D. Hendrickson, *Globalization, Insecurity and Post-War Reconstruction: Cambodia's Precarious Transition*, IDS Bulletin, Vol.32, No.2, Apr. 2001.
25. An interesting example of the kind of problems facing the rebuilding of institutional and regulatory frameworks is the taxation of oil and gas imports from Croatia to Bosnia and Herzegovina. In 1998, the parliament of the BiH Federation passed a decision to introduce taxes on oil and gas imports, but when the law appeared in the official gazette, the relevant articles were missing. This was the doing of public servants under the instructions of government officials from the ranks of Bosnian Croats who were opposed to taxation – some for reasons of political loyalty to the Croat political establishment, others because of their involvement in the oil and gas business. When the problem was eventually identified, local judges were afraid to take the case to court and only under pressure of internationals running the reconstruction programme was taxation legislation enforced. J. Poschl, 'Bosnia and Herzegovina after Five Years of Reconstruction', *WIIW Current Analyses and Country Profits*, Vienna, No.15 (April 2001).
26. P. Stubbs, '"Social Sector" or the Diminution of Social Policy/Regulating Welfare Regimes in Contemporary Bosnia-Herzegovina', mimeo, 2001.

27. A. van Rooy (ed.), *Civil Society and the Aid Industry*, London: Stylus Publishers, 1998, p.43.
28. T. Tvedt, *Angels of Mercy or Development Diplomats – NGOs and Foreign Aid*, Oxford: James Currey, 1998.
29. C. Malena, 'Beneficiaries, Mercenaries and Revolutionaries: "Unpacking" NGO Involvement in World Bank-Financed Projects', *IDS Bulletin*, Vol.21, No.3, 2000.
30. Decentralization in the context of reconstruction in the aftermath of new wars is not without risks as it is at the local level that the power of exclusionary social groups is the strongest. Thus, for example, we see strong opposition to refugee returns in local communities despite an agreement reached at the higher levels of political authority.
31. Howell and Pearce (n.16 above).

Peace Operations Finance and the Political Economy of a Way Out

JEAN DAUDELIN and LEE J.M. SEYMOUR

Two conspicuous features of the contemporary global security problématique need to be explicitly connected: first, diplomatic, humanitarian, developmental and military responses to conflict are hampered by a basic lack of resources; second, these underfunded interventions are increasingly directed at conflicts that thrive on resource abundance. In other words, while the global peace regime is constrained by resource shortfalls, rapacious competition over commodity rents perpetuates local conflict and frustrates peacemaking efforts. In the following pages, we argue that this contradiction must be transcended.

Drawing on recent research into the political economy of conflict and underdevelopment, three main arguments are presented below. First, we show how using local resources promises to expand the scale and scope of activities otherwise inhibited by the international system's inability to provide adequate financing for peace operations and related activities. The second section considers the political economy of resource wars. It explains how control over local resources by external political intermediaries is often a necessary step towards decisively establishing an environment of security and stability, the conditions for confidence building, and eventually, a centre of gravity around which a new authority structure can coalesce. In a third section, we take a long-term, developmental perspective. We argue that external control of key sectors of conflict-affected economies, especially primary industries, is crucial in the interim period between external intervention and the rehabilitation of administrative structures. By managing the reconstruction of local economies, interveners can help consolidate an environment of security and stability supported by sustainable development patterns. Finally, we outline in practical terms the specific mechanisms that would allow peace operations to 'live off the land'.

The Political Economy of Paralysis

To borrow from the Brahimi Report, 'The United Nations was founded, in the words of its Charter, in order "to save succeeding generations from the scourge of war"... Over the last decade, the United Nations has repeatedly failed to meet the challenge, and it can do no better today'.[1] The failings of the global peace regime are multiple and inter-related, with political, organizational and operational dimensions, notwithstanding the inherent complexity of peace operations and the difficult conditions in which they operate. Yet given the weight of economic variables in the interventionist calculus, peacekeeping finance has received relatively little attention, in part due to a preoccupation with the moral, legal and political aspects of the global interventionist regime.[2] In the early 1990s, most notably, efforts to check an expanding peacekeeping budget generated pressures to curtail commitments to, among other places, Rwanda. The genocide that followed brought into sharp focus the yawning gap between supply and demand in international peacekeeping.

At any given time, tens of complex emergencies compete for the limited resources available to address their causes and consequences. Thus, the scope and efficacy of outside interventions invariably reflect the economics of scarcity. Consider recent responses to conflict in the Democratic Republic of Congo. Over seven months after the signature of the Lusaka Protocol, UN Resolution 1291 (2000) authorized the deployment of 500 military observers, to be followed by 5,537 military personnel. Then US Ambassador to the UN, Richard Holbrooke, defended this American-formulated mandate as a response to previously 'unrealistic peacekeeping proposals'.[3] By way of comparison, the UN had approved a 'realistic' NATO-led force of 40,000 for Kosovo in June 1999, a small province of 2 million people versus the 52 million people of the DRC, a country 215 times larger.

Ostensibly, the UN system provides for the financing of authorized missions as peacekeeping is a collective UN responsibility. By rights, there is no reason for missions conducted under UN auspices to face financial shortfalls. The problem does not lie in the sums of money involved: the estimated cumulative cost of peacekeeping from 1948 to June 2001 was just $23.3 billion, and in 2000 expenditure on UN peacekeeping was just $2.6 billion – a drop in the $719 billion ocean of global military expenditure.[4] To put this another way, 'a contribution as small as 0.0002 per cent of GDP would allow a NATO ally to claim the largest peacekeeping burden in terms of GDP'.[5] Nevertheless, the funds to mount consistent and effective responses are systematically withheld from the UN. Part of the problem is procedural, as assessments come at inopportune times in national budgetary cycles. Other states are simply unable to meet commitments due to economic hardship. However, most attention has focused on the United States' practice of regularly withholding payments in order to compel administrative and structural reforms. In the first half of 2001, US arrears hovered at $1.5 billion.[6] As a result, and because shortfalls in the regular budget force the UN to borrow from the peacekeeping account, the Organization owes 72 countries over $1.1 billion for contributions of troops and equipment.[7]

One of the more remarkable features of peacekeeping finance is the way in which the costs of UN missions are concentrated on developed states. In 2000, before an end of the year agreement to reform the scale of peacekeeping assessments, the top five contributors (the United States, Japan, Germany, France and Italy) paid 75 per cent of the peacekeeping budget and 98 per cent of it was borne by just 30 states.[8] Together, the world's remaining 159 states account for the balance of 2 per cent. Reforms to this scale that distribute the burden more broadly were adopted at the end of 2000, introducing a ten-tiered scale assessed as a proportion of GNP with discounts staggered from 7.5 to 90 per cent. By virtue of the disparities in GNP between North and South, however, costs will still be borne overwhelmingly by developed states. One result of this cost distribution is differential, some might even say discriminatory,[9] treatment in the choice of countries to which UN peacekeepers are sent.

The near-universal response to this financial impasse is to implore the international community to 'get serious'. This tendency is exemplified in the Brahimi Report: 'the changes that the Panel recommends will have no lasting impact unless Member States summon the political will to support the United Nations politically, financially and operationally to enable the United Nations to be truly credible as a force for peace.'[10] Realistically, there is little reason to think that so drastic a change in political priorities will take place over anything but the long term. In the meantime, it is incumbent upon those determined to address the causes and consequences of conflict to consider alternative financing modalities.

The Political Economy of Resource Wars

One way in which the cost of conflict management is decoupled from a reliance on the UN and its northern financiers is through the proliferation of Chapter VIII operations that devolve responsibility and expenses to regional organizations – as captured in the fashionable notion of 'African solutions to African problems'. Clearly, however, Africa's regional and subregional organizations can neither mount the multifaceted operations necessary to effectively respond to complex emergencies nor pay for their costs. Without denying the importance of problems such as inadequate training, logistics and equipment, it is obvious that financial aspects figure prominently among the impediments to conflict management in Africa. By way of illustration, the entire annual budget of the OAU, about $30 million, would be insufficient to fund anything but a tiny UN observer mission.[11] International donors have been lukewarm about funding military operations involving countries with dubious human rights records and ambiguous motives. As well, African leaders face domestic political constraints as people question the legitimacy of financing expensive interventions often divorced from local concerns or broader public interests.

For these reasons, many of Africa's recent interventions have been 'self-financing'. Beginning with the series of Nigerian-led, overlapping 'humanitarian' interventions in west Africa, a familiar pattern has emerged characterized by tendencies towards militarized commerce, privatized security and practices reminiscent of economic colonialism. All of these phenomena are evident in the current conflict in the DRC. While such practices have dubious security and development impacts, they have theoretical implications for an investigation into the possibility of harnessing their logic in ways that privilege the public welfare of host communities over the private gain of intervening parties.

Self-financing Interventions in the DRC

Whereas it was previously assumed that ambitious military expeditions were beyond the means of the impoverished states of sub-Saharan Africa, resource exploitation has widened the opportunities for external intervention. In the DRC, the presence of Zimbabwe and Angola, the primary allies of Kabila *père et fils*, has been paid for by mortgaging the DRC's resource wealth. The Zimbabwean Defence Minister was particularly candid in explaining the economics of his country's involvement: 'Instead of our army in the DRC burdening the treasury for more resources which are not available, it embarks on viable projects for the sake of generating the necessary revenue.'[12] Zimbabwe, however, has subsequently encountered difficulties in recouping the costs of intervention through preferential deals for arms sales and Congolese diamonds, gold, cobalt, electricity and agriculture.[13] In the end, the government could not afford the costs of intervention – estimated in February 2000 at $160m in extra-budgetary public spending and $180m in lost equipment.[14] On the opposing side, Uganda's commercial interests have successfully served to underwrite its interventions. President Museveni has argued that 'there is no way that you can link our poverty to our involvement in the Congo... in fact, [it] is part of poverty eradication'.[15] He has a good case. Since participating in the coalition that overthrew Mobutu, entrepreneurial operations in eastern DRC have helped redress the Ugandan economy's balance-of-payment deficit and assisted negotiations with international creditors, all the while lining the pockets of individuals with political and military connections.[16]

Comparative examples can also be derived from private military (that is, 'corporate mercenary') intervention, and ECOMOG[17] missions in Sierra Leone and Liberia. Needless to say, the developmental and security impacts of these operations have been ambiguous at best, and in the case of the DRC outright horrific. Together, these cases highlight a host of problems: subversion of humanitarian ends by economic objectives with ECOMOG; fomentation of local rivalries to further business interests, as in Uganda's role in Hema-Lendu violence in Ituri; tensions in civil–military relations and a breakdown of the command and control structure of armed forces; and troubled relations with the host community as a result of corruption and predation.

Yet these problems derive from the particular means employed and the ends served, rather than from the fact that intervening forces are 'living off the land' *per se*. Sceptics should realize that the potential sums are huge. While it is difficult to establish an accurate picture of the country's natural resource exports, the late Laurent Kabila was said to have been earning around $1 billion a year from diamond and cobalt sales alone.[18] If international authorities could access even a fraction of this it would go a long way towards covering the immense costs of providing security, reconstruction and rehabilitation in the DRC.

Control of Local Resources and the Exercise of International Authority

Transforming the political economy of local resource extraction holds the promise of enabling peace operations financially. But beyond this initial rationale, our proposal is also informed by the dynamics of resource conflicts. As the literature on peace-maintenance has argued, too many recent peacekeeping missions have been compromised by the inability of external intermediaries to effectively exercise political authority.[19] As a solution, peace-maintenance advocates the establishment of an internationally mandated authority inside the war-torn polity in the form of protectorate-like arrangements. Ultimately, however, the process of establishing international authority hinges upon undermining the power and influence of those whose privileged economic and political positions are threatened by the sorts of transformations integral to the success of peacebuilding. In many situations, there is perhaps no better way to suppress the incentives for continued violence than by controlling the conflict commodities themselves.

In examining the correlation between the exercise of political authority and control of local resources, the 'resource wars' of late twentieth-century Africa are particularly instructive. Despite diverse origins and histories, the economic dimensions of conflicts in the DRC, Angola and Sierra Leone manifest a common pattern, as indicated by the following excerpts from a series of 'Expert Panel' reports to the UN on the political economy of conflict:

> [In Angola] UNITA's ongoing ability to sell rough diamonds for cash and to exchange rough diamonds for weapons provides the means for it to sustain its political and military activities.[20]
>
> Diamonds have become an important resource for Sierra Leone's Revolutionary United Front in sustaining and advancing its military ambitions.[21]
>
> The assumption behind the mandate [of the UN panel on illegal resource exploitation in the DRC] is that the parties to the conflict are motivated by a desire to control and profit from the natural resources of the Democratic Republic of the Congo, and that they finance their armies and their military operations by exploiting those resources.[22]

In countries like Angola, Sierra Leone and the DRC, violent armed actors are enmeshed in complex production and exchange relationships that generate incentives for continued violence, instability and underdevelopment.

It is not surprising, then, that the failure of conflict management efforts for all three countries can be explained, in large part, by the inability of external actors to deprive warlords of the resources that sustain their militarized neo-patrimonial networks. Thus, UNITA's exploitation of Angola's diamond and other resources was a key factor in the collapse of both the Bicesse (1991–92) and Lusaka (1994–98) peace processes, both overseen by peacekeeping missions. In the latter case, an understaffed UN mission (UNAVEM III, later named

MONUA) was deployed to supervise a peace agreement at a total cost of over $1 billion. In the division of governmental ministries during the Lusaka peace negotiations, UNITA gained control of the Ministry responsible for overseeing diamond production and marketing.[23] Remarkably, UNITA mined an estimated $1.72 billion worth of rough diamonds before the breakdown of the Lusaka process in late 1998.[24] As with the previous period of internationally supervised peace in 1991–92, these revenues were not used to reinvent UNITA as a legitimate political movement. Instead, when hostilities resumed by late 1998 the movement's diamond-financed military procurement left it better armed than ever.

Similar lessons can be drawn from the Sierra Leone case. The Revolutionary United Front's (RUF) power derives from its links to illicit alluvial mining in the Kono region. Estimates of the RUF's annual diamond production range from $25 to $125 million. Diamonds are the currency of transborder exchanges for arms and other material across the Liberian and Guinean frontiers and, perhaps more importantly, buy the patronage of Liberian President Charles Taylor.[25] True to form, the key failing of ECOMOG and UN missions to the country has been their inability to deprive RUF rebels of the proceeds of this diamond-based war economy. As others have recognized, 'peace in Sierra Leone will remain unsustainable until the economic gains to be derived from criminality and violence are squarely addressed'.[26]

Likewise, empirical examples such as these have informed quantitative, large-*n* studies that have contributed to a growing understanding of the political economy of war. Prominent among these is the work of Paul Collier and colleagues at the World Bank. Their economic theory of conflict places emphasis not on 'the justice of the struggle', but on the ability of rebel organizations to sustain themselves financially.[27] Accordingly, 'peace requires that the intense political conflict continue but that the military option of conducting it should be made infeasible'.[28]

In framing future missions, it is obvious that in the absence of an agreement with belligerents to withdraw from key sites in networks of accumulation and transboundary exchange, or without the coercive capacity to force such withdrawals, the authority of intermediaries is likely to be severely undermined. As argued in the Brahimi Report,

> Would-be spoilers have the greatest incentive to defect from peace accords when they have an independent source of income that pays soldiers, buys guns, enriches faction leaders and may even have been the motive for war. Recent history indicates that,

where such income streams from the export of illicit narcotics, gemstones or other high-value commodities cannot be pinched off, peace is unsustainable.[29]

Clearly, hitherto neglected activities such as policing borders, controlling the export of illicit goods, reducing the influence of criminal syndicates and cracking down on the importation of war material are an essential element in successful peace operations.

An important example of how the military option might be made infeasible by targeting war economies comes by way of Sierra Leone. While UNAMSIL has failed to drive the RUF from the diamond region, private military company Executive Outcomes (EO) has shown how the control of strategic resources by external actors facilitates the establishment of a modicum of security. In fact, EO was able to evict the RUF from key diamond-rich areas with just 150–200 soldiers and government and militia support as part of its successful three-prong operation to (1) expel the RUF from Freetown's environs; (2) stabilize the diamond areas around Koindu (notably, in order for its commercial partners to conduct their own mining operations); and (3) locate and destroy RUF headquarters.[30] With the RUF cast out of mining areas, EO maintained a security presence at economically vital points, thereby cutting into RUF production.[31] Though controversial, it has been argued that 'the involvement of EO in Sierra Leone was in a good cause... [and] EO was certainly cheered on the streets of Freetown for its efforts'.[32]

Still, an equally important lesson from Sierra Leone highlights the dangers of peacekeepers themselves illegally profiting from local resources. The extent of 'military commercialism' in Sierra Leone emerged in a press-leaked unofficial memorandum to the UN from the Indian commander of UNAMSIL, General Jetley. Arguing that 'major players in the diamond racket like Liberia and Nigeria' were undermining his mandate, Jetley suggested that during the ECOMOG mission, 'keeping the Nigerian interest was paramount even if it meant scuttling the peace process'. He continued,

> It is well known that public opinion in Nigeria was against the continued deployment of Nigerian troops as part of ECOMOG in Sierra Leone, however the army was interested in staying... due to the benefits they were getting from illegal mining. Gen Khobe [a senior Nigerian military officer] was known as the 'Ten Million Man,' it is alleged that he received up to $10m to permit the activities of the RUF. The ECOMOG force commander Gen Kpamber was also involved in the illegal diamond mining in connivance with RUF leader Foday Sankoh.

These practices predate UNAMSIL, and can be traced back to the 1990 ECOMOG intervention in Liberia.[33] In the absence of sufficient international support or adequate domestic resources – the US was the major international donor to operations in Liberia with a paltry $10m per year between 1990 and 1995 – and given the deeply-rooted military corruption that plagues many African armed forces, Nigeria and its ECOWAS partners subsidized their protracted engagement through violent accumulation and predation, often in connivance with local factions.

The Political Economy of Peace Maintenance

Clearly, the use of local resources for internationally mandated purposes supposes a degree of professional conduct that was clearly absent in the case of ECOMOG and UNAMSIL. Yet, until the reliance of intervening parties on the resources available in the local economy is made explicit, and strong institutions are devised to oversee such undertakings, one should not be surprised by the prevalence of shady practices. Equally important is putting into place a framework to mitigate the negative characteristics of governance in conflicted rentier states, such as vertical and horizontal corruptions, warlordism and infra-institutionalism. The final thrust of our argument argues that establishing effective interim control over key sectors of the local economy is a necessary step towards bolstering human development and security beyond the departure of international authorities.

Recent research has confirmed strong relationships between (1) a large natural resource base and underdevelopment; (2) underdevelopment and conflict; and (3) peacebuilding failure and natural resource dependence. Indra de Soysa's research on the 'resource curse', for example, provides support for the 'Dutch disease' and 'resource trap' hypotheses linking resource abundance to lower levels of economic and social progress, both of which have significant indirect effects on conflict propensity.[34] Collier likewise confirms that low income and economic decline are both significant risk factors for conflict. Furthermore, in a finding with direct relevance for peace operations, Collier asserts that 'immediately after the end of hostilities there is a 40 per cent chance of further conflict. This risk then falls at around one percentage point for each year of peace'.[35] Finally, another study finds a correlation between a dependence on natural resources and peacebuilding failure.[36]

Several policy implications can be drawn from these findings. First, peace-maintenance operations must address the patterns of governance responsible for the observed confluence of underdevelopment, resource wealth and conflict. It is difficult to see how such systemic reforms can be carried out independent of protectorate-like arrangements, including interim control over resource sectors. Second, it must be realized that promoting good governance, economic growth, and even changing the political culture of a country are lengthy endeavours. The increased probability of renewed conflict in the years and decades following war indicates that the long-term perspective should be paramount in peace maintenance planning.

The difficulty of operationalizing such research is evident in the peace maintenance laboratory that is the United Nations Transitional Administration in East Timor (UNTAET). Arriving in an environment where pre-conflict institutions and markets had collapsed, international agencies operating under the UN's interim administration faced serious humanitarian and developmental challenges. But slowly the pieces of the nation-building puzzle are falling into place. Paradoxically, the most serious challenge to Timor's developmental prospects is probably the offshore petroleum industry on which the country has, in large part, staked its economic prospects.[37] The UN administration has laid the groundwork for this industry by exercising control over the oil sector through the governing trusteeship arrangement. Though development agencies still expect to be engaged well past the transition to independence, they now see an oil-abundant Timor as a prospective model of small-state, sustainable development. To this end, the World Bank Trust Fund for East Timor has run several small projects on integrity in government and good governance, in addition to advocating a zero-tolerance approach towards corruption.[38] But it remains too early to determine whether or not Timor can escape the perverting effects of the rentier state. Serious long-term challenges are posed by the connections between resource abundance and low levels of economic and human development, aggravated social tensions, poor governance, peacebuilding failure and increased likelihood of conflict.

A Pragmatic Toolbox

This article is not the first to propose alternatives for financing UN operations.[39] Yet the majority of the proposals thus far have involved lofty global governance schemes for independently funding the UN, and often its own standing UN army, by means of levies, taxes, bond issues, lotteries and such; one report identifies up to 20 such proposals.[40] In his *An Agenda for Peace*, Boutros-Ghali proposed levies on arms sales and international air travel, authorization to borrow from the Bretton Woods Institutions and tax exemptions for private contributions to the UN.⁴¹ Significantly, such proposals were ruled out as neither 'practical nor desirable' in the Volcker and Ogata Report authored by an expert advisory group convened by Boutros-Ghali himself.⁴² While it would be unwise to dismiss these measures out of hand, the impediments to their adoption currently appear insurmountable. The requisite levels of administrative complexity and international cooperation required appear beyond reach.

We contend that relying on the resources of the country where the operation takes place offers a practical solution to the problems of financing peacekeeping missions. Obviously, this involves thinking imaginatively, and will not occur without the support of key actors in organizations such as the United Nations and its agencies, and the international financial institutions. Yet with a mix of creativity and pragmatism, one can envisage a number of sources of revenue. A list of such financing options, by no means exhaustive, is surveyed below.

Transforming Conflict Commodities, Escrow Accounts and Trust Funds

One possibility, and for our purposes the most germane, involves the use of commodity revenues to directly offset the costs of peace operations through a scheme whereby the UN assumes control of a share of revenues from a key resource, perhaps in cooperation with a private sector operator. While the precise modalities need specification, part of the proceeds could be put towards directly financing peace operations. The closest example of such a mechanism is found in the UN's quasi-protectorate, East Timor. UNTAET signed, on behalf of the future East Timor government, a memorandum of understanding with Australia over royalty sharing from oil and gas exploitation in the offshore Timor Gap Zone of Co-operation. In October 2000, UNTAET received its first monthly royalty payment, worth over $3 million, for oil exploitation in the Timor Sea. The project could provide up to $150 million per year by 2010.⁴³

To create the conditions for future development, a portion of resource revenues derived by peace operations administrators could be placed in offshore escrow accounts or trust funds. These could then be released when institutions are in place to secure the equitable and economically sensible allocation of funds. Recommendations for an oil trust programme along such lines have been moved concerning oil exploitation in Sudan,⁴⁴ and there is a similar precedent – admittedly problematic – in the 'oil for food' programme whereby Iraq's oil revenues are managed by the UN Office of the Iraq Programme and apportioned between humanitarian spending, administrative costs and war-related compensation (with the latter incidentally representing the largest share by far).[45] Perhaps the best example comes by way of the World Bank's participation in Chad's Doba basin oil exploitation. In response to criticism of potential environmental and conflict impacts, the World Bank conditioned its involvement in the project on strict accounting standards, transparency mechanisms, definitions of how revenues would be allocated and the setting up of instruments to ensure these conditions were adhered to – essentially denying government discretion over the allocation of revenues once the project comes on line in 2004.[46] Despite these efforts, as opponents feared $4 million from the project's entrance fee was spent on arms, though these monies are not specifically part of the World Bank arrangement.[47]

Comparable arrangements could be extended to any conflict in which resource rents fuel conflict or are themselves the object of contention, assuming that the particular commodity is legal (whatever the merits of legalizing the international drug trade, the prospects for international supervision of the opium trade in Afghanistan and Burma, or cocaine trade in Colombia, remain slim). Indeed, UN deployment could be conditioned on such an agreement. The alternative is the perpetuation of the sort of absurd arrangements witnessed in UNAVEM III in Angola. As the mission struggled to fund peace operations, UNITA mined hundreds of millions worth of diamonds and the Angolan government earned $2.6 billion from oil royalties in 1996 alone, spending just 0.8 per cent of revenues on the peace process versus 35 per cent on defence.[48]

Tax and Customs Revenue

In situations where international authorities provide interim administration, including functions such as border control and tax collection, the practice of funding peace operations through local resources is already established. In Kosovo, for instance, almost half of the United Nations Mission in Kosovo's (UNMIK) budget is derived from local collection, primarily via customs and tax revenues. The Central Fiscal Authority's budget forecasts that local sources will account for 70 per cent of spending by the end of 2001.[49] This self-financing generates sustainability and decreases the mission's dependency on international donors whose miserly contributions have periodically kept UNMIK at the brink of insolvency.[50] Further, it shows that tapping the local economy – even in ways that have complicated the relationship between UNMIK, the Former Republic of Yugoslavia and the international community – need not be held hostage by international sensitivity to perceived violations of sovereignty.

Asset Seizure

Tracing and then seizing illegitimately earned assets is another possible source of revenue (if 'local' resources are taken to include those cached in offshore banking facilities).[51] A 1998 report from the UN Secretary-General recognized the potential in this area, calling for the development of 'international legal machinery to facilitate efforts to find, attach and seize the assets of transgressing parties and their leaders'.[52] The stakes are in many cases substantial: Nigeria's Abachas, for example, are estimated to have looted some $4 billion from public funds – monies that could indirectly support their country's important regional role in the maintenance of peace and security. If the UN began to act pre-emptively, in order to preclude the common practice of concealing funds in anticipation of sanctions, these resources could be funnelled back to deserving populations through peacekeeping, humanitarian, developmental and other efforts.

Individual/Corporate Responsibility and International Law

Another closely related recommendation from the Secretary-General is the idea of making warring parties more accountable for their actions by holding them financially liable under international law for the costs of reconstruction and rehabilitation.[53] In one case, Bosnian women were successful in a lawsuit against Bosnian Serb leader Radovan Karadžić in US courts. The women were awarded $745 million in damages, and a similar verdict held Karadžić liable for $4.5 billion in the deaths of 39 people.[54] Admittedly, the scope for enforcing such provisions is limited, as is the prospect for the victims actually receiving compensation.

Yet multinational corporations, complicit in an increasing number of conflicts, are subject to legal jurisdictions through which these funds could be recovered. De Beers Centenary AG knowingly abetted conflict in Angola by placing diamond buyers on the Zaïrean frontier to purchase stones mined by UNITA in order to stabilize the global supply of rough diamonds throughout the early and mid-1990s. Further, before its very public change of attitude following charges that it dealt in 'blood diamonds', De Beers was credibly alleged to be in violation of the UN sanctions on purchases of diamonds mined by UNITA in resolution 1173 (1998).[55] Elf-Aquitaine (now merged with TotalFina) has likewise been implicated in financing a $5.8 million arms-for-oil deal with Congo-Brazzaville's president Pascal Lissouba.[56]

Similarly, Canada's Talisman Energy has been accused of exacerbating war in Sudan. As a report commissioned by the Canadian government to look into Talisman's involvement argued: 'We cannot but conclude that our own observations and investigations only add to the growing body of evidence and information that identifies Sudan as a place of extraordinary suffering... and that the oil operations in which a Canadian company is involved add more suffering.'[57] Holding these companies responsible for the consequences of their operations could directly fund peace operations, prove a deterrent and improve compliance with UN sanctions.

Legal developments in the United States hint at the potential scope of corporate liability and future directions in American tort law with international ramifications. Innovative use of the 211-year-old Alien Tort Claims Act (ATCA) – the instrument used in the Karadzić cases – has changed the calculations of multinational corporations operating abroad. Chevron is facing a suit under the ATCA for the alleged slaughter of 112 protesting workers in Nigeria in May 1998. An earlier ruling held that oil company Unocal could be held liable for the use of slave labour and the torture of workers in a joint venture with the ruling military dictatorship in Burma/Myanmar.[58] However, a September 2000 decision overturned that ruling, arguing that the company could not be held liable despite knowing about and profiting from slave labour. The case is under appeal.[59]

The Dark Side

Objections to the use of local resources to finance peace-maintenance deserve serious reflection. Despite the apparent radicalism of this proposal, practice is leading theory. There is a pressing need for further research on the implications of local resource use in the financing of peace operations, drawing on experiences in places such as Kosovo and East Timor. This much-needed assessment could only be given a pithy treatment here, and our analysis does not pretend to be complete. Suffice it to say that the consequences of such practices need careful evaluation.

While the context of each intervention will produce variations on the theme of using local resources through ad hoc measures and the customary politics of 'muddling through', there are a number of general principles that should be followed.

First, local resources should benefit the community from which they are drawn. However desirable the goal of an internationally managed funding mechanism, diverting resources from certain communities to finance operations elsewhere will rightly be perceived as illegitimate. Such practices would truly approximate the colonial enterprise: 'While a colonial power draws resources from a colony, an international authority directs resources into a nation.'[60]

Second, locally raised revenues should not be used to replace international financing. The principle (or, more accurately, the fiction) of collective financial responsibility is central to the legitimacy of international peacekeeping, and countries lacking appreciable domestic resources should not be condemned to neglect. Using a territory's resources to provide public goods for the local population should not detract from the nature of international peacekeeping as a sort of global public good through its contribution to world stability and security. Initial practice in Kosovo unfortunately suggests that tax revenues are merely used to sustain operations in the face of decreasing donor support, rather than providing for an expansion of operations. At the very least, it can be hoped either that a greater number of missions could be undertaken as the financial threshold is lowered, or that scarce funds will be released for use elsewhere.

Third, private sector participation in peace maintenance incurs the danger of economic agendas distorting the implementation of the mandate, just as the presence of powers with strategic interests in interventions taints their humanitarian credentials. Accountability and transparency mechanisms, with strong input from local communities, will be necessary to safeguard against such threats. One should keep in mind, however, that without the international action that such arrangements can facilitate, economic interests will continue to operate – through outside the auspices of an internationally mandated authority tasked with ensuring that the security and developmental impacts of corporate activities are given due consideration.

Conclusion

We suspect that many of the proposals above have been read with a degree of cynicism. But what alternatives have we? There are few indications that those with the ability to pay for effective responses to conflict, namely northern states, are becoming more inclined towards intervention (or the bankrolling of intervention) in areas of marginal geo-strategic or economic interest. Yet these areas include most of Africa and Asia, which together account for the preponderance of global conflict. Conversely, southern states, almost without exception, do not have the funds or capacity to independently support regional operations. These financial shortfalls, and the political economy of paralysis they engender, have left populations vulnerable while international conflict managers are condemned to either watch tragedy unfold from the sidelines or conduct operations on a shoestring budget.

We have attempted to show how control over, and exploitation of, local resources are integral components of peace operations and are inherent in the logic of any feasible model of transition, most especially in societies emerging from 'resource wars' and with a history of resource-dependent development. Yet the possibility that even the most comprehensive peace-maintenance operation might fail to bridge conflict resolution and sustainable development should be considered. Again with East Timor – the first country where the UN has acted as an interim sovereign authority, and an unprecedented example of the use of local resources to finance peacebuilding and reconstruction – the success of the transition process is uncertain. Jarat Chopra, who resigned his post as head of the UNTAET Office for District Administration in frustration, observes that despite all the advantages of the mission, 'it still went wrong'.[61] Chopra observes that the UN is ill-suited to administering territories in transition, a belief shared by others.[62] He therefore calls for a broad brokerage framework for the subcontracting of administrative and service provision functions to whichever agency, be it foreign or local, non-governmental or private, has the required capacity. His conclusion on the need for such reforms applies equally to the notion of using local resources: 'This is not a rallying cry for privatisation; it is a marker of practicality.'[63] While privatization fits well with the proposal examined here, it is uncertain whether either set of reforms can improve the dismal record of peace operations in the 1990s. If the UN fails in East Timor, arguably the easiest test case one could hope for, the international community is likely to lose what little enthusiasm it currently has for undertaking such tasks.

NOTES

1. United Nations, *Report of the Panel on United Nations Peace Operations*, A/55/305 & S/2000/809, 17 Aug. 2000, p.viii.
2. The early 1990s, when the UN financial crisis coincided with unprecedented expansion of the peacekeeping budget, provides an exception to this rule. See for example, Susan Mills, *The Financing of United Nations Peacekeeping Operations: The Need for a Sound Financial Basis*, International Peace Academy Occasional Papers on Peacekeeping, No.3, 1989; Shijuro Ogata and Paul Volcker, *Financing an Effective United Nations: A Report of the Independent Advisory Group on UN Financing*. New York: Ford Foundation, Apr. 1993.
3. Richard Holbrooke, 'Testimony before the House Committee on International Relations', Washington DC, 15 Feb. 2000.
4. Figures from the United Nations Department of Peacekeeping and the Stockholm International Peace Research Institute, respectively.

5. Todd Sandler and Keith Hartley, *The Political Economy of NATO: Past, Present and into the 21st Century*, Cambridge: Cambridge University Press, 1999, p.103.
6. United Nations Department of Public Information, DPI/1634/Rev.21a, Sept. 2001.
7. Global Policy Forum, 'Payments Owed by the UN to Member Countries for Peacekeeping Operations: Dec. 2000', accessed at www.globalpolicy.org/finance/tables/pko/0012owed.htm.
8. 'United States Mission to the United Nations, Fact Sheet, UN Peacekeeping Scale of Assessment', updated 10 Jan. 2001 accessed at www.un.int/usa/fact7.htm.
9. See David Malone and Ramesh Thakur, 'Racism in Peacekeeping', *The Globe and Mail*, Toronto, 30 Oct. 2000.
10. United Nations (n.1 above), viii.
11. The UN Observer Mission in Georgia, for instance, has an annual appropriation of $30m to fund 240 international and local personnel.
12. 'Zimbabwe's Costly Congo Adventure', *BBC Africa*, 20 Jan. 2000.
13. See Robert Block, 'Zimbabwe's Elite Turn Strife in Nearby Congo into a Quest for Riches', *Wall Street Journal*, New York, 9 Oct. 1998; David Shearer, 'Africa's Great War', *Survival*, Vol. 41, 1999, pp.89–106.
14. International Crisis Group, *Scramble for the Congo*, pp.60-63 accessed at www.intl-crisis-group.org/projects/africa/d.r.congo/reports/A400130_20122000.pdf.
15. 'Congo war helps fight poverty, says Museveni', *The Monitor*, Kampala, 23 March 2000; quoted in William Reno, 'War, Debt and the Role of Pretending in Uganda's International Relations', Occasional Paper, Centre of African Studies, University of Copenhagen, July 2000.
16. Reno (n.15 above), p.13.
17. ECOMOG stands for 'ECOWAS Monitoring Group'. It was set up by the Economic Community of Western African States (ECOWAS) at its May 1990 Summit in Banjul, Gambia, to intervene in the Liberia's civil war and subsequently moved on into Sierra Leone. Like ECOWAS, ECOMOG is financed and dominated by Nigeria.
18. International Crisis Group (n.14 above), p.54. See also United Nations, *Interim Report of the United Nations Expert Panel on the Illegal Exploitation of Natural Resources and Other Forms of Wealth of the Democratic Republic of the Congo*, S/2001/49, 16 Jan. 2001.
19. Jarat Chopra, *Peace-Maintenance: The Evolution of International Political Authority* New York: Routledge, 1999; and Jarat Chopra (ed.), *The Politics of Peace-Maintenance*, Boulder: Lynne Rienner, 1998.
20. United Nations, *Report of the Panel of Experts on Violations of Security Council Sanctions Against UNITA*, S/2000/203, 10 March 2000, para. 117.
21. United Nations, *Report of the Panel of Experts Appointed Pursuant to Security Council Resolution 1306 (2000), Paragraph 19, in Relation to Sierra Leone*, S/2000/1195, 20 Dec. 2000, para. 1 accessed at www.globalpolicy.org/security/issues/sierra/report/001220.htm.
22. United Nations, *Illegal Exploitation of Natural Resources and Other Forms of Wealth of the Democratic Republic of the Congo*, para. 5.
23. Former RUF leader Foday Sankoh learned from this experience (unlike the international community) in securing the equivalent post, Chairman of the Commission for the Management of Strategic Mineral Resources, under the July 1999 Lomé Peace Agreement.
24. Human Rights Watch, *Angola Unravels: The Rise and Fall of the Lusaka Peace Process*, New York, 1999.
25. United Nations (n.21 above), para. 248.
26. Ian Smillie, Lansana Gberie and Ralph Hazelton, *Heart of the Matter: Sierra Leone, Diamonds and Human Security*, Ottawa: Partnership Africa Canada, 2000, p.14.
27. Paul Collier, 'Economic Causes of Civil Conflict and Their Implications for Policy', World Bank, 15 June 2000, p.4. See also Paul Collier, 'Doing Well out of War: An Economic Perspective', in Mats Berdal and David Malone (eds), *Greed and Grievance: Economic Agendas in Civil Wars*, Boulder: Lynne Rienner for IPA, 2000, pp.91–112.

28. Paul Collier, 'Economic Causes of Civil Conflict and Implications for Policy', 15 June 2000, p.18 accessed at www.worldbank.org/research/conflict/papers/civilconflict.pdf.
29. United Nations (n1. above), p.4. Also Stephen John Stedman, 'Spoiler Problem in Peace Processes', *International Security*, Vol.22, No.2, 1997, pp.5–53.
30. David Francis, 'Mercenary Intervention in Sierra Leone: Providing International Security or International Exploitation', *Third World Quarterly*, Vol.20, No.2, 1999, p.327.
31. Ian Douglas, 'Fighting for Diamonds – Private Military Companies in Sierra Leone', in Jakkie Cilliers and Peggy Mason (eds), *Peace, Profit or Plunder? The Privatisation of Security in War-Torn States*, ISS: Halfway House, 1999, p.183.
32. Smillie, Gberie and Hazelton (n.26 above), p.60.
33. The intervention and the political economy of the Liberian conflict are considered in greater detail in, among others, Christopher Tuck, 'Every Car or Moving Object Gone: The ECOMOG Intervention in Liberia', *African Studies Quarterly*, Vol.4, No.1 accessed at web.africa.ufl.edu/asq/v4/v4i1a1.htm; William Reno, 'The Business of War in Liberia,' *Current History*, May 1996.
34. Indra de Soysa, 'Natural Resources & Civil War: Shrinking Pie or Honey Pot', paper presented to the 41st Annual Convention of the International Studies Association, Los Angeles, 20 March 2000, p.24 accessed at www.wws.princeton.edu/~cis/DESOYSA. PDF See the World Institute for Development Economics Research project on this issue at www.wider.unu.edu/research/research.htm.
35. Paul Collier, 'Economic Causes of Civil Conflict and Their Implications for Policy' (n.27 above), p.6.
36. Michael Doyle and Nicholas Sambinàs, 'International Peacebuilding: A Theoretical and Quantitative Analysis', *American Political Science Review*, Vol.94, No.4, 2000, accessed at www.worldbank.org/research/conflict/papers/peacebuilding/pbapsr_finalv4.pdf.
37. Lee Seymour, 'East Timor's Resource Curse?', *Far Eastern Economic Review*, 30 Nov. 2000.
38. World Bank Trust Fund for East Timor, 'Update No. 6', 9 Feb. 2001.
39. See, for example, A. McDermott, *The New Politics of Financing the United Nations*, New York: St. Martin's, 2000; United States General Accounting Office, *United Nations Financial Issues and US Arrears*, Washington: GAO/NSIAD-98-201BR, June 1998; Ruben P. Mendez, 'Financing the UN and the International Public Sector', *Global Governance*, Vol.3, No.3, 1997, pp.295–304; United Nations, *New and Innovative Ideas for Generating Funds for Globally Agreed Commitments and Priorities*, A/52/203 and E/1997/85, 23 June 1997.
40. Overseas Development Institute, 'Financing for Development', Briefing Paper, Feb. 1996.
41. Boutros Boutros-Ghali, *An Agenda for Peace: Preventative Diplomacy, Peacemaking and Peace-keeping*, A/47/277 and S/24111, 17 June 1992, para. 71.
42. Volcker and Ogata, *Financing an Independent United Nations* (n.2 above), p.23.
43. 'East Timor receives first royalty payment from oil exploitation in Timor Gap', *UN News Service*, 24 Oct. 2000.
44. See Government of Canada, *Human Security in Sudan: The Report of a Canadian Assessment Mission*, January 2000, p.67, accessed at www.dfait-maeci.gc.ca/foreignp/3110186-e.pdf.
45. See www.un.org/Depts/oip.
46. World Bank, 'Chad –(Cameroon) Petroleum Development and Pipeline Project', 23 June 1999, accessed at www.worldbank.org/pics/pid/td44305.txt.
47. 'World Bank Embarrassed as Chad Spends Oil Money on War', *Mail & Guardian*, 1 Dec. 2000; 'World Bank Reassesses Chad Pipeline Deal', *Washington Post*, 5 Dec. 2000.
48. IMF and National Bank of Angola statistics cited in Global Witness, *A Crude Awakening: The Role of the Oil and Banking Industries in Angola's Civil War and the Plunder of State Assets*, London: Global Witness, 2000 pp.7–8.

49. United Nations, 'Report of the Secretary-General on the United Nations Interim Administration Mission in Kosovo', S/2000/1196, 15 Dec. 2000, para. 104–5.
50. 'UN Chief in Kosovo Says Lack of Money Imperils Mission', *New York Times*, 4 March 2000.
51. See Samuel Porteus, 'Targeted Financial Sanctions,' in Berdal and Malone (eds) (n.27 above), pp.173–203.
52. United Nations, *The Causes of Conflict and the Promotion of Durable Peace and Sustainable Development in Africa*, S/1998/318, 11 Nov. 1999, para. 50.
53. Ibid., para. 50.
54. 'Jury returns $4.5 billion verdict against ex-Bosnian Serb general Karadzic', *CNN.com*, 26 Sept. 2000.
55. See Global Witness, *A Rough Trade: The Role of Companies and Governments in the Angolan Conflict*, London, Dec. 1998 accessed at www.oneworld.org/globalwitness/reports/Angola/cover.htm; Action for Southern Africa, *Waiting on Empty Promises: The Human Cost of International Inaction on Angolan Sanctions*, London, April 2000, accessed at www.anc.org.za/angola/actsareportv4.html.
56. 'Barclays held cash for massacre', *The Observer*, London, 28 Nov. 1999; 'Les secrets africains de l'affaire Elf', *Le Monde*, 25 Oct. 1999.
57. Government of Canada (n.44 above), p.67.
58. Michael Bowden, 'Is a 200-Year-Old Pirate Law the Next Wave in Tort Suits?', *Lawyers Weekly*, accessed at www.lawyersweekly.com/pirate.cfm.
59. Ironically, UNOCAL President John Ilme Jr. was co-chair of the first Business-Humanitarian Forum in January 1997 (see www.bhforum.ch).
60. Jarat Chopra, 'Introducing Peace-maintenance', in *Global Governance: Special Issue on Peace-Maintenance Operations*, Vol.4, No.1, 1998, pp.3–6.
61. Chopra, 'The UN's Kingdom of East Timor', *Survival*, Vol.42, No.3, 2000, p.29.
62. James Traub, for example, questions the feasibility of UNTAET's goal, arguing that 'although there is no question of the UN's benevolence, its competence as a colonial master is open to question' ('Inventing East Timor', *Foreign Affairs*, Vol.79, No.4, p.75).
63. Jarat Chopra (n.61 above), p.36.

Post-Conflict Elections: Constraints and Dangers

BENJAMIN REILLY

Elections have become an integral element of many United Nations peacekeeping missions over the past decade. The reason for this is clear: the focus of most UN missions has shifted from one of pure peacebuilding to one of state re-building or, in some cases like East Timor, state creation. In such cases, elections provide an inescapable means for jump-starting a new, post-conflict political order; for stimulating the development of democratic politics; for choosing representatives; for forming governments; and for conferring legitimacy upon the new political order. They also provide a clear signal that legitimate domestic authority has been returned – and hence that the role of the international community may be coming to an end. For all of these reasons, elections have become a central part of many UN peacekeeping missions. In addition, electoral assistance outside peacekeeping missions has become something of a growth industry since the fall of the Berlin Wall and the 'third wave' of democratization has led to a threefold increase in the number of putatively democratic governments around the globe.

Despite this, there has been a considerable variation in the relative success of elections in meeting the broader goals of democratization from country to country and case to case. In some cases, such as Namibia and Mozambique, elections clearly played a vital role in making a decisive break with the past. In others, such as Angola, flawed elections created more problems than they solved. In Haiti, administrative inefficiencies undermined the credibility of the broader electoral process. By contrast, in Cambodia, technically successful electoral processes were soon overwhelmed by the realities of power politics. And in Bosnia, premature elections helped to kick-start the façade of democratic politics, but also helped nationalist parties cement an early grip on political power. While this mistake has been avoided in Kosovo and East Timor, it is still to be seen how elections influence the broader process of peacebuilding in these two critical cases.

What is clear, however, is that in any UN mission, the holding of elections forces critical political choices to be made. Elections represent a key step in a broader process of building political institutions and legitimate government. Elections influence the extent to which the internal politics of fragile new states become stabilized, whether the new political dispensation comes to be viewed as legitimate, and how the rhythm of peaceful democratic politics can evolve and become sustainable. Variations in electoral procedures can also play a key role in determining whether the locus of political competition evolves along extremist or centrist lines, and hence in developing moderate and broad-based political parties.

There are three main areas of variation that are crucial influences on the shape of post-conflict politics in most countries. First, there is the question of timing: should post-conflict elections be held as early as possible, so as to fast-track the process of establishing a new regime, or should they be postponed until peaceful political routines and issues have been able to come to prominence? Second, there is the mechanics of elections themselves: who runs the elections; how are voters enrolled; what electoral formula is used. Third, there is the often underestimated issue of the effect of the elections on political parties. Especially in cases of weak civil society, political parties are the key link between masses and elites, and play an absolutely crucial role in building a sustainable democratic polity. Hence, the interaction between parties and the electoral process is itself crucial. Are the political parties contesting the election narrow, personalized, sectarian or ethnically exclusive entities, using the political process to pursue their wartime objectives? Or are they broad, multi-ethnic, programmatic organizations with real links to the community? How can the former be discouraged and latter promoted?

More generally, there is the overarching issue of under what circumstances elections help to build a new democratic order, and under what circumstances they can undermine democracy and pave the way for a return to conflict. For example, elections are part of the broader process of democratization, but ill-timed, badly designed or poorly run elections can actually undermine the broader process of democratization. This is the overarching theme of this essay.

Timing

As a starting point, the issue of election timing is a crucial, and under-appreciated, variable in election planning. Issues of timing also directly affect administrative choices, electoral system designs and the way political parties form. For example, in some cases timing demands – particularly the need to hold a quick election – have influenced the choice of electoral laws, and these have affected not just the party system but also the broader incentives presented to political actors as part of the election process. Take the case of Angola's 1992 presidential elections held under the Bicesse Agreement of May 1991 as part of the peace process aimed at stopping Angola's long-running civil war. The major parties contesting the election were the political wings of two former liberation movements turned armies: the governing MPLA, led by President Eduardo Dos Santos, and UNITA, led by Jonas Savimbi. Due to the extraordinary nature of the election (the first ever held in Angola) and severe timing pressures, a hastily-drafted electoral law was enacted which included, as part of the presidential election, a run-off between the top two candidates if no-one gained a majority in the first round of voting.

This choice of formula had two impacts. First, it precluded any possibility of power sharing between the two main combatants, as the election itself could only be won by one candidate. Second, it provided an escape hatch for parties weakly committed to the process, who could get an indication of their support levels after the first round of voting. When Savimbi realized after the first round that he was unlikely to win the election, he rejected the election and went back to war. The issues of timing and electoral system choice thus impacted directly on the overall failure of the peace process in Angola. Of course, it is possible that this may have occurred anyway. But the design of the electoral system clearly presented strategic opportunities for candidates to remove themselves from the contest – an incentive that would have been lower under a different set of institutional rules.

Such events may suggest that democracy itself is part of the problem in such highly fraught situations, and that post-conflict situations are too fragile to be exposed to the competitive pressures of the electoral process. But this oft-heard critique ignores several factors. First, elections can be purposively designed to encourage not winner-takes-all outcomes, but the sharing of power between groups. Indeed, many would argue that some form of power-sharing is a primary requirement in post-conflict situations. Second, critics of elections as instruments of democratization often ignore the real need to construct a legitimate governing authority in post-conflict circumstances. Not least because so many of today's conflicts take place within states, the overarching challenge of many UN missions is to build or re-build a sustainable democratic state that can function without direct international involvement. Elections are a crucial element in achieving this. State-building has been a priority issue in both Kosovo and East Timor, for example, where UN missions were confronted with the challenges of attempting to build functioning democracies in societies only recently ravaged by violent conflict and suffering a history of incorporation and oppression by powerful neighbours.

One valid criticism of elections in post-conflict scenarios, however, is that if held too early, they can undermine the nascent democratic order. This has been a fundamental problem of many UN-supervised elections: they have been held too soon and too quickly after peace has been restored. In fact, over the last decade, UN peacekeeping missions appear to have developed a kind of standard operating procedure. Once a minimum level of peace has been obtained (which does not necessarily mean a full ceasefire agreement), and a basic level of infrastructure is in place, the next step is usually to hold some kind of parliamentary elections – often within a year or two of the start of the mission – followed by a rapid hand-over to the newly-elected authorities, and an even more rapid departure of UN troops and personnel. Thus in Kosovo there was strong pressure on the OSCE, the body tasked with organizing elections in the region, to hold elections as quickly as possible, regardless of whether the social conditions that exist there are conducive to the cut and thrust of open electoral politics or not. A similar pressure to hold 'instant elections' was present in East Timor, where the UN Transitional Administrator, Sergio de Mello, argued that postponing elections beyond 2001 would be 'difficult', arguing that 'you can't hold back the horses' of political development indefinitely. In both cases, national elections were held in the second half of 2001.

But if held too early, elections in fragile situations can easily undermine the longer-term challenge of building a sustainable democracy. Elections in conflictual situations can act as catalysts for the development of parties and other organizations which are primarily (and often solely) vehicles to assist local elites gain access to governing power. They can promote a focus on regional, rather than national, issues. They can serve to place in positions of elected authority leaders committed to exclusionary visions of the country – leaders who are, in many cases, the very same ones who started or fought in the conflict in the first place. This generals-to-politicians transformation has been a recurring problem in the Balkans, where nationalist parties and elites have attempted to use the political process to continue to press their sectarian aims. Early elections also tend to elicit more extreme reactions from voters than an election held after a period of state rebuilding. This is one of the perverse realities of post-conflict elections: the *sine qua non* of the democratic process, elections, can also be its undoing.

The timing of elections can also impact directly on the shape of the political party system, and on the degree of coordination between local and national-level elites. For example, a major goal in building a sustainable democracy should be the creation of parties which are broad-based, have strong links to local communities, and campaign on a national platform. But in post-conflict situations, many political parties are not broad-based vehicles for presenting competing policy and ideological platforms, but rather narrowly-focused, personalized elite cartels. In other cases, political movements are often merely thinly-disguised variants of the armies which fought in the original conflicts, as exemplified in Bosnia by the growth of nationalist parties like the (Croat) HDZ, (Serb) SDS and (Bosniac) SDA, respectively. This problem also afflicts former liberation movements, such as East Timor's Fretilin, or the Kosovo Liberation Army, as they attempt to transform themselves into mainstream political organizations. Either way, holding elections too early in the transition period can have the perverse effect of blocking the development of more aggregative and programmatic political parties – institutions which are now widely accepted to be important facilitating agents for successful democratization.

A second issue is the coordination of election timing with sub-national elections. Some scholars argue that in a new democracy, holding national elections before regional elections generates incentives for the creation of national, rather than regional, political parties[1] – and hence that the ideal process of election timing is to start at the national level and work one's way down. Others such as Diamond believe that simultaneous national and local elections 'can facilitate the mutual dependence of regional and national leaders. The more posts that are filled at the regional and local level ... the greater the incentive for regional politicians to coordinate their election activities by developing an integrated party system'.[2] This was the situation at Indonesia's 1999 elections, with identical party-based ballots being presented to voters at simultaneous elections for national, provincial and local assemblies, which greatly strengthened the nascent party system. In recent years, however, UN practice has been the opposite: to start with municipal elections and work up, as in Kosovo. This approach is particularly suited to 'state-building' elections, which can help develop party politics from the ground up. In general, the comparative evidence suggests that this bottom-up approach to electoral timing is probably the best way to encourage the development of party politics and to inculcate voters in the routines of electoral politics.

A more immediate problem often comes not from the domestic realm but from the approach taken by the international community itself. International policy makers, not least at the UN, have typically viewed elections as a punctuation point in a peacekeeping mission, which can usher in not just a new government but also provide a convenient exit point for international involvement. Thus Cambodia's 1993 election, the culmination of the biggest UN peacekeeping mission to date, was followed by a rapid departure of the UN and other international forces from Cambodia – a departure which did little to translate the results of an exemplary electoral process into solidifying a fragile new polity. Soon after, a 'coup' by the 'second prime minister', Hun Sen, against the most popular elected party, FUNCINPEC, saw Cambodia return to its familiar politics of intimidation and authoritarian rule. Elsewhere, rushed elections (for example, in Liberia) with little in the way of broader political support, have undermined the legitimacy of the election process, creating further problems for future democracy-building efforts.

The wider obsession in the 1990s with elections as a form of conflict resolution is perhaps the most obvious manifestation of this 'quick-fix' mentality. The world is littered with elections, often conducted at the behest of the international community, which only served to inflame and politicize the root causes of conflict. Given this, it is not surprising that elections held too early in the process of state rebuilding (or 'premature elections', as they have become known) often have the opposite results to those intended. The December 1991 Algerian elections, which were aborted after the fundamentalist Islamic Salvation Front won the first round of voting, and which led to the suspension of the constitution and the strengthening of military rule, were one case in point. In Burundi, the June 1993 elections undermined prospects for democracy by fuelling an ethnic 'retribalization' of party politics, which inflamed pre-existing Tutsi–Hutu tensions not just in Burundi but in neighbouring Rwanda as well. In both cases, early or ill-thought-through elections appeared to undermine the broader path of democratic development.

There are, however, powerful pressures, both domestic and international, for early elections to occur as part of the process of state rebuilding in post-conflict societies. For one thing, given the risk-averse nature of the international community when it comes to peacekeeping commitments, such elections can (as noted above) provide a clear 'exit strategy' for international involvement. But supporting the difficult process of transforming a poor, traumatized and war-ravaged society into a well-functioning democracy requires more than the presence of a few hundred UN officials for 18 months, with an election at the end. It means, quite simply, being prepared to invest substantial time and money in an open-ended process of social and political development. With the exception of the Balkans, which benefits from its location in Europe (and where observers are talking about an international presence in the region for *decades*), there are few post-conflict societies anywhere in the world where international actors have the inclination to pursue such an open-ended strategy. In most cases, the roving eye of the international media and the major western governments moves on to other, more fashionable, issues.

A second-best alternative to such open-ended commitment is not to rush into immediate elections following a peace deal, but rather to encourage local involvement for a few years until some of the basic elements of a pluralistic party system and a functioning state have been established. This was the approach taken by the UN in both East Timor and Kosovo, where local-level democratization and security-building has taken precedence over the early holding of a national poll, and where national consultative bodies of local leaders have been introduced *without* an electoral process. In East Timor, for example, the UN developed a National Consultative Council, made up of representatives of East Timor's government-in-waiting, into a form of unelected legislature, which included representatives of youth, church and women's groups. In Kosovo, national elections were postponed in favour of municipal polls, where the stakes are much lower and the responsibilities of elected officials were focused on service delivery rather than national issues. In both cases, the evidence suggests that, by involving local actors in the process of governing while lengthening out the transition to full-blown national elections, a more mature and responsible form of party politics has begun to be developed. This approach has much to recommend it for future operations.

Electoral Mechanics

The mechanics of the electoral process can have a profound – and often profoundly misunderstood – impact on the success or failure of post-conflict democratization. Electoral mechanics can be divided into two main areas: the electoral *system* – that is, the formula by which votes are converted into seats, including the way ballot papers are laid out and the structure of electoral districts, and the electoral *administration* – such as the electoral management body, the provisions for voter registration, boundary delimitation and the like. Between them, these two areas comprise some of the most important variables influencing the success or failure of post-conflict elections, and indeed for democratization more generally.

While electoral systems have attracted a voluminous academic literature, issues of electoral administration remain under-studied by scholars and under-rated in general in terms of their effect on post-conflict polities. Voter registration, for example, is a perennial area of concern, not least because nearly all post-conflict elections take place in an environment where basic census and other records are missing. The construction of a comprehensive register of voters is thus often a first step in the bureaucratic process of state-building. It is also often an enormously time-consuming, logistically-challenging and resource-intensive process: in Cambodia, for example, the voter registration period took almost a full year before the election and demanded huge amounts of time, personnel and money. Because electoral districts and polling places are often drawn and allocated on the basis of voter registration records, this process usually impacts on these areas too.

However, probably the most important administrative decision concerns the composition of the body managing the elections, and specifically whether the elections are run by the government of the day or whether some form of Independent Electoral Commission is established, and whether such a body is composed of political parties or non-partisan civil servants. The world-wide trend is definitely towards independent electoral commissions staffed by non-partisan civil servants; indeed, since the world's largest democracy, India, adopted this model at independence it has been widely adopted around the world. However, the influence of the United States is important here, as the US form of electoral administration is based around political appointees and party representatives, and many post-conflict democracies have also adopted this model. The comparative evidence suggests that this is a mistake, and that independent commissions run by apolitical civil servants are definitely to be preferred. Party-based commissions have an almost inevitable tendency to split along party lines. In Haiti, for example, the Provisional Electoral Council was made up of representatives of the political parties, but was also deeply divided along party lines, and internal mistrust and divisions prevented it from working efficiently.[3] In Cambodia, by contrast, a non-partisan electoral commission was widely seen as one of the outstanding elements of the entire UN mission. Non-partisan commissions were also a prominent and successful part of UN missions in Namibia and in East Timor.

The danger of using party-based electoral administrations was graphically demonstrated by Indonesia's transitional elections in 1998. Amid the flowering of new political movements that often accompanies a democratic opening, a requirement that both the government and opposition political parties must be represented on the General Elections Commission (KPU), resulted in a deadlocked and unwieldy body of no less than 53 persons, most of them party representatives (including some individuals who were also candidates for the election). Consequently, during the preparation for one of the most important transitional elections of the 1990s, the body charged with running the elections – the KPU – became almost completely dysfunctional, being deeply divided along party lines and unable to take even basic decisions (at one stage, fist-fights broke out between different members of the commission). After the elections, which were administratively flawed, the Indonesians moved quickly to discard the party-based KPU and replace it with a much smaller, non-partisan body of 11 non-party and non-government representatives, many of them academics.

Electoral processes also need to be sustainable. While the UN plays an important 'vector' role in spreading new practices and technologies, there is a distinction between the ideal electoral technology and the capacity of a recipient country to handle that technology in a sustainable manner. A number of internationally-financed and run elections over the past decade have introduced a level of electoral technology which was clearly unsustainable for the host country, and could not be replicated in their second, locally-run elections. Cambodia and Mozambique both fall into this category. Highly expensive levels of basic equipment and staffing is a common problem; an over-reliance on sophisticated information technology more suited to a First World country than a Third World one is another (a typical example is the use of computerized electoral rolls in countries where electric power is unreliable). Building a *sustainable* electoral administration needs to be the over-riding aim in such situations, even where this means using more basic technology or equipment. Similarly, donors need to think hard about the relative merits of funding expensive one-off international election observation missions (otherwise known as 'electoral tourism') versus the longer-term benefits of directly supporting the domestic electoral administration and local observer groups. The latter is less glamorous but usually has a much greater pay-off in actually assisting the consolidation of a new democracy.

While these and other issues of electoral administration continue to receive inadequate attention, the design of electoral systems, by contrast, has long been recognized as one of the most important institutional choices for any political system. Electoral systems can be purposively designed to achieve particular outcomes, and serve to structure the arena of political competition, including the party system.

The great potential of electoral system design for influencing political behaviour is thus that it can reward particular types of behaviour and place constraints on others. This is why electoral system design has been seized upon by many scholars as one of the chief levers of constitutional engineering to be used in mitigating conflict within divided societies. As Arend Lijphart notes, 'If one wants to change the nature of a particular democracy, the electoral system is likely to be the most suitable and effective instrument for doing so'.[4] As well as their suitability for engineering, electoral rules also serve to structure the arena of political competition during election campaigns. This has important behavioural consequences for both voters and candidates. Because elections represent a primary arena of political competition in many new democracies, and different strategies of cooperation or antagonism between the players can increase or decrease their prospects for success, the electoral system is also a key mechanism in shaping wider political practices, and can have an effect far beyond the elections themselves.

Electoral systems also have a direct impact upon politics in societies divided along ethnic, religious, ideological or other lines. Donald Horowitz, for example, argues that 'the electoral system is by far the most powerful lever of constitutional engineering for accommodation and harmony in severely divided societies, as indeed it is a powerful tool for many other purposes'.[5] Lijphart says that 'the electoral system has long been recognized as probably the most powerful instrument for shaping the political system'.[6] Timothy Sisk writes that electoral systems 'play an important role in "engineering" the results of democratic voting, and along with other institutional choices can have a profound impact on the nature of political parties and the general character of democracy'.[7] Beyond this consensus on the importance of electoral systems, however, there is profound disagreement among theorists as to which electoral systems are most appropriate for divided societies.

Two schools of thought predominate. The scholarly orthodoxy has long been that some form of proportional representation (PR) is all but essential if democracy is to survive the travails of deep-rooted divisions. For example, Arthur Lewis's study of the failure of post-colonial democracy in countries such as Ghana, Nigeria and Sierra Leone in the late 1950s and 1960s prompted him to argue that divided societies need PR to 'give minorities adequate representation, discourage parochialism, and force moderation on the political parties'.[8] Such arguments foreshadowed, in part, the electoral recommendations of 'consociational' approaches to managing ethnic cleavages in divided societies, which emphasize the need for divided societies to develop mechanisms for elite power-sharing if democracy is to be maintained. In terms of electoral systems, consociationalists argue that some form of proportional representation is all but essential for divided societies, as this enables all politically-significant ethnic groups, including minorities, to form ethnically-based parties. Their prescriptions for electoral system design often focus on the need for party list PR, usually in large districts. This is based on the tendency of PR to produce multi-party systems and hence multi-party parliaments, in which all significant segments of the population can be represented, and on the empirical relationship between proportional electoral rules and 'oversized' or grand coalition governments, which are a fundamental feature of the power-sharing approach on which consociationalism is based. The use of large, multimember electoral districts is particularly favoured, because it maximizes proportionality and hence the prospects of multiple parties in parliaments, which can then form the basis of a cross-ethnic government coalition.[9] PR election rules are thus important of themselves – because they are likely to facilitate proportional parliamentary representation of all groups – and also an important component of wider consociational prescriptions that emphasize the need for grand coalitions, group autonomy, and minority veto powers.

In contrast to this orthodoxy, an alternative approach sometimes typified as 'centripetalism' maintains that the best way to mitigate the destructive effects of ethnicity in divided societies is not to simply replicate existing ethnic divisions in the legislature, but rather to utilize electoral systems that encourage cooperation and accommodation between rival groups, and therefore work to break down the salience of ethnicity rather than foster its representation in parliament.[10] Drawing on theories of bargaining and cooperation, centripetalism advocates institutional designs that encourage opportunities for dialogue and negotiation between opposing political forces in the context of electoral competition. By privileging cooperative campaign strategies with increased prospects of electoral success, candidates representing competing (and sometimes violently opposed) interests are presented with incentives to negotiate for reciprocal support, creating an 'arena of bargaining' where vote-trading arrangements can be discussed.[11]

Centripetalist approaches advocate the use of electoral rules which encourage 'vote-pooling' and 'preference swapping' in order to encourage inter-ethnic bargaining and promote accommodative behaviour. At the core of this approach is the need to make politicians reciprocally dependent on the votes of members of groups other than their own.[12] The most reliable way of achieving this aim, according to proponents of the centripetal approach, is to offer sufficient electoral incentives for campaigning politicians to court voter support across ethnic lines. For example, some electoral models – such as preferential systems like the alternative vote (in Fiji) or the single transferable vote (Northern Ireland) – permit (or even require) voters to declare not only their first choice of candidate on a ballot, but also their second, third and subsequent choices amongst all candidates standing. Parties that succeed in negotiating preference-trading agreements for reciprocal support with other parties will be rewarded, thus strengthening moderate voices and the political centre. This gives them strong institutional incentives both to engage in face-to-face dialogue with their opponents, and to negotiate on broader policy issues than purely vote-seeking ones. The overall effect is thus to reorient electoral politics away from a rigid zero-sum game to a more fluid, complex and potentially positive-sum contest. The success of 'pro-peace' forces at Northern Ireland's breakthrough 1998 election was dependent to a significant extent on such vote-transfers towards the moderate middle and away from extremists. Fiji's transitional 1999 election also utilized centripetal procedures, as did the transitional 1990 election in Estonia. Sri Lanka and Papua New Guinea are other examples of countries in which centripetal electoral systems have or will be used.

Regardless of whether consociational or centripetal approaches (or some mixture of the two) are favoured, there is widespread agreement amongst many scholars that some type of power-sharing government featuring all significant groups is an essential part of democracy-building in divided societies. In particular, multi-ethnic coalitions are favoured by both consociationalist and centripetalists as desirable institutions for divided societies. This form of the power-sharing model is most often associated with proportional elections, as PR is the surest way of guaranteeing fair results and minority representation. Lewis, for example, argues that 'one of the advantages of proportional representation is that it tends to promote coalition government'.[13] Yet the comparative evidence from our cases suggest that power-sharing has been less stable and less in evidence in post-conflict elections than many scholars would have predicted. In most cases, moreover, proportional elections have resulted in majority rule: Namibia, Mozambique, Liberia are all examples of this. In each case, however, the largest party would probably have won an even greater majority had alternative institutional designs been employed.

It is instructive to note that almost all of the major transitional elections conducted in recent years, including almost all of those held under UN auspices, have utilized some form of PR. In fact, transitional elections in Chile (1989), Namibia (1989), Nicaragua (1990), Cambodia (1993), South Africa (1994), Mozambique (1994), Bosnia (1996, 1998, 2000), Kosovo (2001) and East Timor (2001) all used a form of regional or national list PR for their founding elections. In fact, party-list PR has become the de facto norm of UN parliamentary elections. In presidential systems, this has usually been combined with some form of run-off election for the presidency. Only Haiti in 1995, which used a run-off system for its parliamentary elections, has deviated from the PR norm (and there the record of this system was mixed, to say the least: in Haiti, as in Angola, some losing candidates trailing after the first round of voting chose to boycott the second round, thus undermining the legitimacy of the process as a whole).

As would be expected from their widespread use, PR systems have many advantages for transitional elections in new democracies: they are fair, transparent and provide a clear correlation between votes cast in the election and seats won in parliament. By bringing minorities into the process and fairly representing all significant political parties in the new legislature, regardless of the extent or distribution of their support base, PR is often seen as an integral element for creating an inclusive and legitimate post-authoritarian regime. But the adoption of such systems for post-conflict elections has usually been dictated more by administrative concerns, such as the need to avoid demarcating individual electoral districts and to produce separate ballot papers for each district, than these wider political issues. Indeed, in many post-conflict elections, national PR systems are the only feasible way to hold an election quickly, as a uniform national ballot can be used, no electoral districts need be demarcated, and the process of voter registration, vote counting and the calculation of results is consequently simplified.

However, national PR systems also have some disadvantages, as they provide no geographic link between voters and their representatives, and thus create difficulties in terms of political accountability and responsiveness between elected politicians and the electorate. In addition, many new democracies – particularly those in agrarian societies – have much higher demands for constituency service at the local level than they do for representation of all shades of ideological opinion in the legislature. It has therefore increasingly been argued in Namibia, South Africa, Cambodia and elsewhere that the proportional systems used at the first transitional elections should be modified to also encourage a higher degree of *geographic accountability* – such as by having members of parliament represent territorially-defined districts and service the needs of a constituency. A popular choice in recent years has been for 'mixed' electoral systems, in which part of the legislature is elected on a national level by proportional representation, and some is elected at a local level from single-member districts, so that both the proportionality and accountability are maximized. For example, the August 2001 elections for East Timor's 88-member constituent assembly – the body tasked with drawing up the country's first constitution – used a mixed system, with 75 of the assembly's seats elected on a nationwide basis by proportional representation, and 13 seats (one for each of the electoral districts) elected by first-past-the-post.

There are also variations within PR systems that need to be considered. For example, the precise kind of PR formula used can influence the extent to which minor parties are represented, or major parties are advantaged. For example, the use of a 'Hare' divisor at the provincial level in Cambodia, rather than using a 'Largest Remainder' system nationwide, had a major political effect: minor parties who would have gained seats had one national constituency been used fell short, while the two major parties – the Cambodian People's Party and Funcinpec – both gained 'seat bonuses' as a result of these (apparently minor) system choices. Overall, an additional ten parties would have gained representation had the election been held on a national rather than a provincial basis.[14] In Namibia, by contrast, a highly proportional national PR system was introduced – despite concerns voiced by the United Nations Institute for Namibia that parties should 'reject any PR system that tends to fractionalize party representation'.[15] The final Namibian electoral system was one of the most proportional in the world: with no legal thresholds in place, a party needed less than one per cent of the vote to gain election.

As such cases suggest, it is impossible to divorce the shape of the party system, and prospects for post-election power-sharing, from the design of the electoral system. All three are mutually entwined to a large extent. For example, different types of electoral formula can encourage or retard different types of party constellations, and can also influence the extent to which post-conflict parties are broad-based and moderate entities, drawing cross-communal support, or whether they are (as in Bosnia) merely former armies in a new guise – wolves in sheep's clothing. Proportional representation, while fairly representing all views, can also enable small extremist parties to gain crucial footholds in power. In support of this contention, some comparative studies have found that smaller 'district magnitude' – the number of members elected from each electoral district – is the crucial institutional variable in blocking the rise of 'fringe' or extremist parties and encouraging the development of a broad-based party system, suggesting that less proportional systems are to be preferred.[16]

Other technical considerations can also have major implications. Take the case of designing list PR systems for ethnically-divided societies: because such systems can utilize one standard national ballot paper and do not require electoral districts to be drawn or voter rolls to be demarcated on a geographical basis, they are by far the simplest system for electoral administrators – and, arguably, voters – facing first-time elections in new democracies. But in Bosnia, the application of PR has also been seen to undermine the process of democratization by disengaging politicians from voters and, worse, permitting the development of hard-line nationalist political parties, who can achieve electoral success by making narrow, sectarian appeals to their core ethno-political base. Indeed, early Bosnian elections have served to emphasize that under such conditions, the surest route to electoral victory under PR is to play the ethnic card – with disastrous consequences for the longer-term process of democratization.

Because of these concerns, the Bosnian elections of November 2000 therefore utilized an 'open list' PR system, in which voters could choose not just between parties but also between candidates within parties, with the expectation that this would encourage greater identification with and responsiveness from elected politicians. But – as anyone familiar with the use of the same system in the deeply ethnically-torn country of Sri Lanka could have advised – this was a risky move in a divided society where ethnic affiliation remains the primary basis of voter choice. In Sri Lanka, parties that have attempted to field a multi-ethnic candidate list have found that such 'open lists' can undermine, rather than promote, multi-ethnic government: Sinhalese voters will, if given the chance, deliberately move Tamil candidates placed in a winnable position on a party list to a lower position. This may well have been a problem in South Africa as well, had not the electoral system used been a 'closed' list, which allowed major parties such as the ANC and the NP to place ethnic minorities and women high on their party list. In Bosnia, the 2000 elections saw a wave of victories for extremist parties and candidates, a wave of victories that the 'permissive' open list PR electoral system only served to encourage, as it contained no real incentives for inter-ethnic cooperation or moderation.

Political Parties and Power-sharing

Transitional democracies, particularly those moving from a deep-rooted conflict situation, typically have a greater need for inclusiveness and a lower threshold for the robust rhetoric of adversarial politics than their established counterparts. Similarly, the stable political environments of most Western countries, where two or three main parties can often reasonably expect regular periods in office via alternation of power or shifting governing coalitions, are very different from the type of zero-sum politics which so often characterize divided societies. This is one of the reasons that 'winner take all' electoral systems like first-past-the-post have so often been identified as a contributor to the breakdown of democracy in the developing world: because such systems tend to lock out minorities from parliamentary representation they can, in situations of ethnically-based parties, easily lead to the total dominance of one group over all others.[17] Democracy, under these circumstances, can quickly become a situation of permanent inclusion and exclusion, a zero-sum game, with frightening results.

But there are also distinctive elements of political parties in post-conflict situations that appear to transcend institutional considerations. Because of the underdeveloped and deeply divided nature of most post-conflict societies, elections often have the effect of highlighting societal fault-lines and hence laying bare deep social divisions. In such circumstances, the easiest way to mobilize voter support at election time is to appeal to the very same insecurities that generated the original conflict. This means that parties have a strong incentive to 'play the ethnic card' or to take hard-line positions on key identity-related issues, with predictable consequences for the wider process of democratization. Post-communist elections in Yugoslavia in the early 1990s, for example, resulted in the victory of extremist nationalist parties, committed to (and achieving) the break-up of the federation. The 1993 elections in Burundi, which were supposed to elect a power-sharing government, instead mobilized population groups along ethnic lines and served as a catalyst for ethnic genocide a few months later. Similarly, Bosnia's 1996 and 1998 elections effectively served as ethnic censuses, with parties campaigning on ethnic lines and voters reacting to heightened perceptions of ethnic insecurity by electing hard-line nationalists to power, greatly undermining the process of democracy-building.

For this reason, scholars and policy makers alike have frequently identified the need to build broad-based, cross-regional and multi-ethnic political parties in fragile multi-ethnic states, particularly those susceptible to separatist appeals. Horowitz, for example, has advocated the need for broad multi-ethnic parties or coalitions of parties as a key facilitating factor in avoiding ethnic conflict.[18] Similarly, Huntington argues that fractionalized and ethnically or regionally exclusive party systems are extremely damaging for democratic prospects and are, consequently, found widely in the failed democracies of the Third World.[19] A 26-nation study of democracy in developing countries concluded that 'a system of two or a few parties, with broad social and ideological bases, may be conducive to stable democracy'.[20] Diamond sums up the prevailing view of many scholars, arguing that 'political parties remain important if not essential instruments for representing political constituencies and interests, aggregating demands and preferences, recruiting and socializing new candidates for office, organizing the electoral competition for power, crafting policy alternatives, setting the policy-making agenda, forming effective governments, and integrating groups and individuals into the democratic process'.[21] By contrast, under the conditions of 'polarized pluralism', featuring competition between extremist movements, the logic of elections changes from one of convergence on median policy positions to one of extreme divergence.[22] Politics becomes a centrifugal game. Such fragmented party constellations are empirically much more likely to experience violence and the breakdown of democracy than more moderate multipartism based on a few 'catch-all' political parties.[23]

For this reason, there is an increasing focus in the policy world – which has yet to be adequately digested by scholars – on the need to build broad-based, programmatic political parties in new democracies, and to avoid the narrow, personalized and sectarian parties and party systems that have undermined so many new democracies. Particularly in societies split along ethnic lines, cross-regional and multi-ethnic parties that compete for the centre ground appear to be a – and perhaps the – crucial determinant of broader democratic consolidation and peacebuilding. For this reason, new democracies around the globe have, over the past few years, experimented with an unusual array of institutional approaches to encourage the development of sustainable political parties and party systems.

There are several ways of doing this. First, *party rules* governing the formation, registration and campaigning of political parties can be enacted which encourage parties to be cross-regional and cross-ethnic in their composition. This was the approached used successfully at Indonesia's transitional 1999 elections, where to qualify to compete in the election, political parties must have established a branch structure in more than half of Indonesia's 27 provinces, and within each of these provinces must also have established branches within over half of all regions and municipalities. The Indonesian drafters stated clearly that their aim was to discourage political groups based on ethnicity or region that could form the basis of secessionist claims, and to encourage the development of broad-based organizations campaigning on a national platform.[24] The results from the 1999 election were encouraging for these expectations, as the main electoral contest did indeed appear to take place between three large cross-regional parties, and the level of ethnic violence associated with the elections was much lower than had been feared (although it appears to be rising again in the post-election period). Variations on this approach have also been used in several other Asian and West African countries.

Second, *electoral systems* can be designed to enable voters to rank-order choices between candidates ('preferential voting'), a process that has been shown to help sustain centrist parties. This was the approach used at Northern Ireland's breakthough 1998 'Good Friday agreement' elections, which utilized a single transferable vote form of electoral system that enabled voters to indicate secondary choices on their ballot. Analyses of these elections have found that the use of a transferable ballot enabled 'pro-peace Republican and Unionist voters to give their first vote to their communal party, but to transfer their 'secondary' votes to pro-agreement non-sectarian parties (thus advantaging the 'moderate middle' of non-ethnic parties). Vote transfers overwhelmingly flowed from sectarian parties on both sides towards the pro-agreement but non-sectarian middle.[25] Pro-agreement parties on both sides of the sectarian divide benefited from such vote transfers, which – among other things – were ultimately crucial in converting a bare 'anti-agreement' unionist voter majority into a bare 'pro-agreement' unionist parliamentary majority. Evans and O'Leary, for example, conclude that the principal reason that a workable assembly emerged from the 1998 elections 'was the adoption, or re-adoption, of the single transferable vote … voters' lower-order preferences kept the Assembly on-track by reducing the numbers of seats that the anti-Agreement unionist parties won in the election'.[26]

Third, *distribution requirements* can be enacted which require parties or individual candidates to garner specified support levels from across different regions, rather than just their own. The best-known example of this type of cross-regional engineering has been in Nigeria. Nigeria's February 1999 presidential elections which swept Olesegun Obasanjo to power took place under laws which contained a so-called 'distribution requirement': instead of the usual majority vote requirement, successful candidates had to obtain not just a majority of the vote, but also not less than one-quarter of the vote cast in at least two-thirds of the states of the federation. The intention behind this kind of distribution requirement – first introduced in 1979 and since adopted in two other African countries as well – was to ensure that the winning candidate gained cross-ethnic support across the country rather than just in one part. Again, a primary aim was to counter the secessionist tendencies that may have been unleashed by the electoral process under different rules. From the 1999 presidential election, the preliminary evidence is encouraging: Obasanjo ran on a cross-ethnic platform and in fact gained greater votes outside his own region than within it (precisely because, it appears, he campaigned on a cross-regional multi-ethnic platform).

Fourth, the 'rules of the game' can be constructed in such a way as to encourage, or require, parties to put forward *multi-ethnic lists of candidates*, thus encouraging multi-ethnicity *within* parties. In countries as varied as Lebanon, Singapore and South Africa, the 'rules of the game' encourage parties to present multi-ethnic candidate lists to the voters. In Lebanon, for example, election is dependent, at a practical level, on being part of a mixed list of candidates representing different religious groups. In most cases, candidates must compete for election against other members of their own group. Electors choosing between party lists must thus make their choice on the basis of criteria other than ethnicity. In Singapore, most MPs are elected from multi-member districts known as 'Group Representative Constituencies', which each return between three and six members from a single list of party or individual candidates. Of the candidates on each party or group list, at least one must be a member of the Malay, Indian or some other minority community. Moving from a compulsory to a voluntary model of multi-ethnic candidate lists, the closed-list proportional representation system used in South Africa's 1994 elections enabled the major political parties to voluntarily adopt a multi-ethnic candidate composition – thus enabling the major 'black' party, the ANC, to place white and coloured members at winnable places on their candidate list.

Finally, *external interventions* can be used to try to stimulate the development of a meaningful party system where none exists. In Kosovo, for example, the OSCE devoted substantial resources to introducing a network of 'political party service centres', intended to support the territory's nascent political groupings by providing them with logistical and material assistance and, by implication, helping them move towards becoming functioning, policy-oriented political parties, rather than the narrow and personalized vehicles for ethnic extremists that were evident in Bosnia. The party service centres aim to help strengthen the organizational capacity of Kosovo's political parties, to assist them in developing their policy platforms and preparing for election campaigns. They have a particular focus on assisting parties that have demonstrated that they are viable and have a popular mandate. In Papua New Guinea, which has a weak and fragmented party system that has destabilized executive government, a new law tries to strengthen the party system by encouraging newly elected MPs to build stable coalitions in parliament, and by granting the resulting 'parliamentary parties' monetary and administrative support. The law also provides for a by-election if an MP votes against their own party leader in a parliamentary confidence vote. Both the Kosovo and Papua New Guinea approaches can be seen as 'top down' inducements to organize and build sustainable parties.

Conclusion

It seems trite to reiterate what has been said many times before: democratization is a long-term process of social and political development, rather than a short-term event run by the international community. But we forget this at our peril. The impact that external interventions can have on democratization – particularly in post-conflict situations – is largely limited to the design and construction of hardy institutions; the provision of adequate security and infrastructural conditions; as well as a modest input into the norms and routines of a first election. Beyond that, democracy is a domestic game, and its longer-term outcomes are very much the preserve of local actors and conditions. International interventions are crucial in putting in place the short-term conditions for a transition to democratic rule, but their longer-term impacts are necessarily limited.

Given this, the most important contribution that the international community can make is to help establish coherent and robust political institutions, rather than to engage in broader attempts at social engineering. Because institutions structure the routines of behaviour in which political actors engage, they are crucial elements, over the longer term, in helping to build a moderate and sustainable political culture, in which routines of cooperation and accommodation come to be accepted as the norm rather than the exception. But such routines have to be allowed to develop organically within a facilitating institutional framework. The role for the UN and other external actors should ultimately be to make sure that such a framework is the best and most appropriate that can be devised. Such a limited focus is necessarily a modest endeavour – but a worthy one nonetheless.

ACKNOWLEDGEMENTS

This essay draws upon the author's research for a project on the UN and democracy organized by Roland Rich of the Centre for Democratic Institutions at the Australia National University and the UNU Peace and Governance Programme. Thanks to Edward Newman of the United Nations University and Robin Ludwig of the United Nations Electoral Assistance Division for their helpful comments on an earlier draft of this paper.

NOTES

1. J. Linz and A. Stepan, *Problems of Democratic Transition and Consolidation: Southern Europe, South America, and Post-Communist Europe*, Baltimore: Johns Hopkins University Press, 1996, pp.98–107.
2. L. Diamond, *Developing Democracy: Towards Consolidation*, Baltimore: Johns Hopkins University Press, 1999, p.158.
3. S. Nelson, 'Haitian Elections and the Aftermath', in K. Kumar (ed.), *Postconflict Elections, Democratization and International Assistance*, Boulder, CO: Lynne Rienner Publishers, 1998, p.76.
4. A. Lijphart, 'Electoral Systems', in S.M. Lipset (ed.), *The Encyclopedia of Democracy*, Congressional Quarterly Press, Washington DC, 1995, p.412.
5. D.L. Horowitz, *A Democratic South Africa? Constitutional Engineering in a Divided Society*, Berkeley: University of California Press, 1991, p.163.
6. A. Lijphart, 'The Alternative Vote: A Realistic Alternative for South Africa?', *Politikon*, Vol.18, No.2, 1991, p.91.
7. T. Sisk, 'Choosing an Electoral System: South Africa Seeks New Ground Rules', *Journal of Democracy*, Vol.4, No.1, 1993, p.79.
8. W.A. Lewis, *Politics in West Africa*, London: George Allen & Unwin, 1965, p.73.
9. A. Lijphart, 'Electoral Systems, Party Systems and Conflict Management in Segmented Societies', in R.A. Schreirer (ed.), *Critical Choices for South Africa: An Agenda for the 1990s*, Cape Town: Oxford University Press, 1990, pp.10–13.
10. T. Sisk, *Democratization in South Africa: The Elusive Social Contract*, Princeton: Princeton University Press, 1995; B. Reilly, *Democracy in Divided Societies: Electoral Engineering for Conflict Management*, Cambridge: Cambridge University Press, 2001.
11. Ibid.
12. D.L. Horowitz, *Ethnic Groups in Conflict*, Berkeley: University of California Press, 1985; D.L. Horowitz, *A Democratic South Africa? Constitutional Engineering in a Divided Society*, Berkeley: University of California Press, 1991.
13. Lewis (n.8 above), *Politics in West Africa*, London: George Allen & Unwin, 1965, p.79.
14. My thanks to Michael Maley for the data on this point
15. L. Cliffe, *et al.*, *The Transition to Independence in Namibia*, Boulder CO: Lynne Rienner Publishers, 1994, p.116.
16. See J. Willey 'Institutional Arrangements and the Success of New Parties in Old Democracies', *Political Studies*, Vol.46, No.3, 1998, pp.651–68 (Special Issue).
17. The classic argument on this remains W.A. Lewis (n.8 above).
18. See Horowitz, *Ethnic Groups in Conflict* (n.12 above).
19. See Samuel P. Huntington, *The Third Wave: Democratization in the Late Twentieth Century*, Norman: University of Oklahoma Press, 1991.
20. See L. Diamond, J. Linz, and S.M. Lipset, 'Introduction: What Makes for Democracy?', in Diamond, Linz, and Lipset (eds), *Politics in Developing Countries: Comparing Experiences with Democracy* (Second Edition), Boulder: Lynne Rienner, 1995, p.35.
21. L. Diamond, 'Introduction: In Search of Consolidation', in L. Diamond, M.F. Plattner, Y. Chu and H. Tien (eds), *Consolidating the Third Wave Democracies*, Johns Hopkins University Press, 1997, p.xxiii.

22. See Giovanni Sartori, *Parties and Party Systems*, Cambridge: Cambridge University Press, 1976.
23. See G. Bingham Powell, *Contemporary Democracies: Participation, Stability, and Violence*, Cambridge, MA: Harvard University Press, 1982.
24. John McBeth, 'Dawn of a New Age', *Far Eastern Economic Review*, 17 Sept. 1998.
25. See B. Reilly, *Democracy in Divided Societies: Electoral Engineering for Conflict Management*, Cambridge: Cambridge University Press, 2001.
26. G. Evans and B. O'Leary, 'Northern Irish Voters and the British–Irish Agreement: Foundations of a Stable Consociational Settlement?', paper presented at the American Political Science Association Annual Meeting, Atlanta GA, Sept, 1999, pp.3–4.

Current International Civil Administration: The Need for Political Legitimacy

SALLY MORPHET

This essay examines the three current international transitional civil administrations in Bosnia, the Federal Republic of Yugoslavia and East Timor, as well as the former UN Transitional Administration in Eastern Slavonia, Baranja and Western Sirmium (UNTAES) in Croatia. It argues that transitional civil administrations are more likely to achieve political legitimacy, nationally and internationally, as well as in the long (and short) terms, if the states involved base their peacebuilding work on international legal standards and norms. These standards also need to be mirrored in the establishment of acceptable – and accepted – frameworks of law at the national level. As Hurrell has argued, '[s]tates need international law and institutions both to share the material and political cost of protecting their interests and to gain the authority and legitimacy that the possession of crude power can never on its own secure'.[1]

The essay argues that UN member states were able to set up East Timor's transitional civil administration with only certain procedural difficulties because UN member states conformed to international legal standards and norms in this respect. In contrast, states involved in setting up both current civil administrations in former Yugoslavia (as well as the previous UNTAES) were hampered by the fact that certain decisions on, for instance, the right of self-determination – made by concerned governments during and after the break-up of former Yugoslavia – 'were breaches of law'.[2] It is worth recalling that UN members have not normally accepted secession: indeed, the UN Operation in the Congo (ONUC) was launched in 1960 to prevent secession. These uncertainties, the essay argues, have particularly affected the previous and current civil administrations within former Yugoslavia and made it more difficult for the governments involved to establish an appropriate framework of law at the national level and to build up local capacity. This has hampered efforts to bring about political and economic change, as such change must be underpinned by the use of international and national legal norms. Not surprisingly, the Office of the High Representative (OHR) and the UN Interim

Administration Mission (UNMIK) have a more complex relationship with the UN than does the UN Transitional Administration in East Timor (UNTAET).

The essay begins by looking at the peacebuilding successes and failures of these four civil administrations, with a focus on legal issues and local capacity building. It argues that the contribution of civil administration to peacebuilding needs to be considered in terms of wider contextual factors such as Germany's decision not to apply international law on recognition, or the fall of President Milosevic. It then discusses the legal and practical problems raised by governmental disregard of certain international legal norms within former Yugoslavia, the particular problems regional actors encounter in dealing with civil administration and the rest of the world community, and the usefulness of thinking about past experience of civil administration in preparing exit strategies.

Four Civil Administration Missions in Former Yugoslavia and East Timor: Similarities and Differences

Peacebuilding was defined by the UN Secretary-General in 1997 as 'the various concurrent and integrated actions undertaken at the end of a conflict to consolidate peace and prevent a recurrence of armed confrontation', or, putting it differently, the achievement of peace with sufficient justice, reconciliation and development in the state concerned.[3] For the purpose of this contribution, peace is seen as necessarily allied with a concern for justice, both long and short term. This includes rectificatory and distributive justice as well as the restoration and recreation of the rule of law.[4] Reconciliation and development cannot be brought about without tackling the root causes of conflict within national and international legal frameworks (which should complement each other), as well as a concern for the equality and dignity of every human being. Moreover, the West's concerns with managing conflict and reducing suffering have to take other cultures' notions of justice and morality into account.[5] The following discussion will examine these questions in the context of four civil administrations: UNAMET/UNTAET; UNTAES; the OHR; and UNMIK.

UNAMET and UNTAET: East Timor

Following Portuguese withdrawal in 1974, and despite a UN Security Council resolution in April 1976 (on which Japan and the United States abstained) calling on all states to respect the territorial integrity of East

Timor, the inalienable right of its people to self-determination and the withdrawal of Indonesian forces, East Timor was integrated into Indonesia. After numerous attempts to resolve the problem through talks between UN Secretaries-General and the Portuguese and Indonesian governments, in 1999 the governments asked the Secretary-General to ascertain the views of the East Timorese population on autonomy options for East Timor within the state of Indonesia.

The UN Mission in East Timor (UNAMET) was set up unanimously by the Security Council in June 1999 to organize this consultation and to oversee a transition period pending the implementation of the decision. In August almost 80 per cent of the East Timorese voted for independence. This precipitated great violence from pro-integration militias and some Indonesian security forces. Many East Timorese were killed and over half the population was displaced. Strong diplomatic efforts were used to ensure Indonesian withdrawal from East Timor. In September the Security Council unanimously authorized a Chapter VII multinational force (INTERFET) to restore peace and security and to protect UNAMET. Indonesia and Portugal responded by transferring authority over East Timor to the United Nations (similar action had been taken in West Irian in 1962–63),[6] which, through a unanimous Chapter VII resolution, established a UN Transitional Administration.

UNTAET was mandated to provide security and maintain law and order; to establish an effective administration; to assist in the development of civil and social services; to ensure coordination of various assistance efforts; to support capacity building for self-government; and to assist in building conditions for sustainable development. It was also to provide transitional governance and public administration, including an international police element, humanitarian assistance, emergency rehabilitation, and military security.

Legal Framework and Issues

The November 1999 regulation on the authority of the interim administration vested all legislative and executive authority, including the judiciary, in UNTAET: in exercising these functions the UN Administrator 'shall consult and cooperate closely with representatives of the East Timor people'.[7]

Nevertheless, the administration has inevitably become embroiled in local controversies. One major legal challenge that particularly affects the rural population is the question of property rights to large areas of commercial and agricultural land.[8] Numerous land titles were distributed in the past to Chinese, Indonesians and certain Portuguese companies. The East Timorese within the administration, however, did not want UNTAET to conduct a land survey or issue temporary titles based on land use, as they wanted an independent government to pursue this reform. Others, however, feared that influential politicians might manipulate the process to their advantage thus making it difficult to attract foreign investment for as long as the issue remained unresolved.[9]

Local Capacity Building

Capacity building started off badly because of the pressures of setting up INTERFET and UNTAET. There was a 'significant loss of continuity in planning and leadership, in communication between New York and Dili, and in the transmission of in-theatre knowledge and experience from UNAMET to UNTAET'.[10] No political–military campaign plan was drafted and the previous genuine contacts with East Timorese were not maintained. One result was that the main pro-independence National Council of Timorese Resistance began 'to reconstitute its structures through village elections' in efforts to maintain its de facto effective control of towns and the countryside.[11]

Despite this the local population welcomed the UN in November 1999. However, there were disagreements about how to proceed within the UN structure. As Chopra argues, UNTAET was preoccupied 'with control at the expense of the local community's involvement in government'[12] and tried to reject a World Bank project on Community Empowerment and Local Government (CEP) because of fears 'that any national legislation governing local administration would amount to a form of official recognition of these local authorities'.[13]

Soon after his arrival (from the Balkans), the Transitional Administrator, Sergio De Mello, chose not to integrate Timorese into the administration's transitional structure. Local consultation was initially engaged through a National Consultative Council (NCC) set up in December 1999. Some East Timorese began to believe UNTAET was purposely resisting Timorese participation in order to safeguard UN influence, while, at the same time, was failing to take measures to address unemployment, food distribution and the lack of reconstruction.[14] These frustrations were eased when in July 2000 a National Council was set up to 'facilitate broader participation in policy-making'.[15] The Council included representatives of districts, civic organizations, political parties and religious groups. At the same time UNTAET reorganized itself 'to resemble more closely the future government and to increase the direct participation of the Timorese'.[16] The National Council had seven standing committees (equivalent to cabinet portfolios), the majority of which were held by East Timorese. East Timor's largest pro-independence group, the Revolutionary Front for an Independent East Timor (Fretilin), gained the largest number of seats in the important August 2001 election. It needs to join forces with either the left wing Social Democratic Association, or the new Democratic Party (supported by the younger generation) to pass a new constitution by the required two-thirds majority.

Assessment

That it is important to think about contextual factors surrounding an operation was aptly highlighted by the clear lesson that 'Indonesia should not have been entrusted with the maintenance of security during and after the UNAMET ballot'.[17] The police and military components that worked in an advisory capacity for UNAMET were simply insufficient.

Furthermore, there seems to have been a major cultural and information gap between the East Timorese people and the international agencies arriving in East Timor. As the Working Group for Study and Examination, Yayasan HAK, recommended in January 2000: 'the general goal must be to empower people, not to treat them as thoughtless objects'; coordination was needed with the people in general and national NGOs, with a focus on 'concrete practical activity'; people have to be adequately informed 'about the allocation of the funding granted by the World Bank'; and there should have been 'clarification and dissemination of information as to the time' these agencies were to stay in East Timor.[18]

Basically, the underlying international legal framework in which UNTAET was set up and operated was clear-cut and similar to UNTEA in 1962–63. UNTEA provided for the administration of West Irian, which was to be transferred from the Netherlands to the UN and from the UN to Indonesia. UNTEA had full powers to legislate for the territory, to guarantee civil liberties and (very important) property rights.[19]

All major parties concerned had the political will (and the political legitimacy) to help ensure East Timorese independence. However, UNTAET has had failures in local capacity building. It took some time to initiate an appropriate dialogue with the representatives of the East Timorese people. UNTAET's mandate is clear, but surprisingly does not focus directly on the importance of information strategies. Continuing challenges include the uneasy relationship between justice and reconciliation, property rights, diplomatic relations with Indonesia, refugee repatriation, militia strategy and language policy.[20]

CURRENT INTERNATIONAL CIVIL ADMINISTRATION

UNTAES: Croatia

UNTAES provides useful clues for understanding the role and performance of current civil administrations within former Yugoslavia. It was authorized by a unanimous Chapter VII Security Council resolution in January 1996 to deal with the aftermath of Croatian army attacks on Serbs in UN Protected Areas within Croatia in 1995. These resulted in more than 170,000 Serbs leaving the area. An agreement was reached between the Croatian Government and the local Serb authorities, supported by the FRY (both President Tudjman of Croatia and President Milosevic of the FRY wanted a solution to the problem[21]) to facilitate peaceful reintegration of Eastern Slavonia into Croatian territory.

The Basic Agreement of November 1995 referred to the right of return and security for refugees and displaced persons, and the right to recover and receive compensation for property. The new administration's military component was mandated to monitor the voluntary and safe return of refugees and displaced persons to their homes of origin in cooperation with the UN High Commission for Refugees (UNHCR), and to contribute to the maintenance of peace and security in the region. The civilian component was to establish and train a temporary police force, undertake civil administrative and public service tasks, facilitate refugee returns, organize elections and certify results.

Assessment

The civil administration component of UNTAES was set up according to normal legitimate procedures. UNTAES continued to have support on the ground as well as backing from the Security Council. Nevertheless, one can question whether the mandate fully, uncompromisingly and effectively reaffirmed the basic rules designed to regulate contemporary international order,[22] given the uncertainties about much of the international legal approach to former Yugoslavia. One can also question whether UNTAES really 'helped to address, and often resolve, important practical issues, such as citizenship, energy supply, road and railway links, pensions, health insurance, education, ownership, currency, judiciary system, employment, housing, border controls, telephone and postal services, administration, ethnically mixed police forces, the amnesty, national service exemptions and the April 1997 local elections'.[23] Many of these issues were not only of a practical, but of a legal nature and remained unresolved.

The useful UN *Lessons Learned* on UNTAES is even less optimistic.[24] To be fair, there were gains: the Administrator was able to maintain authority over both the civilian and military components and had the power (subsequently expanded) to overrule decisions of the local administration. And much local Serb/Croat cooperation was achieved through the establishment of Joint Implementation Committees and through the organization of marketplaces. Local people were seen as an important resource for the consolidation of the UN's work after the Mission's eventual withdrawal. Nevertheless, the report suggests that UNTAES could have paid more attention to local capacity building. New thought must be given to 'transformations' of local actors within peacebuilding.[25] The concomitant public information strategy was well controlled and directed. Local languages were used.

On the down side, major problems regarding Croatian property, amnesty and citizenship laws, which discriminated against Serbs, were not resolved. The final Croatian Amnesty law of May 1996 lacked clarity in terms of penal enactment. Key legal issues that remained unresolved at the close of UNTAES' mandate included obligations regarding property-related issues, tenancy rights, funding for the Joint Council of Municipalities, and full implementation of the Amnesty law. Progress was also lacking on guarantees of the right to remain in the region; equal access to reconstruction grants; help for refugees and displaced persons; and, most important of all, the protection of rights of people (often the above) belonging to minorities in accordance with accepted international standards. Unfortunately, the Human Rights Monitoring Unit did not even become fully functional until August 1997. This was compounded by the fact that the Transitional Police Force did not always opt for proactive policing, while its professionalism was sometimes weakened by minority allegiances. Even more worrying, if civil administration is meant to succeed in the long term, was the growing harassment and intimidation of Serbs after UNTAES left, committed by Croat authorities and by displaced Croats attempting to reclaim their homes.[26]

The *Lessons Learned* study notes that 43 agreements aimed at integrating public institutions were signed. It suggests that 'the final judgement [on the success of the Mission] would depend on whether the Croatian Government would implement the various agreements and work towards national reconciliation'.[27] Genuine reconciliation would only be attained if significant progress at national and grassroots levels was recorded on the future of refugees and displaced persons, including equal treatment in the areas of housing and access to reconstruction grants and loans as well as to property compensation, as guaranteed under the law. The international community had to continue long-term monitoring. It was also imperative to develop a national reconciliation strategy and programme that went beyond elections: however, no such programme was accepted until October 1997.[28]

The relative short-term success of UNTAES (compared to the experience so far of that of the OHR and UNMIK) may well relate to contextual factors surrounding the Mission: it was politically supported by Milosevic and Tudjman, accepted unanimously by the UN Security Council, worked within a framework of some political recognition of borders and, most important of all, its mandate was both less ambitious and less confused. The long-term prospects for proper integration of the Serb minority, however, remain disturbing.

The Office of the High Representative: Bosnia

Former Swedish Prime Minister Carl Bildt was appointed High Representative for Bosnia (which had become a UN member in May 1992) at the first conference of the Peace Implementation Council (PIC) in London in December 1995, immediately following the US-organized Dayton Agreement. He was designated as the Chairman of the PIC, which oversees implementation of the 1995 Dayton peace accord that ended the war in Bosnia. The Agreement was endorsed later in the same month in the unanimous SCR 1031, which also agreed to Bildt's designation. UN authorization was avoided because of United States reservations about UN involvement.[29]

Bildt had earlier outlined his plans for the job. Requisites were a clear mandate, sufficient resources and the opportunity to operate on both the Bosnian and the international levels, and to rely on the existing UN civilian structure. Other important issues were the return of refugees, ensuring structures for economic cooperation as well as a civilian police operation.[30] However, a clear mandate was not achieved. Bildt was not given overall control of the military, although he was mandated to monitor the implementation of the Dayton Agreement. Other bodies were also involved. The Organization for Security and Cooperation in Europe (OSCE) was in charge of elections. Economic issues were the preserve of the EU and World Bank. The UN was given responsibility for the new International Police Task Force (IPTF), which was given a stronger mandate than previous UNCIVPOL operations.

Legal Framework and Issues

The OHR was authorized through Dayton and not through the UN, although the UN has become steadily more engaged with it. Regular OHR reports to the UN Security Council, since March 1996, were specifically requested in a unanimous Chapter VII resolution in

December. This unusual authorization demonstrates differences over the status and role of Bosnia within the international community of states, which were also exemplified by the debate over whether the FRY was or was not (after a Security Council resolution in September 1992) a member of the UN.[31]

This underlying uncertainty continued to make it difficult for the OHR, as for UNTAES, to find acceptable solutions to major legal issues, particularly property laws. OHR proposals had to comply with Dayton besides 'being in line with European or international practice' as well as 'Bosnia's own legal and constitutional principles'.[32] Within the Federation battles raged over the powers of the common institutions versus the powers of the two/three entities and the use of law by local authorities to prevent minority refugee returns. In the spring of 1997 Bildt found himself employing the strategy of 'blocking the military, the secession and the domination [by Serbs and/or Croats] option' so 'we could contain the development of Bosnia within the Dayton framework. ... This I knew was going to be a difficult balancing act between tendencies towards setting up a semi-protectorate and acceptance of local deals which might not always be what we would have liked to see'.[33]

He also became involved in economic regeneration to ensure that economic development 'supported the political endeavours for which I did have overall responsibility'.[34] As he notes, economic reforms, an effective currency system and freedom to do business and set up companies implied a legal system 'that would establish the prerequisites for a free economy, an effective banking structure, clear rules for property rights, and sound and stable public finances to ensure payment of essential public investments'.[35] By the spring of 1997 the Steering Board had come to see the OHR as 'not simply an implementing agency on the ground, but very much a strategy-shaping operation they could not do without'.[36]

Local Capacity Building

Like his successors, Bildt found it difficult to achieve reconciliation within Bosnia. His first report to the Security Council (March 1996) drew attention to one of the key factors, the lack of political will to carry out the agreements in Bosnia. He failed in his initial attempt to keep Sarajevo multi-ethnic and considered that he had been betrayed 'by the Muslim leaders in general, and by Izetbegovic in particular'.[37] The problems continued. After Bildt left in 1997, the PIC agreed at Bonn that the OHR could use his final authority in theatre regarding the interpretation of the Peace Agreement in order to facilitate the resolution of difficulties. This he could pursue by making binding decisions on certain specific issues (that is, he was given UNTAES-like powers).[38] The subsequent unanimous SCR 1144 (also in December) expressed its support for the conclusions of the PIC.

His successors have continued similar policies besides using their additional powers: the fifteenth report of the High Representative to the UN Secretary-General, covering end-June to end-October 1999, noted that the first decision of the new High Representative was to seek to ensure that publicly-funded broadcasting in Republika Srpska, a key factor in communicating with the local population, was free from political bias or interference. The sixteenth report[39] (October 1999–April 2000) reported that the High Representative and the OSCE Head of Mission cooperated in dismissing 22 public officials throughout Bosnia for serious and persistent obstructions of the Dayton Accords: these officials were also barred by the Provisional Elections Commission. The action had received widespread public support.

Assessment

Bildt suggests 'that any future peace implementation mission has a lot to learn from the experiences we made breaking new ground. There must be a unity of political efforts, a clear will to back political intentions with military might and a realization that peace is in essence a political process'.[40] Interestingly, he made no reference to the UN, law, justice or the concerns of the local population. This perhaps demonstrates the fact that he and his successors considered that they could not rely on the backing of the international community of states in the UN, which might have lent increased political legitimacy to his Mission. G-8 backing alone was clearly not sufficient.

The Bosnian civil administration must in the long term be considered in the wider context of the fact that the local population remains uncertain about ultimate legal boundaries between the states of former Yugoslavia and the lasting qualities of the Dayton framework. This makes it even more difficult to resolve the complex legal questions underlying the political and economic order within and outside Bosnia. One critic suggests that '[t]he support given to the nationalist parties at present stems not so much from the lack of alternatives but the inability of alternative political groups and opinions to gain a broader hearing when the dominant concern is for the security of the entity itself and the jobs and homes that are dependent on a secure political settlement'.[41]

Missions have often been judged by their mandate performance, facilitation of conflict resolution, conflict containment and limitation of casualties.[42] The OHR and its military counterpart, SFOR, have had more success with conflict containment and limitation of casualties than conflict resolution. The OHR has found it difficult to work with many of the local people: this has led to the increase of its 'protectorate'-like powers and concern about the accountability of civil administrators.[43] Exit strategies following the resumption of peace, reconciliation and development seem distant despite the fact that the first OHR was appointed in 1995. United States ambivalence about the UN and the OHR – and its support for the G8 – is also reflected in the historical development of UNMIK.

UNMIK: Kosovo FRY

The Security Council established the UN Interim Administration Mission in Kosovo by a Chapter VII resolution in June 1999. It was a direct result of the NATO bombing over Kosovo in the spring of 1999, which itself followed the FRY's campaign to expel Albanians from Kosovo. This was 'the first time a major use of destructive armed force had been undertaken with the stated purpose of implementing UN Security Council resolutions but without Security Council authorization'.[44] This was the fifth UN Security Council resolution on Kosovo on all of which China had abstained (Russia abstained on two). All agreed that the principles of the solution to Kosovo's plight should be based on the territorial integrity of the FRY. The G8 Foreign Ministers, however, in their list of principles endorsed by and attached to SCR 1244 called for:

> a political process towards the establishment of an interim political framework agreement providing for substantial self-government for Kosovo, taking full account of the Rambouillet accords and the principles of sovereignty and territorial integrity of the Federal Republic of Yugoslavia and the other countries of the region, and the demilitarization of UCK.

They also called for the establishment of an interim administration 'to provide transitional administration while establishing and overseeing the development of provisional democratic self-governing institutions to ensure conditions for a peaceful and normal life for all inhabitants in Kosovo'.

The resolution authorized the UN Secretary-General to establish such an administration. UNMIK's responsibilities included organizing elections; supporting key economic infrastructure reconstruction and humanitarian aid; assuring the safe and unimpeded return of all refugees and displaced persons; and maintaining civil law and order including establishing local police forces. Interestingly, the UN was given executive authority over policing in both Kosovo and East Timor, rather than its normal function of assisting in the development of local police forces and of monitoring their behaviour.[45]

Legal Framework and Issues

The range of authority of the transitional administration can be seen in the first Regulation for Kosovo (July 1999), which served as the precedent for East Timor.[46] It stated that '[a]ll legislative and executive authority with respect to Kosovo, including the administration of the judiciary, is vested in UNMIK and is exercised by the Special Representative of the Secretary-General [SRSG].' It also noted that 'all persons undertaking public duties or holding public office in Kosovo shall observe internationally recognized human rights standards'.

The structure of this Mission and its leadership was somewhat similar to that of the OHR. UNMIK's four pillars presided over by the SRSG comprised:

- Humanitarian Assistance (the responsibility of the UNHCR).
- Civil Administration – the UN.
- Democratization and Institution Building – the OSCE.
- Reconstruction and Development – the EU.

The first pillar was phased out at the end of June 2000. A new pillar, on Police and Justice, was removed from the second pillar and set up in May 2001 to provide greater focus, centrality and coordination. Neither the Commander of KFOR nor the SRSG were given authority over the other.

The disputes between local Serbs and Albanians were exacerbated over applicable Yugoslav law. The Albanians finally agreed to the law in force before 22 March 1989 (that is, before Milosevic had abrogated the Province's legal autonomy providing for self-administration). The Serbs, however, protested against this legislation and called it an 'encroachment on Yugoslav sovereignty'.[47] Legal issues including property rights also came to the fore. UNMIK proposed a standard registry of property claims, to redress legal measures on property taken in recent years that discriminated against any ethnic group and to rebuild property and cadastral records.

All these efforts were hampered by a vacuum within law enforcement. Even one year after the deployment of the Mission, the international police force was still only at 77 per cent of its authorized strength. This meant 'that vengeance' by Albanians 'could be enjoyed with virtual impunity'.[48] Some security was achieved at the cost of Albanian/Serb segregation. The overall security vacuum embraced not only the police force but also the judiciary and prison system. The question of which law was applicable was compounded by the unwillingness of local judges, prosecutors and the population to cooperate in the area of criminal justice, and to remain biased towards Serbs or Albanians. The SRSG therefore decided in February 2000 to appoint international judges and prosecutors. Nevertheless, many problems continued,[49] indicating a need for justice in a much broader sense.

Local Capacity Building

Unfortunately, UNMIK took several months to deploy. This meant that it had 'a difficult time establishing its authority and replacing self-appointed authorities with legitimate and representative bodies'.[50] The SRSG began by attempting local consultation by setting up a Kosovo Transitional Council[51] which was subsequently replaced by a Joint Interim Administrative Structure (JIAS). This arrangement included an Interim Administrative Council (IAC), which would recommend amendments to applicable law and propose policy guidelines to administrative departments.[52] Representatives of all major political parties and ethnic groups met on a weekly basis to provide input into UNMIK decision making. Despite these efforts, the municipal elections in October 2000 were boycotted by the Kosovo Serbs and almost all Roma and Turks.[53] Political circumstances finally improved after the fall of Milosevic in the same month. UNMIK and the FRY instituted a regular dialogue and agreed to open an UNMIK office in Belgrade.[54] By March 2001 the Mission was able to shift its focus away from relief-intensive efforts to political and economic capacity building.

Assessment

UNMIK, like the OHR, had more success with conflict containment and limitation of casualties than actual conflict resolution. It found it difficult to work with certain local people (and sometimes with their counterpart organizations). The Mission was set up in the context of a number of international legal problems. These include the lack of authorization of NATO's bombing campaign and the status of the FRY within the UN. Ambiguities over the future of Kosovo were also reflected in UNMIK's mandate, as Rambouillet allowed for its secession without FRY consent.[55] Information remains crucial. Both UNMIK and the OHR recognize the key importance of setting up appropriate legal systems, particularly for property disputes (for both economic and political purposes). Both have failed to find appropriate answers. Some suggest the fact that so many different – and diverse – organizations involved is at the root of many bureaucratic problems, despite the fact that they are all ultimately managed by member states of the organizations concerned.

International Law and Former Yugoslavia

Many international lawyers suggest that a number of decisions made during the conflict in former Yugoslavia on such subjects as requirements for statehood, the application of the right of self-determination, recognition of seceding states, the imposition of sanctions and the treatment of the FRY's UN membership 'represent a derogation from the rules of international law'.[56] This may have happened because of the increased pressure on regional actors to deal with major problems of international peace and security in the post-Cold War world of the 1990s. Some of them clearly lacked the necessary experience. For instance, the original members of the influential Badinter Commission, a Legal advisory body on recognition, self-determination and succession to the International Conference on Former Yugoslavia, were constitutional court judges rather than international lawyers.[57]

A number of European leaders, for instance, subscribed to the view 'that self-determination is a right that authorizes minorities to break away'.[58] This is contested by many international lawyers who insist that there is neither a right of secession nor that minorities are entitled to the right of self-determination.[59] The right of self-determination (the UN Charter only refers to the principle of self-determination[60]) was asserted through the same Article 1 of the two major human rights Covenants on Civil and Political Rights (ICCPR) and on Economic, Social and Cultural Rights (ICESCR), which came into force in 1976. It has never been used to assert that minorities have the right of self-determination. However, it has correctly been used to suggest that East Timor has the right of self-determination, which, as one judge on the International Court of Justice has argued, follows from the principle of territorial integrity.[61]

As one practising international lawyer (who was on Bildt's staff in Bosnia) has noted, '[t]he EC member states' approach to recognition in the case of the states of the former Soviet Union and former Yugoslavia was unusual ... [and] not in line with previous state practices'. Moreover, '[t]here has often been tension between law and policy in connection with the former Yugoslavia. It may from time to time have seemed that international law has been given short shrift by policy makers'.[62] Civil administrators in Bosnia, Croatia and the FRY have found this underlying tension has not helped promote long-term practical solutions to their problems.

Regional Actors and the World Community of States

Actors dealing with former Yugoslavia have included the G7 (G8 including Russia), which gives political direction to the OHR, as well as the more regionally oriented European Union, European Commission, NATO and the OSCE. These states represent the Western political dominance that replaced the politics of the Cold War.[63] Concerns by Western European states that Russia might come to the aid of Serbs in former Yugoslavia also imposed constraints on their actions *vis-à-vis* former Yugoslavia.

Although these organizations were legally bound in their actions by Chapter VIII of the UN Charter, they did not consistently act according to those obligations – even though states' responsibilities under the Charter prevail over those of any other agreement including NATO. Germany, for instance, was determined to recognize Croatia and Slovenia prematurely irrespective of the fact that this did not conform to international legal standards.[64] Short-term views (and supposed gains) tempted some actors to underestimate the political legitimacy that they could have derived from working within the parameters of the UN and international law. Unfortunately, this legacy has repeated itself in the context and conduct of post-war civil administration. It is extremely important for states (and groups of states) to commit themselves 'to legal processes and to taming the unequal political order within which those processes are embedded'.[65]

Rights of Persons Belonging to Minorities

Ted Robert Gurr has convincingly argued that the slowdown in ethnic warfare after the early 1990s was partly due to the intervention of domestic and international peacemakers and a number of committed protagonists who tried to ensure autonomy for minorities through the implementation of international standards of individual and group rights.[66] Asbjorn Eide's 1993 report is, for instance, based on the premise that international human rights law is above all concerned 'with the equality and dignity of every human being'.[67] It therefore sets limits to the collective rights of both majorities and minorities. The

State should not be the 'property' of one ethnic, religious or linguistic group whether majoritarian or minoritarian. In discussing minority problems in times of transition, he suggests that 'fear of the future, insecurity in terms of protection both of identity and from discrimination, has created grounds for political mobilization by ethnic entrepreneurs which has caused some of the worst tragedies in Europe since the end of the Second World War'.[68]

Why have these ideas not flourished in the new states within former Yugoslavia? Is it the case because these states failed to achieve both peace and justice? The experiences of UNTAES, the OHR and UNMIK have shown how difficult it is for civil administrators to develop local civil society and ensure the expression of the will of all the people within the state. This can only be accomplished if appropriate regimes for persons belonging to minorities have been devised.

Many agree that minorities were not victimized within former Yugoslavia.[69] Carl Bildt has suggested that, '[h]ad genuine and credible guarantees of minority rights been extracted from Croatia as a precondition for recognition, not only would the prospect for peace in Bosnia have been dramatically improved, but the way would also have been paved for a settlement in Kosovo'.[70] Instead, Croatia was recognized despite the fact that the Badinter Commission had stated that it had not made the required constitutional changes regarding its treatment of minorities.[71] In the final analysis, the European Community's decision to grant recognition to secessionist republics turned out to be extremely problematic for both persons belonging to minorities within former Yugoslavia as well as the civil administrators who had to address the consequences of intergroup struggle after some violence had ended.[72]

Secession

It is not surprising that the NATO's bombing campaign in support of Kosovo's struggle against Belgrade has attracted particular attention from the international community of states. Under Article 53 of the UN Charter no enforcement action should be taken by regional bodies without authorization from the Security Council. NATO's action against the FRY was not explicitly authorized by the Security Council. Any resolution recommending Kosovo's secession presented to the Security Council would probably be vetoed by China, Russia and, possibly, France, who would be likely to argue that this would be against Charter principles. Generally most UN states are committed to territorial integrity and a conservative interpretation of the right of self-determination. One lawyer has, however, suggested that the Security

Council has the authority to make decisions regarding the governance of a territory; that there could be 'situations in which the Security Council would be justified in directing a permanent change in some aspect of the status, boundaries, political structure, or legal system of territory within a state, if the Council should determine that doing so is necessary to restore and maintain international peace and security'.[73]

The Need for Future Research on Civil Administration

Future research must embrace the lessons that can be learned from past examples of civil administration. Were these administrations able to contribute to peace, reconciliation and development? Many of these provided governmental civil administration, that is, the exercise of some or all executive powers within government. Not all were set up by the UN. They include the UN Operation in the Congo (1960–64) and the UN Temporary Executive Authority in West Irian (UNTEA 1962–63) and its security force (UNSF) in West Irian. Further examples are the UN Transition Assistance Group (1989–90) in Namibia and the UN Transitional Authority in Cambodia (1992–93).

Civil administrations increasingly embrace people's civil administration (the development of civil society and the expression of the will of the people through the organization and conduct of elections as well as information management).[74] Examples include the second UN Verification Mission in Angola (1991–95); the UN Operation in Mozambique (1992–94); and the UN Observer Mission in El Salvador (1991–95). In these missions, the interface between law, politics and economics is becoming increasingly important.[75]

Research needs to focus on how legal issues have been handled in the context of civil administration. As already noted, the most relevant example for East Timor is UNTEA, which provided for the transfer of administration of West Irian from the Netherlands to the UN, and then and from the UN to Indonesia. UNTEA had full powers of legislation, the provision of civil liberties and protection of property rights.[76] A number of Missions were deeply involved in the interpretation and application of national law. UNTAG's concern with gaining the public trust, and thus establishing itself as a legitimate authority was important, as was its concern to ensure that the South African administrator-general repealed all remaining discriminatory or restrictive laws.[77] UNTAC had the power to issue restraining orders in disputes about property claims.[78] In contrast, ONUSAL was not given the mandate for institutional reform of the judiciary: this meant that in that respect, its impact was minimal.[79]

Future research should, in a comparative fashion, include cases outside the UN context. For instance, the League of Nations was involved with the interim administration of the German Saar and Colombian Leticia, as well as with plebiscites 'arranged and conducted by inter-allied commissions, which usually took governmental charge of the territories in question for the relevant period'.[80] The League's Mandate territories,[81] the post-First World War occupation of Germany (and, indeed German administration in many European countries during the Second World War), and the post-Second World War occupations of Germany and Japan also need to be scrutinized.[82]

It would furthermore be helpful to discuss the treatment of minority populations by governments of the post-Yugoslav states.[83] Finally, consideration could be given to the territories put under UN trusteeship, as well as the 32 plebiscites, referenda and elections held under the supervision or observation of the UN in both trust and non-self-governing territories between 1956 and 1990, some of which fall into the category of people's civil administration.[84] It is important to acknowledge that civil administration *per se* is, historically, not unusual[85] and often has provided possibilities for real change in the long term. Having said that, however, more work needs to be done to analyse and understand – and eventually learn from – factors for success and failure.

Exit Strategies

Alvaro de Soto and Graciano del Castillo noted in 1995 that the decision to end a peacekeeping operation, while of course honouring the mission's commitments and mandate, is as important as the original decision of deployment. They suggest the test of an exit scenario should be 'whether peace-related reforms have advanced enough to make the process durable, indeed irreversible – that is, whether the structures and institutions put in place ensure that potential conflicts will be resolved by peaceful means rather than by resorting to arms, and that potentially explosive problems, such as threats posed by disgruntled former combatants, have been defused'.[86]

Much of the same reasoning also applies to civil administrations. UNTAET needs to maintain a continuing and even more effective dialogue with the new East Timorese government, members of civil society and UN member states. Such dialogue must focus on the future of East Timor, and the future provision of international aid and monitoring. The OHR, UNMIK and all states within the international community need to face the unfinished legal business underlying previous attempts to grapple with former Yugoslavia's problems. Of significant importance will undoubtedly be the resolution of the situation in Kosovo. Will UN member states (or other smaller groups of states directly involved in the resolution of Kosovo future status) authorize Kosovo's secession if the FRY does not agree? If they do, this could be a potentially dangerous precedent.

The three current civil administrations discussed in more detail here need to find solutions to basic national legal problems (made more complex by the underlying legal uncertainties in former Yugoslavia) in areas such as property rights; amnesty laws; citizenship; the right to remain in the region; and discrimination against persons belonging to minorities. In doing so, they must ensure that sufficient attention is given to the three distinct dimensions of justice – rectificatory, distributive and the rule of law.[87]

Conclusion

This contribution has considered three current administrations and one previous civil administration (three in former Yugoslavia and one in East Timor). It has tried to demonstrate how vital it is that states involved in peacebuilding missions and UN agencies are aware of the importance (both politically and economically) of conforming to standards of international and national law. This is particularly important in the context of the rights of persons belonging to minorities. States also need to be concerned with rectificatory and distributive justice (nationally and internationally) in both the short and long terms.

Civil administrations are more likely to succeed in carrying out their mandate and in achieving political legitimacy (which allows them to have a lasting effect) if they have been set up appropriately through the UN and if those managing administrations take their accountability seriously. They will find it difficult to achieve political legitimacy if they build on inadequate legal foundations. The normal legal criteria for the recognition of states needs to be followed (this was not the case in former Yugoslavia). These criteria have usually included the fact that states should only be recognized if they have, and seem likely to continue to have, a clearly defined territory with a population, a government that is able to exercise effective control of that territory, and independence in their external relations. UN resolutions may also be relevant.[88]

The OHR and UNMIK (as well as UNTAES in the past) continue to be partially crippled by the underlying insecurity within Bosnia, Croatia and the FRY. This has been exacerbated by ambiguous mandates as well as an inappropriate legal and political approach towards persons belonging to minorities despite the fact that much useful research in this area is available. UNTAET, despite its real problems, is more likely to fulfil its much less ambiguous mandate than either the OHR or UNMIK. This essay also argues that regional states and their organizations need to prepare themselves particularly carefully if they wish to contribute to successful peacebuilding. They must ensure that their short-term political concerns do not take precedence over norms of international and national law. They also need to be aware what appropriate research is available and what might usefully be commissioned. If these basic requirements are met, their civil administrations might be able to secure political legitimacy and, thus, the authority that is necessary to address, and hopefully resolve, many of the political and economic challenges that lie at the core of their mandates.

ACKNOWLEDGEMENTS

The opinions expressed are the author's own, and should not be taken as an expression of official United Kingdom policy.

NOTES

1. Andrew Hurrell, 'Conclusion: International Law and the Changing Constitution of International Society', in Michael Byers (ed.), *The Role of Law in International Politics, Essays in International Relations and International Law*, Oxford University Press, 2000, p.331.
2. Miroslav Baros, 'The UN's Response to the Yugoslav Crisis: Turning the UN Charter on its Head', *International Peacekeeping*, Vol.8, No.1, spring 2001, p.58.
3. Rama Mani, 'Contextualising Police Reform', *International Peacekeeping*, Vol.6, No.4, winter 1999, pp.20–21.
4. Rama Mani, 'The Rule of Law or the Rule of Might? Restoring Legal Justice in the Aftermath of Conflict', in Michael Pugh (ed.), *Regeneration of War-Torn Societies*, London: Macmillan, 2000, p.90. See also Ruth Wedgwood and Harold Jacobson (eds), 'Foreword to Symposium: State Reconstruction after Civil Conflict', Hansjörg Strohmeyer, 'Collapse and Reconstruction of a Judicial System: The United Nations Missions in Kosovo and East Timor', Michael J. Matheson, 'United Nations Governance of Postconflict Societies', *American Journal of International Law*, Vol.95, No.1, Jan. 2001; Mark Plunkett, 'Reestablishing Law and Order in Peace-Maintenance', in Jarat Chopra (ed.), *The Politics of Peace-Maintenance*, Boulder: Lynne Rienner, 1998; Timothy A. Wilkins, 'The El Salvador Peace Accords: Using International and Domestic Law Norms to Build Peace', in Michael W. Doyle, Ian Johnstone and Robert C. Orr (eds), *Keeping the Peace: Multidimensional UN Operations in Cambodia and El Salvador*, Cambridge: Cambridge University Press, 1997.
5. Hugh Miall, Oliver Ramsbotham and Tom Woodhouse, *Contemporary Conflict Resolution*, London: Polity Press, 1999, p.63.
6. Sally Morphet, 'Organizing Civil Administration in Peace-Maintenance', in Jarat Chopra (ed.), *The Politics of Peace-Maintenance*, Boulder: Lynne Rienner, 1998, pp.45–6.
7. Report of the Secretary-General on the United Nations Transitional Administration in East Timor, Addendum, S/2000/53/Add.1, 8 Feb. 2000, p.2.

8. Catherine Scott, *East Timor Transition to Statehood*, London, CIIR Comment, 2001, pp.21–44.
9. 'East Timor Starting from Scratch', *IISS Strategic Comments*, Vol.7, No.8, Oct. 2001, p.2.
10. Jarat Chopra, 'The UN's Kingdom of East Timor', *Survival*, Vol.42, No. 1, autumn 2000, p.28.
11. Ibid., p.32.
12. Ibid., p.30.
13. Ibid., p.31.
14. Ibid.
15. Report of the Secretary-General on the United Nations Transitional Administration in East Timor, S/2000/738, 26 July 2000, p.1. See also Astri Suhrke, `Peacekeepers as Nation-builders: UN Dilemmas in East Timor', *International Peacekeeping*, Vol 8, No.4, Winter 2001, p.17.
16. Ibid, p.1.
17. James Cotton, 'Against the Grain: The East Timor Intervention', *Survival*, Vol.43, No.1, spring 2001, p.136.
18. Working Group for Study and Examination Yayasan HAK, Dili, East Timor 10/01/2000.
19. Morphet (n.6 above), p.45.
20. Catherine Scott, *East Timor Transition to Statehood*, London, CIIR Comment, 2001, pp.21–44.
21. Carl Bildt, 'Peace Journey The Struggle for Peace in Bosnia', in London: Weidenfeld & Nicolson, 1998, pp.134–35.
22. Pjer Simunovic, 'A Framework for Success: Contextual Factors in the UNTAES Operation in Eastern Slavonia', *International Peacekeeping*, Vol.6, No.1, spring 1999, p.128.
23. Ibid, p.137.
24. Lessons Learned Unit, UN Department of Peacekeeping Operations, *The United Nations Transitional Administration in Eastern Slavonia, Baranja and Western Sirmium (UNTAES) Lessons Learned*, July 1998, pp.3–50.
25. Beatrice Pouligny, 'Peacekeepers and Local Social Actors: The Need for Dynamic, Cross-Cultural Analysis', *Global Governance*, Vol.5, No.4, Oct.–Dec. 1999, pp.403–24.
26. Bildt (n.21 above), p.390.
27. Lessons Learned Unit (n.24 above) p.37.
28. It would be interesting to study the OSCE monitoring reports that were supposed to be done after the Mission left in January 1998. Lessons learned from these Missions should perhaps be revisited every five years or so. Did, for instance, the death of President Tudjman improve the situation in Eastern Slavonia? It appears it did not. UNTAES' public information strategy and the use of the Administrator's powers both only worked in the short term.
29. Bildt (n.21 above), p.117.
30. Ibid., pp.113–14.
31. Michael C. Wood, 'Participation of Former Yugoslav States in the United Nations and Multilateral Treaties', in Jochen A. Frowein and Rudiger Wolfrum (eds), *Max Planck Yearbook of United Nations Law Vol.1*, London: Kluwer Law International, 1997, p.247. The FRY was admitted into the UN in November 2000.
32. Bildt (n.21 above), p.311.
33. Ibid., p.343.
34. Ibid., p.244.
35. Ibid., p.243.
36. Ibid., p.358.
37. Ibid., p.198.
38. Eighth Report from the High Representative for Implementation of the Peace Agreement on Bosnia and Herzegovina to the Secretary-General, S/1998/40, 16 Jan. 1998, p.4.

39. Sixteenth Report from the High Representative to the Secretary-General, S/2000/376, 4 May 2000, pp.2-3.
40. Bildt (n.21 above), p.386.
41. David Chandler, *Bosnia Faking Democracy After Dayton*, London: Pluto Press, 1999, p.199.
42. Duane Bratt, 'Assessing the Success of UN Peacekeeping Operations', *International Peacekeeping*, Vol.3, No.4, winter 1997, p.79.
43. Ralph Wilde, 'From Bosnia to Kosovo and East Timor: The Changing Role of the United Nations in the Administration of Territory', *ILSA Journal of International and Comparative Law*, Vol.6. No.2, spring 2000, p.471.
44. Adam Roberts, 'NATO's Humanitarian War over Kosovo', *Survival*, Vol.41, No.3, autumn 1999, p.102.
45. Espen Barth Eide and Tor Tanke Holm, 'Postscript: Towards Executive Authority Policing? The Lessons of Kosovo', *International Peacekeeping*, Vol.6, No.4, winter 1999, p.211.
46. UNMIK/REG/1999/1 25/07/99, at www.un.org/peace/kosovo/pages/regulations/reg1.html.
47. Alexandros Yannis, 'Kosovo under International Administration', *Survival*, Vol.43, No.2, summer 2001, p.34.
48. Ibid., p37.
49. Ibid., p.38. See also Steven Powles, Bar Human Rights Committee, *The Times*, 7 March 2000.
50. Ibid., p.34.
51. Report of the Secretary-General on the United Nations Interim Administration Mission in Kosovo, S/1999/987, 16 Sept. 1999, p.1.
52. Report of the Secretary-General on the United Nations Interim Administration Mission in Kosovo, S/1999/1250, 23 Dec. 1999, pp.1–2.
53. Report of the Secretary-General on the United Nations Interim Administration Mission in Kosovo, S/2000/1196, 15 Dec. 2000, p.1.
54. Report of the Secretary-General on the United Nations Interim Administration Mission in Kosovo, S/2001/218, 13 Mar. 2001, p.1.
55. Marc Weller, 'The Rambouillet Conference', *International Affairs*, Vol.75, No.2, April 1999.
56. Baros (n.2 above), p.58.
57. Dominic McGoldrick, 'Yugoslavia – The Responses of the International Community and of International Law', in M.D.A. Freeeman with R. Halson (eds), *Current Legal Problems 1996, Volume 49, Part 2: Collected Papers*, Oxford: Oxford University Press, p.381.
58. Rosalyn Higgins, *Problems & Process of International Law and How We Use It*, London: Clarendon Press, 1994, p.124.
59. Ibid., pp.111–28, McGoldrick (n.57 above), pp.385–6 and Baros (n.2 above).
60. Article 1.2.
61. Higgins (n.58 above), p.127.
62. Wood (n.31 above), p.237 and p.256.
63. In addition, the Organization of the Islamic Conference played an important part in the International Conference on Former Yugoslavia.
64. McGoldrick (n.57 above), p.383.
65. Hurrell (n.1 above), p.347.
66. Ted Robert Gurr, *Peoples Versus States Minorities at Risk in the New Century*, Washington DC: US Institute of Peace Press, 2000, pp.275–88.
67. Asbjorn Eide, *Possible ways and means of facilitating the peaceful and constructive solution of problems involving minorities*, Report for the Sub-Commission on Prevention of Discrimination and Protection of Minorities, E/CN.4/Sub.2/1993/34, 10 Aug. 1993.
68. Ibid.
69. Baros (n.2 above), p.49.

70. Bildt (n.21 above), p.374.
71. Baros (n.2 above), p.63.
72. Ibid., pp.46–9.
73. Matheson (n.4 above) p.85.
74. Morphet (n.6 above), pp.41–3.
75. Jenny Pearce, 'From Civil War to "Civil Society": Has the End of the Cold War Brought Peace to Central America?', *International Affairs*, Vol.74, No.3, July 1998.
76. Morphet (n.6 above), pp.45–6.
77. Ibid., p.47.
78. Ibid., p.51.
79. Wilkins (n.4 above), p.272.
80. Alan James, 'The Peacekeeping Role of the League of Nations', *International Peacekeeping*, Vol.6, No.1, spring 99, pp.54–60.
81. See, in particular, the problems raised in the context of Palestine, in Susan Silsby Boyle, *Betrayal of Palestine: The Story of George Antonius*, Boulder: Westview Press, 2001.
82. Samuel H. Barnes, 'The Contribution of Democracy to Rebuilding Postconflict Societies', *American Journal of International Law*, Vol.95, No.1, Jan. 2001, p.91.
83. Baros (n.2 above), p.49.
84. Morphet, (n.6 above), p.58.
85. See the useful, wide-ranging discussion of all this in Ralph Wilde, 'From Danzig to East Timor and Beyond: The Role of International Territorial Administration', *American Journal of International Law*, Vol.95, No.3, July 2002, pp.583–606.
86. Alvaro de Soto and Graciano del Castillo, 'Implementation of Comprehensive Peace Agreements: Staying the Course in El Salvador', *Global Governance*, Vol.1, No. 2, May–Aug. 1995, pp.202–3.
87. Mani (n.4 above), p.1. See also Mark Plunkett (n.4 above).
88. See British House of Commons written answer of 16 November 1989.

Refugees and Post-Conflict Reconstruction: A Critical Perspective

B.S. CHIMNI

Recent decades have seen more internal than international conflicts, and these have involved the displacement of large numbers of people both within and across states. The end of a conflict has therefore come to be associated with the return home of refugees and internally displaced persons, and a return to normality, peace and stability. The return of displaced persons also lends greater legitimacy to the subsequent democratic and state-building process.

Today, the return of refugees also coincides with the disinclination of states to host refugees. The current geopolitical agenda prevalent in many developed states of the North is at odds with the admission and recognition of refugees. Developing countries, on the other hand, seek to return refugees for other reasons, be they the end of the original political context (for example, support for national liberation struggles), the social and economic burden of hosting refugees, environmental degradation, and the possibility of social conflict. The refugees themselves wish to return, as 'the alternative is to languish in camps and to live indefinitely off handouts, or to suffer from harassment, round-ups, arbitrary detention, extortion and even deportation'.[1] In other words, 'repatriation is conceived as an escape route from conditions of deprivation'.[2] Of course, going back 'home' also means regaining citizenship rights and, for the first generation of refugees, meeting an emotional need.[3] But, as will become clear, refugees will be able to regain citizenship rights and feel at home only if the pre-conditions for sustainable return prevail.

Despite the absence of suitable conditions for return in many cases, there continues to be a strong focus on the repatriation of refugees. Thus, over the last decade, the Office of the United Nations High Commissioner for Refugees (UNHCR) has been under great pressure to facilitate and promote the return of refugees to the country of origin even when conditions are far from ideal. It has led to various forms of pressure or duress being brought to bear on refugees to return.[4] For instance, 'despite a well-established legal principle that refugee repatriation should take place on a wholly voluntary basis and in conditions of safety and dignity, a substantial proportion of Africa's most recent returnees have gone back to their homes in conditions which do not meet these standards'.[5]

The current stress on repatriation has also meant a research focus on ensuring early return. Unsurprisingly, legal experts have given relevant texts suitable interpretations[6] and social scientists have, in a bid to legitimize involuntary return, grounded return in the discourse of human rights.[7] In contrast, 'little information is available about what has happened to those refugees who have returned home...few authors have attempted to investigate the *experiences of the returnees themselves*'.[8] This is a matter of some concern because if repatriation brings to an end the 'refugee cycle', 'it also coincides with the beginning of a new cycle'.[9] To put it differently, the sustainable return of refugees demands that the long-term problems of returnees be addressed, at a time when UNHCR is *reducing* its support in this area. As a result, the organization 'has been unable to assess the longer-term consequences of its interventions'.[10]

A deeper concern arises from the absence of any systematic theoretical and legal framework that allows the various elements of the reconstruction, reintegration and peacebuilding strategies of international organizations or states to be derived from a critical and integral understanding of the problems that characterize 'post-conflict' societies or of refugees who return to them. The result is an array of measures that have rarely been arrived at in consultation with refugees and returnees, and which often work at cross-purposes with each other. Moreover, they have often been assembled in the matrix of a neo-liberal vision which, among other things, does not focus on the international causes of internal conflicts and excludes the possibility of building a participatory 'post-conflict' state. In brief, the basic problem with current policies relating to the return and reintegration of refugees to 'post-conflict' societies is the poverty of epistemology deployed to identify suitable measures that will go to promote 'sustainable return'. This is the latent, albeit running, theme of this contribution, which is divided into four further parts. The next part critically examines the concepts of a 'post-conflict society', 'peacebuilding' and 'sustainable return'. This is followed by an analysis of specific problems that returnees face, such as housing and property rights, the presence of land mines, and the issue of disarmament, demobilization and reintegration of former combatants. The next section examines the role of UN agencies such as UNHCR and the Security Council (UNSC) and the problems of coordination arising from numerous UN agencies being involved in peacebuilding. Finally, the conclusion makes a number of recommendations.

Conceptual Clarifications

What is a 'Post-Conflict' Society?

Since the early 1980s, when the increased flow of refugees from the South to the North in a non-Cold War context began, the solution of voluntary repatriation has come to be designated by the UNHCR as the 'ideal solution'.[11] But by the 1990s states became increasingly impatient with the standard of 'voluntariness' which they felt constrained return in less than ideal conditions, in particular to societies embroiled in internal conflicts. This invited a research focus on repatriation under conflict and yielded the somewhat convenient conclusion that most refugees return spontaneously to their country of origin and that they do so even when the conflict has not ended. The real issue of whether the policies of host states left the refugees with any alternative did not receive adequate attention.[12] Be that as it may, the movement of spontaneous refugees still left large numbers of refugees in host states. Therefore, at some point, the distinction between spontaneous and involuntary returns had to blur.

The need to legitimize return called for the invention of new and flexible conceptual categories. One such concept is that of a 'post-conflict' society. Its elastic nature is best illustrated with reference to a World Bank review in 1998 of its activities in 'post-conflict' countries that included Angola, Bosnia, Burundi, Cambodia, Rwanda and Uganda – all of which, as Crisp points out, 'continue(d) to experience high levels of social conflict, violence, human rights abuse and large-scale population displacement'.[13] Indeed, the World Bank itself admitted that 'drawing a line between 'conflict' and 'post-conflict' is difficult'.[14] The UNHCR also accepts that it may be 'misleading' to talk of 'post-conflict situations' when there are still 'periods of intense if sporadic fighting', but continues to use the term 'post-conflict'.[15] According to Macrae, what is problematic is that UNHCR does not indicate the criteria for describing a particular situation as one of transition or determining when it is going to end.[16]

What is the meaning and purpose of blurring the distinction between war and peace? These appear to be fourfold: first, and most obvious, it legitimizes involuntary repatriation of refugees. Second, the representation of conflict situations as normal allows donor states to disengage from them.[17] Third, the assumption of normalcy allows structural adjustment programmes to be launched by the international financial institutions (IFIs).[18] Fourth, it helps circumscribe the meaning of 'peacebuilding' by equating it with a rudimentarily accountable state. This last conclusion calls for further elaboration.

Meaning of 'Peacebuilding'

'Peacebuilding', according to UNHCR, refers 'to the process whereby national protection and the rule of law are re-established. More specifically, it entails an absence of social and political violence, the establishment of effective judicial procedures, the introduction of pluralistic forms of government, and the equitable distribution of resources'.[19] Likewise, the UN Secretary-General has noted that 'peacebuilding may involve the creation or strengthening of national institutions, monitoring elections, promoting human rights, providing for reintegration and rehabilitation programmes, and creating conditions for resumed development'.[20] But in the absence of serious effort on the part of the international community to assist 'post-conflict' societies (as has been the experience from Afghanistan to Rwanda) the possibilities of reconstruction and peacebuilding are dim. The UN Secretary-General has himself noted in this regard the lack of support for a number of key reconstruction and development projects in post-conflict societies.[21] Although a dozen bilateral agencies are said to have created 'peacebuilding funds', 'only a small proportion – less than 15 per cent – of all emergency assistance is being devoted to anything like reconstruction or peacebuilding'.[22] To put it differently, the developed North appears to have successfully disengaged from post-conflict situations even as it incessantly talks of 'peacebuilding'.

This has compelled post-conflict societies to turn to IFIs for succour. But, unfortunately, the IFIs prescribe conditions that, in the final analysis, tend to reproduce the general environment that is vulnerable to conflict. So often the meaning of 'an accountable post-conflict state' turns out to be a state that can come to terms with the legitimacy crises and social protest generated by the implementation of a neo-liberal adjustment programme and greater integration into the world economy. In the circumstances, formal compliance with the norms of liberal democracy changes very little.[23] The parties that participate in 'post-conflict' elections either lack any alternative programme to neo-liberalism or do not have the resources to push it through. In most cases 'there is a pathological fixation on aping World Bank and IMF prescriptions'.[24] The contesting political parties are, in other words, not interested in the dismantling and reconstruction of 'the unstable, non-hegemonic, violent, exploitative and inefficient neocolonial state'.[25] The state continues to be repressive and its resources continue to be privatized. There is therefore little possibility of implementing a reconstruction agenda which pays heed to peoples' needs and frames policies with their participation. Instead, the state continues to manipulate divisions within society, making the renewal of conflict a distinct possibility.

Unfortunately, even those concerned with the protection of returnees are now hoping to closely collaborate with the IFIs.[26] The UNHCR has initiated 'a common dialogue' with the World Bank in order to develop a coherent approach to reintegration and the funding instruments required to finance this strategy.[27] This is difficult to understand, for the World Bank can only provide leadership on macroeconomic and external debt issues. Furthermore, the UNHCR 'lacks the legal or ethical framework offered by international refugee law or equivalent humanitarian principles to guide its interventions in this area of its work'.[28] This framework is necessary for as the UNHCR itself concedes, 'structural adjustment programmes may in the...short run exacerbate the causes of conflict'.[29] According to UNHCR, 'it is unrealistic to ask countries like Rwanda, Somalia or Sierra Leone to embrace an "orthodox" adjustment programme to rebuild their devastated economies when healing the deep scars of war and genocide alone is such a daunting task'.[30]

Even the UN Secretary-General appears to recognize the potentially negative role of IFIs in creating conditions of conflict in Africa. He has therefore pleaded with the IFIs to ease the conditionality that normally accompanies loans in order to initiate 'a "peace-friendly" structural adjustment programme'.[31] Indeed, the World Bank has assessed its own experience in post-conflict situations and concluded that conventional wisdom can turn into folly during post-conflict periods. Criticisms arose from inside (and outside) the Bank that 'too much emphasis was put on a rapid pace of reforms in Haiti, Rwanda, and Uganda, as opposed to concentrating on maintaining low inflation and a convertible currency, and approaching other reforms more incrementally'.[32] The World Bank thus concluded that an emphasis on immediate and widespread privatization in post-conflict situations 'may well not enhance the prospects for sustained, equitable development, and may even make them worse'.[33] How then are conditions of 'sustainable return' to be created without heavy doses of non-conditional development aid?

Ensuring 'Sustainable Return'

'Sustainable return' is, in any case, more than simple development. It has been described as 'a situation where – ideally – returnees' physical and material security are assured, and when *a constructive relationship between returnees, civil society and the state is consolidated*.[34] It calls for four kinds of insecurities to be addressed, namely physical insecurity, social and psychological insecurity, legal insecurity and material insecurity.[35] The absence of conditions that ensure security on all these fronts could compel the refugee to seek asylum again. The elimination of these insecurities anticipates 'peacebuilding' and 'reconciliation' leading to 'reintegration'. 'Reconciliation' 'refers to the consolidation of constructive social relations between different groups of the population, including parties to the conflict'.[36] The relationship between reconciliation and reintegration is critical, as reconciliation has to precede reintegration.[37] 'Reintegration' is described as 'a process which enables formerly displaced people and other members of their community to enjoy a progressively greater degree of physical, social, legal and material security'.[38]

This holistic understanding points, first, to the need to view repatriation and reintegration as an integral process in order to ensure sustainable return. In its General Conclusion on International Protection of 1994, the Executive Committee of the UNHCR stressed the fact that 'for repatriation to be a sustainable and thus truly durable solution to refugee problems it is essential that the need for rehabilitation, reconstruction, and national reconciliation be addressed in a comprehensive and effective manner'. If this understanding is correct, it only goes to underline the limits of the role of the UNHCR in creating conditions of sustainable return; it possesses neither the human nor material resources to undertake this task. It also calls for a coordinated response by UN agencies.

Some Problems of Return

Second, 'sustainable return' requires that problems relating to property and housing rights, landmines, and disarmament, demobilization and reintegration combatants be resolved.

Housing and Property Rights

It has been aptly observed that 'housing and property restitution has emerged as one of the most important components of post-conflict reconciliation and rehabilitation'.[39] Indeed, 'property problems are at the heart of the return process'.[40] There is today a general obligation placed upon states of origin to safeguard the property rights of the returnees. On 26 August 1998, the UN Sub-Commission on Prevention of Discrimination and Protection of Minorities adopted

Resolution 1998/26 entitled *Housing and Property Restitution in the Context of the Return of Refugees and Internally Displaced Persons*. The resolution recognized that 'the right of refugees and internally displaced persons to return freely to their homes and places of habitual residence in safety and security forms an indispensable element of national reconciliation and reconstruction and that the recognition of such rights should be included within peace agreements ending armed conflicts'.[41] It urged states to 'develop effective and expeditious legal, administrative and other procedures' including 'fair and effective mechanisms designed to resolve outstanding housing and property problems'. It also called upon the UNHCR and UNHCHR to 'develop policy guidelines to promote and facilitate the right of all refugees'. This resolution has been affirmed in subsequent years.[42]

Yet, thousands of returnees cannot return to their original homes or recover their property or receive compensation in lieu of it. This is because the issue of enforcement has not always been sufficiently addressed. Peace agreements that have made a provision for return of housing and property rights have not included effective enforcement mechanisms. Thus, even though the Dayton Accord established the Commission on Real Property Claims of Refugees and Displaced Persons (CRPC),[43] it is reported that of the 50,000 claim certificates issued by the CRPC only a small minority of them, three percent according to the International Crisis Group, resulted in the claimant actually recovering his property.[44] Therefore, minority returnees have found it difficult to return to their original homes despite changes in national property laws.[45] On the other hand, compensation has not been paid as it was not 'compatible with the overall strategy of trying to reverse effects of ethnic cleansing by encouraging return to minority areas'.[46] In brief, despite the effort to develop appropriate norms on the international plane it is difficult to see housing and property disputes being resolved in a fair and free manner in post-conflict societies. Property issues are central political issues.[47] The lesson it points towards is the need to devise effective preventive strategies as 'post-conflict societies' are hostile spaces for the restoration of property rights.[48]

Women and Property Rights

The particular concerns of women with respect to property and housing rights call for special and explicit attention in peace agreements.[49] Women's rights to land, housing and property need to be more firmly established as human rights. But 'because gender inequality or structural inequality based on gender is rarely seen as a *cause* of armed conflict, it does not find a place in the reform agenda'.[50] The neo-liberal solution of relying on the market does not provide the answer for 'women cannot purchase land, housing and property...because they are poor, economically marginalized and have no access to capital. And, of course, women cannot access capital without land as collateral to secure a loan or to generate an income'.[51] To begin with there is a need to adopt gender-sensitive legislation. Second, United Nations agencies and governmental and non-governmental aid agencies must re-examine their programmes through a gender lens and then 'coordinate and re-structure efforts to ensure that women's interests and entitlements with respect to land, housing and property play a defining role in their work plans and activities'.[52] Third, in keeping with the understanding that repatriation and reintegration should not be viewed as separate processes, women's organizations can be established in refugee camps even before the conflict has ended or it is time to return.

Removal of Landmines

Landmines represent a key obstacle to the return of refugees and displaced persons and to reconstruction activities. This has been the experience of returns to all post-conflict societies including Cambodia, Afghanistan, Mozambique and Angola. The UN General Assembly has, for example, noted the 'devastating consequences and destabilizing effects of the use of anti-personnel landmines on Cambodian society' and called for greater contributions from donor countries.[53] It has also expressed concern 'about the problem of millions of anti-personnel landmines and unexploded ordnance as well as the continued laying of new landmines in Afghanistan, which continue to prevent many Afghan refugees and internally displaced persons from returning to their villages and working in their fields'.[54] The answer lies in first, devoting greater funds to de-mining operations. Second, de-mining should be stressed in the terms of reference of peacekeeping operations.[55]

Disarmament, Demobilization and Reintegration (DDR)

The UN Secretary-General has noted that 'the effective disarmament, demobilization and reintegration of former combatants can be crucial to the success of a peace process, but without some degree of predictability of funding for such operations, the entire enterprise risks failure'.[56] The former HCR, Sadako Ogata, called for 'more decisive action by the Security Council'.[57] She identified two problems that need to be addressed: first, the need to clarify the roles and responsibilities of all actors involved in DDR-related activities, and second, that without a greater focus on reintegration, the disarmed and demobilized soldiers could turn to more financially rewarding military activities.[58] The UNSC has therefore recognized that adequate and timely funding for disarmament, demobilization and reintegration is critical to the successful implementation of a peace process.[59] Taking all these recommendations into account, the UN Secretary-General proposed to 'include comprehensive disarmament, demobilization and reintegration programmes...for future peace operations...so that the Security Council can consider including aspects of the disarmament, demobilization and reintegration programmes in the operations' mandates and the General Assembly can review proposals for funding demobilization and reintegration programmes, in the start-up phase, through the mission budgets'.[60] These are moves in the right direction. However, it needs to be recognized that the effectiveness of DDR measures depends on the success in enhancing income-generating activities. In its absence, DDR could actually lead to the deterioration of the law and order situation.[61]

United Nations, Repatriation and Return: Multiple Roles

What is the role that the United Nations system should play in ensuring sustainable return to post-conflict societies? At present, as the UN Secretary-General has noted, 'virtually every part of the United Nations system, including the Bretton Woods institutions, is...engaged in one form of peace-building or another'.[62] Indeed, the UN acts, in a sense, as a surrogate state until 'peacebuilding' has been successfully achieved. However, we will confine ourselves to discussing the role of the UNHCR, UNSC and UNDP and underline the need for greater coordination. Subsequently, we will stress the need to evolve a law of responsibility of international institutions.

UNHCR and Sustainable Return: The Limits of Involvement

It was in 1985 that the Executive Committee of the UNHCR noted the legitimate concern of the High Commissioner for the consequences of refugee return. At this time, 'legitimate concern' was interpreted primarily in relation to protection, in particular to the adherence by states of origin to given guarantees and amnesties to returnees.[63] The reasons for UNHCR non-involvement in returnee reintegration until the early 1990s are sixfold. First, as the exile bias prevailed in the first decades of its existence there was little opportunity for UNHCR to be involved in such activities. It was only after voluntary repatriation became the central preoccupation of UNHCR in the post-Cold War period and the UNDP declared the 1990s as the decade of returnees that 'the concept of returnee aid and development began to gain currency among those administering development aid and those responding to humanitarian needs'.[64] Second, in the 1960s and 1970s, when refugees did return in large numbers in Africa it was often a result of the de-colonization process and the newly independent state did not shy away from the responsibility of meeting the concerns of returnees. Third, even when the state demurred in these times the UNHCR thought it squarely the task of the state of origin to ensure the 'reintegration' of returnees. Fourth, in the 1990s refugees were returning to the poorest of countries that were in no position to respond to the needs of returnees; according to the World Bank, in this period, 16 of the 20 poorest states were post-conflict countries.[65] Fifth, in this period UNHCR became increasingly involved with internally displaced persons. Finally, the involvement in returnee integration was necessary to the strategy of promoting the return of refugees. In the words of Crisp, 'the genius of the returnee aid and development strategy was that...it was unambiguously intended to promote and consolidate the solution of voluntary repatriation'.[66] Thus, for example, in 1996 UNHCR spent US$214 million on reintegration, nearly double the levels in 1994.[67]

Yet, the UNHCR is neither a development agency nor is it equipped in material and intellectual terms to address the problem of the development of post-conflict societies. Understandably then, the scope of returnee aid has been confined to achieving the objective of establishing minimum material and social conditions in which the return of refugees can be promoted. The strategy was exemplified by Quick Impact Projects (QIPs) executed by UNHCR to help the reconstruction and reintegration process. QIPs are essentially 'emergency development' projects that do not take into account the long-term problems of recurrent costs and sustainability. This weakness of QIPs merely reflects the 'outer limit' of UNHCR's mandate. It is involved in an activity that takes it far away from its protection role. Furthermore, there is often the assumption that UNHCR's multilateral partners would be willing and able to build on activities initiated by UNHCR. Unfortunately, this is often not the case.[68] Moreover, as the former HCR has pointed out, the UNHCR has been 'very frustrated by lack of funding in the post-emergency phase in places like Rwanda, Liberia and Bosnia'.[69]

This has led to attempts at collaboration with the World Bank on the reconstruction of 'post-conflict societies'. But the attempt to collaborate with the World Bank, as has already been pointed out, overlooks the fact that at least one cause of internal conflict is the 'international financial institutions imposed programmes that exacerbated inflation, land scarcity, and unemployment'.[70] The international community therefore needs to ensure that there are enough funds available that are not subject to the traditional conditionality imposed by IFIs. More significantly, it has to urgently address the inequities in the international economic system that *inter alia* translate into low primary commodity prices and huge debts for poor Third World countries.

The UN Security Council and Post-Conflict Peacebuilding: Two Statements

Through a presidential statement on the subject of post-conflict peacebuilding in 1998, the Security Council outlined its approach to peacebuilding. First, it recognized 'the importance of the post-conflict peace-building efforts of the United Nations...with due involvement of all United Nations bodies'. In particular, it welcomed the role played by the Secretary-General in this field. Second, it encouraged the Secretary-General 'to explore the possibility of establishing post-conflict peace-building structures as part of efforts by the United Nations system to achieve a lasting peaceful solution to conflicts, including in order to ensure a smooth transition from peacekeeping to peace-building and lasting peace'. Third, it noted 'the value of including, as appropriate, peace-building elements in the mandates of peacekeeping operations'. It agreed with the UN Secretary-General that 'relevant post-conflict peace-building elements should be explicitly and clearly identified and could be integrated into the mandates of peacekeeping operations'.[71] Fourth, the UNSC recognized 'the need for close cooperation and dialogue between the bodies of the United Nations system, in particular those directly concerned in the field of post-conflict peace-building, in accordance with their respective responsibilities and expresse[d] its willingness to consider ways to improve such cooperation'.[72]

In February 2001, subsequent to a debate on the subject, another presidential statement was issued on the need for a comprehensive and integrated approach to peacebuilding. The Security Council presidential statement noted that 'the quest for peace requires a comprehensive, concerted and determined approach that addresses the root causes of conflicts, including their economic and social dimensions'.[73] It also pointed out that peacebuilding called for 'short and long-term actions tailored to address the particular needs of societies sliding into conflict or emerging from it' and 'should focus on fostering sustainable institutions and processes in areas such as sustainable development, the eradication of poverty and inequalities, transparent and accountable governance, the promotion of democracy, respect for human rights and the rule of law and the promotion of a culture of peace and non-violence'. The Security Council expressed 'its willingness to consider ways to improve its cooperation with other United Nations bodies and organs directly concerned by peace-building, in particular the General Assembly and the Economic and Social Council which have a primary role in this field'. Of course, all the activities were to be initiated with 'the consent and cooperation of the authorities of the State concerned', where it exists.

As statements go these are fine. But it will all eventually depend on how these are interpreted by the international community. While the UNSC does talk of root causes of conflicts, it can merely address, and that too in a limited way, the internal causes of conflicts. But as we have suggested, without recognizing the *international* causes of internal conflicts, peacebuilding is impossible in the long run. Here the Security Council statement emphasizes the 'comparative advantage' of the actors involved in peacebuilding, meaning thereby that IFIs will continue to play a key role in devising economic policies. This is deeply problematic unless these institutions change their approach and conditionality.

Second, as Murphy has noted, the components of the mandates have 'become unrealistic'.[74] Between 1991 and 2000, of the 36 peacekeeping operations launched by the United Nations, 31 related to intra-state peacekeeping.[75] The intra-state peacekeeping operations were laden with complex and extensive mandates: the tasks assigned ranged from assisting in the process of reconciliation to the clearing of landmines to demobilizing and disarming combatants.[76] According to one student of peacekeeping: 'Problems may become more intractable when peacekeeping is stretched…to address the social, economic and a variety of problems of governance … UN peacekeeping should not be viewed as a magic wand capable of solving all problems without reference to intricacies on the ground, the capabilities of the Organization, etc'.[77]

While the difficulties involved may not call for a complete rejection of the instrument of peacekeeping to realize a variety of tasks it clearly points to the problems and limits of such deployment. There is a need to closely study situations where peacekeeping has been effective in achieving particular tasks. Thus, for example, we need to know how UN peacekeepers were successful in Mozambique in demobilizing 80,000 troops and recovering 155,000 weapons. On the other hand, why did it cost the loss of 148 lives in Somalia?[78]

Third, if the mandate of operations in intra-state peacekeeping is to be as comprehensive as is envisaged by the Security Council and the Secretary-General then there is a need, in order to lend legitimacy to them, to expand the membership of the UNSC. Its democratization will allow a more representative body to address the issues concerned with a greater degree of authority and understanding.

Need for Coordination Among UN Agencies

The greater need for coordination among UN agencies is a recommendation that any report on UN activities can hardly resist. The recent Presidential Statement of the UNSC has underlined the need for 'an integrated operation response through mutual consultation; joint monitoring of peace-building activities; and establishing repertories of best practices and lessons learned in the area of peace-building'.[79] According to the UNDP, a key actor in the reconstruction and peacebuilding, 'a consensus is falling into place on the urgency of improved coordination during post-conflict situations, partly as a result of pressure created by several well-publicized incidents' such as the shelter programme in Rwanda.[80] In the case of the UNDP, coordination is called for because, first, it 'tends to focus on long-term development issues. ... It is not institutionally well equipped to undertake the speedy and local-level rehabilitation activities which are required when large numbers of people suddenly return to areas which have been devastated by war'.[81] Second, it does not target individuals but state structures. Third, its mandate has not included any protection role, albeit in recent agreements with the Office of the UN High Commissioner for Human Rights. UNDP has sought to integrate human rights and sustainable development into its work.[82] However, it does not have the institutional capacity to tackle contentious protection issues. In view of these constraints the UNDP needs, as it itself recognizes, to work more closely with UNHCR representatives on reintegration efforts.[83] In brief, it 'should formulate and distribute an overall policy statement on its role in post-conflict situations'.[84]

Need for Law on Responsibility of International Institutions

In order to ensure effective peacebuilding and sustainable return, the international institutions responsible for well-defined activities must be made more accountable for their actions. For example, in instances when the acts and omissions of an international institution lead to the violation of human rights it should be held responsible in international law. For example, the UNHCR should incur responsibility in international law for violating its mandate. Unfortunately, this is not the case today.[85] Thus, it is not responsible in international law if it 'incorrectly declares that a source state is safe for return, closes a camp and permits or facilitates the repatriation of the refugee population who suffer persecution on return'.[86] The law on the subject of responsibility of international institutions is still undeveloped. This situation needs to be urgently rectified as it does not stand to reason that states are held responsible for the violations of human rights but the international institutions they establish are not.

Conclusions and Recommendations

The fate of post-colonial 'post-conflict' societies does not permit the luxury of a purely theoretical critique. We must conclude by making suggestions on how to improve policies relating to repatriation and return and identify measures that will help create a sustainable society.

First, there should be a clear definition of the role of UNHCR in the return and reintegration process. Legal and ethical guidelines should be spelt out in this regard. A greater role should be assigned to the UNHCR's Department of International Protection in the repatriation process. The voluntary nature of repatriation must be ensured.

Second, the planning for repatriation must begin long in advance. The repatriation and reintegration of refugees should not be seen as two separate tasks but be addressed in an integrated manner. Responsible phasing out from an existing reintegration programme must be ensured.

Third, the key issues of housing and property rights need to be effectively addressed. A central problem that needs to be tackled is that of enforcement. Therefore, provision should be made in peace accords and national laws for the effective enforcement of housing and property rights. The problems that women have in securing housing and property rights call for particular attention so as to make productive resources available to them.

Fourth, de-mining must be included in the agenda of peacekeeping operations, and greater resources devoted to it so as to render return safe and sustainable.

Fifth, there must be a focus on reintegration of disarmed and demobilized soldiers. DDR programmes must also be integrated into the mandate of peacekeeping operations and more funds must be devoted to them. Since its success depends on income-generating activities, effective steps need to taken in this direction.

Sixth, the UN Security Council must outline its own role and that of peacekeeping in peacebuilding. It should ensure that peacekeeping mandates are not overly expansive. A more democratic Security Council would lend greater authority and legitimacy to the tasks assigned to peacekeeping operations.

Seventh, there is a need for dialogue and coordination among UN agencies in the pursuit of peacebuilding and reintegration activities. The UNDP needs to clarify if it has a protection role and what it is to be. There is also an urgent need to develop the law of responsibility with respect to international organizations.

Eighth, more non-conditional financial assistance should be made available to undertake developmental activities. The IFIs must ensure *peaceful* structural adjustment programmes.

Last, but not the least, since the United Nations system virtually seeks to (re)produce a sustainable society and state, it must closely interrogate the epistemological assumptions it makes to realize it. There is, among other things, a need to revisit and rethink the concepts of 'post-conflict societies', 'peacebuilding' and 'sustainable return'. Even better, the UN must effectively move 'from a culture of reaction to a culture of prevention'. In this context, the *international* causes of internal conflicts need to be identified and addressed. Only then will it become possible to prevent refugee movements in the first place, while creating suitable conditions for post-conflict returnees.

NOTES

1. G. Kibreab, 'Revisiting the Debate on People, Place Identity and Displacement', *Journal of Refugee Studies*, Vol.12, 1999, pp.384–411 at p.390.
2. G. Kibreab, 'Rejoinder', *Journal of Refugee Studies*, Vol.12, 1999, pp.422–9 at p.423.
3. Ibid., pp.425 and 405.
4. GA Doc. A/AC.96/887 (1997) Executive Committee of the High Commissioner's Programme: Forty-eighth session: Annual Theme: Repatriation challenges, p.1.
5. J. Crisp, ' Africa's refugees: Patterns, Problems and Policy Challenges', New Issues in Refugee Research, UNHCR Working Paper No.28, August 2000, p.16.
6. James C. Hathaway, 'The Meaning of Repatriation', *International Journal of Refugee Law*, Vol.9, No.4, 1997, pp.551–8.
7. G.J.L. Coles, 'Approaching the Refugee Problem Today' in G. Loescher and L. Monahan (eds), *Refugees and International Relations*, Oxford: Oxford University Press, 1989, pp.373–410.
8. F. Cornish, K. Peltzer and M. MacLachlan, 'Returning Strangers: The Children of Malawian Refugees Come "Home"?', *Journal of Refugee Studies*, Vol.12, No.3, 1999, pp.237–64 at p.265, emphasis in original.
9. R. Black and K. Koser (eds), *Refugee Repatriation and Reconstruction*, New York: Berghahn Books, 1999, pp.11–12.
10. Ibid. Nevertheless, in the past few years it has undertaken a more systematic survey of returnees and their concerns and issued guidelines on returnee monitoring. See UNHCR (2000) A/AC.96/ 930 Executive Committee of the High Commissioner's Programme: Note on International Protection, para. 51.
11. B.S. Chimni, 'From Resettlement to Involuntary Repatriation: Towards a Critical

History of Durable Solutions to Refugee Problems', UNHCR Working Paper No.2, February 1999.
12. Barry N. Stein and Fred C. Cuny, 'Repatriation Under Conflict', *World Refugee Survey 1991*, pp.15–21.
13. J. Crisp, 'The "Post-Conflict" Concept: Some Critical Observations', PRU Discussion Paper, 21 Aug. 1998, p.2 (on file with the author).
14. World Bank (Aug.1999) Post-Conflict Fund: Guidelines and Procedure.
15. UNHCR operational framework for repatriation and reintegration activities in post-conflict situations. Geneva: UNHCR, Division of Operational Support, Reintegration Section, 1999, p.xvii, emphasis added.
16. Joanna Macrae, 'Aiding Peace...and War: UNHCR, Returnee Reintegration, and the Relief–Development Debate', New Issues in Refugee Research, Working Paper No.14, Geneva: UNHCR, 1999, p.15.
17. Crisp, 1998 (n.13 above), p.3.
18. Ibid.
19. *The State of the World's Refugees: A Humanitarian Agenda*, Oxford: Oxford University Press, 1997, p.159.
20. K. Annan, *The Causes of Conflict and the Promotion of Durable peace and Sustainable Development in Africa*, New York: United Nations, 1998, p.14.
21. Ibid.
22. Inter-Agency Standing Committee, *Global Humanitarian Assistance 2000: An Independent Report Commissioned by the IASC from Development Initiatives*, Geneva: IASC, 2000, p.51.
23. J.O. Ihonvbere, 'The State, Constitutionalism and Democratization', *Seminar* 490, June 2000, pp.21–32 at p.24.
24. Ibid.
25. Ibid., p.25.
26. 'By the end of the decade, UNHCR was collaborating closely with the World Bank. This cooperation has focused particularly on trying to establish mutual understanding of each organisation's mandate and programming modes, through joint training and secondment of staff. J. Wolfensohn and S. Ogata, 'Letter regarding a framework for cooperation between United Nations High Commissioner for Refugees (UNHCR) and the World Bank', Washington and Geneva, World Bank and UNHCR, 17 Apr. 1998.
27. The Roundtable co-convened by the two organizations at the Brookings Institution in early 1999 was a first step in trying to facilitate a system-wide discussion on these issues and has been followed up by subsequent meetings and papers. See UNHCR and World Bank, *Report on the roundtable on the gap between humanitarian assistance and long-term development*, Washington DC: Brookings Institution, 1999.
28. Macrae (n.16 above).
29. UNHCR (1998) EC/48/SC/CRP.15, Oversight Issues: Reintegration.
30. UNHCR (1999) Executive Committee of the High Commissioner's Programme, Standing Committee, 14th meeting, EC/49/SC/INF.2, 14 January 1999: The Security, Civilian and Humanitarian Character of Refugee Camps and Settlements.
31. Annan (n.20 above).
32. Cited in *Sharing New Ground in Post-Conflict Situations: The Role of UNDP in Support of Reintegration Programmes*, New York: UNDP, Jan. 2000, p.49.
33. Ibid.
34. UNHCR 1998 (n.29 above), emphasis added.
35. *The State of the World's Refugees 1997* (n.19 above), pp.154–60.
36. Ibid., p.159.
37. UNHCR 1998 (n.29 above).
38. *The State of the World's Refugees, 1997* (n.19 above), p.159.
39. S. Leckie, 'Introduction: Land and Property Issues', *Forced Migration Review*, Apr. 2000, pp.4–5 at p.4.

40. Catherine Phuong, '"Freely to Return": Reversing Ethnic Cleansing in Bosnia-Herzegovina', *Journal of Refugee Studies*, Vol.13, No.2, 2000, pp.165-83 at p.169.
41. Economic and Social Council, E/CN.4/Sub.2/Res/1998/26, 26 August 1998: Housing and property restitution in the context of the return of refugees and internally displaced persons- Sub-Commission resolution 1998/26.
42. See generally Bret Thiele, 'Recent Developments in United Nations Policy on Housing and Property Restitution for Refugee Return', *Refuge*, Vol.19, No.3, Dec. 2000, pp.3-7.
43. Its mandate, as laid down in Article XI of Annex 7 of the Dayton Accord, is as follows: The Commission shall receive and decide any claims for real property in Bosnia and Herzegovina, where the property has not voluntarily been sold or otherwise transferred since 1st April 1992, and where the claimant does not now enjoy possession of that property. Claims may be for return of the property or for just compensation in lieu of return.
44. Phoung (n.40 above), p.169. See also Lene Madsen, 'Homes of Origin: Return and Property Rights in Post-Dayton Bosnia and Herzegovina', *Refuge*, Vol.19, No.3, Dec. 2000, pp.8-17.
45. Madsen, ibid., p.10 ff.
46. Ibid., p.170.
47. Catherine Phoung, 'At the Heart of the Return Process: Solving Property Issues in Bosnia Herzegovina', *Forced Migration Review*, 2000, pp.5-8 at pp.6-7.
48. On preventive strategies see UNGA A/55/985, 7 June 2001: Prevention of armed conflict: Report of the Secretary-General.
49. UNCHS (Habitat) United Nation Centre for Human Settlements, Land Management Series No. 9: *Women's Rights to Land, Housing and Property in Post-conflict Situations and During Reconstruction: A Global Overview*, p.55. For an overview of the international legal framework on women's housing and property rights see pp.22-32. www.unchs.org/tenure/Publication/Womrights/pub_1.htm.
50. Ibid., p.44.
51. Ibid., p.3.
52. Ibid., p.6.
53. UNGA Res. A/RES/53/145, 8 March 1999: Adopted on the report of the Third Committee (A/53/625/Add.2) 53/145. Situation of human rights in Cambodia.
54. UNGA A/54/63 S/1999/171, 12 February 1999: Comprehensive review of the whole question of Peacekeeping Operations in all its aspects: Enhancement of African Peacekeeping Capacity-Report of the Secretary-General.
55. *An Agenda for Peace: Preventive Diplomacy, Peace-Making and Peace-Keeping*, New York: United Nations, 1994.
56. UNSG, Report of the Secretary-General on the Work of the Organization GAOR: 55th session Supp.No.1 (A/55/1) (2000), para. 72.
57. Sadako Ogata, 'Briefing to the Security Council', New York, 10 Nov. 2000. Text available at www:\\http.unhcr.ch
58. Ibid.
59. United Nations S/2000/108, 20 Oct. 2000, Report of the Secretary-General on the implementation of the report of the Panel on United Nations peace operations Contents, para. 26.
60. Ibid.
61. UNDP, Management Development and Governance Division, Bureau for Development Policy: *Governance in Post-Conflict Countries*. http://magnet.undp.org/Docs/crisis/monograph/Monograph.htm.
62. Ibid., para. 21.
63. Conclusion No.40 (XXXVI)-1985: Voluntary Repatriation. Adopted by the Executive Committee of the UNHCR.
64. Ibid.
65. World Bank, *Post-Conflict Fund: Guidelines and Procedure*, Washington, DC: World Bank, Aug. 1999.

66. Crisp (n.5 above).
67. Macrae (n.16 above).
68. UNHCR 1998 (n.29 above), 'Tajikistan provides a clear example of an unworkable gap between the expectations of UNDP and UNHCR in the field of reintegration. UNDP did not continue many of the projects that UNHCR had initiated with grass-roots community actors'.
69. Ogata (n.57 above).
70. OAU Report of the International Panel of Eminent Personalities asked to investigate the 1994 Genocide in Rwanda and the Surrounding Events (2000) www.oauoua.org/Document/ipep/ipep.htm, para. 15.
71. For Secretary-General's view to this effect see Annan (n.20 above), p.15.
72. UNSC (1998) S/PRST/1998/38, 29 December 1998, Statement by the President of the Security Council.
73. Security Council SC/7014, 4278th Meeting (AM) 20 February 2001: Presidential Statement. The text is available at www.un.org/News/Press/docs/2001/sc7014.doc.htm. All subsequent quotations are from this source.
74. C.S.R. Murthy, 'United Nations Peacekeeping in Intrastate Conflicts: Emerging Trends', *International Studies*, Vol.38, No.3, July–Sept. 2001, pp.207–29 at p.219.
75. Ibid., p.211
76. Ibid., p.215.
77. Ibid., p.221.
78. Ibid., pp.219–20.
79. Ibid.
80. A top United Nations priority in the country, the shelter programme attracted dozens of agencies, including Habitat, International Federation of the Red Cross (IFRC), UNDP, UNHCR and numerous NGOs. By 1997, however, 'the UN agencies were unanimous in describing the shelter programme ... as disastrously uncoordinated ...[and drawing] insufficiently on the advice of the technical agencies. ... The result ... is large numbers of houses standing empty, while shelter needs continue to be high', UNDP (n.32 above), p.40.
81. *The State of the World's Refugees, 1997* (n.19 above), p.166.
82. Human Rights Watch (2000), *Burma*, www.hrw.org/hrw/reports/2000/burma/
83. Ibid.
84. UNDP (n.32 above), p.53.
85. G. Gilbert, 'Rights, Legitimate Expectations, Needs and Responsibilities: UNHCR and the New World Order', *International Journal of Refugee Law*, Vol.10, 1998, pp.349–88 at p.377.
86. Ibid., p.382.

Demobilization, Reintegration and Peacebuilding in Africa

KEES KINGMA

Demobilization and reintegration assistance are generally seen as important efforts in post-war situations. The 1998 report by UN Secretary-General on 'The Causes of Conflict and the Promotion of Durable Peace and Sustainable Development in Africa' lists 'the reintegration of ex-combatants and others into productive society' as one of the priorities of post-conflict peacebuilding.[1] In early 2000, the UN Secretary-General issued a report on 'The Role of United Nations Peacekeeping in Disarmament, Demobilization and Reintegration' which reiterates the importance of demobilization and reintegration in peacebuilding.[2] And the Brahimi Report referred to demobilization and reintegration as key to post-war stability and to reducing the likelihood of conflict recurring.[3]

A number of countries in Africa have in the past two decades experienced processes of demobilization and reintegration associated with the resolution of violent conflicts. Some of these took place in the context of a peacekeeping operation, but not all of them. The experiences in Angola, Eritrea, Ethiopia, Liberia, Mozambique, Namibia, Sierra Leone, South Africa, Uganda and Zimbabwe have all been different, within their distinct political and socio-economic contexts. Nevertheless, they also have similarities. Disarmament, demobilization and reintegration have been features of at least 15 peacekeeping operations in the past decade. More than a dozen UN agencies and programmes, as well as international and local NGOs, fund these programmes.[4]

Demobilization and reintegration of ex-combatants,[5] one of the key components of conversion,[6] could potentially create significant opportunities for sustainable peace and human development. Demobilization usually also implying a reduction of military expenditure through a decline in the number of soldiers can allow for more development-oriented spending, and thereby increased levels of human development. Lower budget deficits can also have a positive effect, particularly on investment and employment opportunities, through lower interest rates and/or lower inflation. Able-bodied people might shift to more economically productive activities. Demobilization would also allow for more sustainable resource use and decreased income and asset disparities. However, research on several demobilizations in Africa has shown that the savings as a result of demobilization are slow in coming and often not as high as expected, while the actual direct costs of the demobilization and reintegration support have been shown to be high.[7] Moreover, the complex processes of demobilization, resettlement and reintegration can also result in new social and political conflicts. Even if the conversion is managed smoothly at the technical level, it might cause social tensions.

A considerable body of literature exists on the demobilization and reintegration experiences in various African countries. However, little research has been conducted on the sustainability of the demobilization and reintegration efforts in the early 1990s, and the longer-term role of demobilization and reintegration in peacebuilding. This essay explores the extent to which the demobilization has had an impact on peacebuilding processes in Africa, and particularly on causes of (further) conflict. Have the demobilization, resettlement and (sometimes lack of) reintegration processes led to new conflicts, or rekindled old ones? The next section will present general characteristics of demobilization and reintegration assistance in Africa. The third section presents a discussion of the concept of peacebuilding. In the fourth section, the key analysis of the ways in which the demobilization and the resettlement and reintegration of ex-combatants have had (or could still have) an impact on the recurrence or development of conflicts is presented. The main conclusions will be drawn in the final section.

Demobilization and Reintegration: Terminology and Experiences

The term 'demobilization' has different meanings depending on the context in which it is used.[8] As used here, it refers to the process of significantly reducing the number of personnel under arms and in military command structures. In some cases, demobilization also incorporates the process of dissolving opposition forces sometimes after their integration into (new) regular armed forces. The demobilization itself is only the first part of the conversion process. After demobilization, 'resettlement' of ex-combatants in the location where they prefer to live usually follows; and finally, there is 'reintegration' in which they find a new and productive role in civilian life. The last phase is basically open-ended. Although reintegration is essentially a single but complex process that also involves the family of the demobilized, a distinction is often made between different components of reintegration: economic, social and political. The process also has psychological aspects, as most ex-combatants go through a process of adjusting attitudes and expectations, and many are still dealing with traumatic experiences related to the war.

The word reintegration is in some cases a misnomer, as not all ex-combatants return to their area of origin. Sometimes their skills have more relevance and marketable value in other places. In certain situations, after the ending of the war, villages from which soldiers or guerrilla fighters came sometimes no longer exist. And in cases where the ex-combatants have committed atrocities in or near their own communities (as happened at times in Mozambique), they would not be able to return to these communities. Some of the soldiers demobilized in Rwanda in the late 1990s did not live inside the country before the war. More generally, we should note that ex-combatants and their societies have often been considerably transformed by wars, especially in countries where the conflict has lasted for a long time, such as in the Eritrean liberation war. In several countries, many combatants have no memory of the pre-war times.

In some cases demobilization took place after one of the fighting parties had gained a victory, while in others the demobilization followed a negotiated peace settlement. In several cases it was not only regular soldiers who needed to be demobilized, but also ex-guerrilla fighters and members of militia groups. This added to the complexities and political sensitivities of the exercises. The observed cases of demobilization usually involved a large number of different actors (see Figure 1), with each having their different roles and interests. It should also be noted that, particularly after wars, some other relevant processes and policy interventions occurred simultaneously, such as democratization, economic stabilization, infrastructural rehabilitation and repatriation of refugees.

Successful post-war demobilization and resettlement require good data for planning purposes, effective logistics and management, and substantial resources for shelter, registration, transport and the provision of basic needs.[9] Given the specific circumstances in the various countries, the procedures of the actual demobilization exercises varied considerably. Generally, once the decision to demobilize was taken, practical plans needed to be worked out and financing obtained. In several cases, such as Ethiopia in the 1990s, Namibia and South Africa, the demobilization required that several groups of combatants needed to be repatriated from neighbouring or other countries.

In most of the African countries that implemented demobilization and reintegration programmes, post-war economic conditions were

FIGURE 1
POSSIBLE ACTORS IN DEMOBILIZATION PROCESSES

1. Demobilized combatants (male and female; ex-child soldiers; ex-government soldiers and ex-guerrillas)
2. Associations of demobilized combatants
3. Families of ex-combatants
4. Communities in which ex-combatants resettle
5. Other groups trying to reintegrate (e.g. returned refugees and internally displaced people)
6. Local business community
7. Government agencies
8. Armed forces, and other security forces
9. Local NGOs
10. The UN and its agencies
11. Donor agencies
12. International NGOs

Source: Kees Kingma (ed.), Demobilization in Sub-Saharan Africa, p.41.

such that these activities could not be funded solely by national resources. Governments and NGOs had limited capacity and resources. Indeed, in some countries, for example Mozambique and Uganda, the international community played an active role in supporting the demobilization, resettlement and reintegration process. In others, however, governments conducted most of the activities themselves. For example, in Eritrea in the mid-1990s, the new government funded and conducted most of the demobilization and reintegration support itself. The government had clear ideas on how it wanted to conduct the exercise and it wanted to shape development cooperation on the basis of 'partnership and mutual responsibility, rather than the classical unequal donor-recipient relation'.[10] It was unable to receive sufficient commitments from external donors and accumulated a large domestic debt to fund the exercise.

The post-war demobilization and reintegration support efforts that were more or less completely implemented achieved in different countries fairly mixed results. Some have been implemented rather systematically, while others merely happened spontaneously. Some were conducted rather smoothly; many faced considerable problems in their implementation. In terms of impact, some had a beneficial effect on peace and human development, while others had a neutral or negative effect on these processes. There have also been some outright failures to demobilize. In Angola in the early and mid-1990s demobilization was tried twice. But for several reasons, both efforts failed and the country slipped back in full-scale war in late 1998. The demobilizations in Eritrea and Ethiopia in the mid-1990s were initially quite successful. However, they were completely reversed after the outbreak of war in May 1998.[11]

The Concept of Peacebuilding

To assess the contribution of demobilization and reintegration to peacebuilding, it is important to reflect briefly on this emerging concept. *An Agenda for Peace*, published by the United Nations in 1992, defined post-conflict peacebuilding as 'action to identify and support structures which will tend to strengthen and solidify peace in order to avoid a relapse into conflict'.[12] It was thus defined as a set of actions that would change institutional structures. Since then, the use of the concept has evolved, with various contributions. The literature that has since appeared has shown large variations in the usage of the term.[13] The term has been used both in a narrow and a broad sense, and considerable differences have appeared with regard to the different dimensions of peacebuilding. Henning Haugerudbraaten[14] identifies in the literature six dimensions of peacebuilding, on which there are different views: the aim, the means, the time aspects, the main actors, the process or activities dimension, and the way it is organized. He warns against using too narrow or too broad a definition. In the latter case, it could become superfluous if it becomes too closely associated with quite well established concepts, such as 'development' or 'nation-building'. The concept of peacebuilding has thus far not been widely, nor very precisely, used in the African context by academics or policy makers.

After most peace agreements or other processes of terminating armed conflict, the actual conflict (or the sources of conflict) still exists. In this essay, 'peacebuilding' is defined as the processes and interventions that reduce or take away entirely the root causes of a conflict. In a post-war situation such a movement towards positive peace implies that a relapse into violent conflict is less likely. This definition includes the promotion of good governance and non-violent conflict resolution mechanisms.

Figure 2 indicates that peacebuilding incorporates several different processes and might be influenced by many different structural factors and policy interventions. These processes are, for example, democratization, economic development and demilitarization. Structural factors that could have an impact on the success or failure of peacebuilding are such things as: the security situation in and around the country, the protection of human rights, and the institutional capacity of the state to design and implement economic, social and other relevant policies. Peacebuilding requires not only justice and the absence of violence, but also institutions capable of facilitating economic activity, mediating conflicts, providing security and managing the diverse interests of groups in society.

The process of peacebuilding can be supported through a broad set of policies and programmes such as measures to stabilize the economy, rehabilitate infrastructure, strengthen food-security systems and support the broad-based revival of economic production. Other measures might include capacity building, land reform or redistribution of other property to disadvantaged groups. Measures related more directly to the war could include the monitoring of a ceasefire or peace accord, emergency relief operations, support to resettlement and reintegration of ex-combatants, demining and other micro-disarmament measures. Relief activities should take the longer-term development requirements into account, while development efforts could help to reduce the frequency, intensity and impact of shocks, which will in turn reduce the need for future relief assistance. All these efforts can play a direct role in creating a sense of confidence and well-being among people.

The processes, as well as the factors and interventions which might support or inhibit peacebuilding, can be political, economic, social, cultural or psychological. Figure 2 shows that some of the processes, factors and policies are crosscutting and embody several dimensions. For example, the reintegration of ex-combatants into civilian life has inter-related economic, political, social, cultural and psychological aspects.

Figure 2 does not attempt to be complete. An issue such as leadership, for example, is critical in post-war peacebuilding. However, it is hard to pinpoint in this framework. The indicators of some of the processes or structural factors are of course also simplified. For example, the process of democratization in a post-civil war situation is highly complex. On the formal side it might imply for example the drawing-up of a new constitution, establishment of political parties (or transforming warring factions into parties) and elections for different levels of government. This involves numerous local processes, and might involve an international dynamic in cases where an election is supported and monitored by the UN, individual countries or regional organizations. Democratization also implies informal processes such as the reorganization of civil society, the (re-)emergence of NGOs, the expansion of diverse media, increased political participation at various levels, and the strengthening of local conflict resolution mechanisms.

The concept of peacebuilding as presented here could potentially contribute to bridging the artificial divide between 'security' and 'development' discourses. It might provide more substance to the

FIGURE 2
THE CONCEPT OF PEACEBUILDING

Peace and Human Development

Peacebuilding

	Political	Economic	Social/Cultural/Psychological
Processes	Democratization* (formal and informal) State/nation-building Demilitarization*	Economic development* State/nation-building Demilitarization & conversion*	Reconciliation Empowerment Demilitarization*
Structural factors (may support or inhibit peacebuilding)	CMR (patterns/role of armed forces) Security* Political (human) rights Law & order State/capacity/'good governance'	CMR (defence industry) Economic security Socio-economic (human) rights Law & order State capacity	CMR (new perceptions/roles) Human security Human rights Law & order
Policy/Programmes (may support or inhibit peacebuilding)	Structural adjustment Repatriation* Demobilization & reintegration support Disarmament & demining* Redistribution	Structural adjustment Repatriation* Demobilization & reintegration support Disarmament & demining* Redistribution Rehabilitiation infrastructure*	Education/health care Repatriation* Demobilization & reintegration support Redistribution Psycho-social assistance for trauma healing

(* strong regional implications)

Source: Peter Batchelor and Kees Kingma, 'Demilitarisation and Peace-building in Southern Africa' (Introduction to results of collaborative research), forthcoming, Ashgate, 2002.

so-called new thinking on security, which has risen to prominence since the end of the Cold War.[15] Increased security and stability, for example, are more likely to lead to progress in human development. On the other hand progress in human development is a prerequisite for sustainable peacebuilding.

Reintegration and the Recurrance or Development of Conflict

On the basis of the demobilization and reintegration experiences in Africa,[16] the following section will analyse ways in which the resettlement and reintegration of ex-combatants has had (or could still have) an impact on the recurrence or development of conflicts. The factors that lead to conflicts or affect peacebuilding in general can of course occur in combination, and often occur as part of a vicious cycle. Their effects are also more likely to be felt if there is already some instability or tension in the country or specific location involved.

Political and Institutional Environment

The progress and impact of demobilization and reintegration depend to a large extent on the political and institutional environment in which they occur. The presence of a functioning state and legal system is one of the central requirements for peacebuilding. Laurie Nathan[17] argues that for the process of demilitarization to lead to positive peace in Africa, the security vacuum that both state and non-state actors try to fill by violent means needs to be filled by legitimate political structures. In the post-war situations reviewed, the state is generally weak or fragile. The strengthening of state capacity and law and order, and the development of processes of democratic decision making and non-violent conflict resolution, are therefore necessary to prevent slipping back into war and the demobilization falling apart.

In cases where there is barely a state nor any external power to keep parties to their agreement, demobilization has little chance of success. Ideally, the state would guide and protect the processes of demobilization and resettlement. During the demobilizations in Mozambique and Namibia, the UN played such a role. The failure of demobilization efforts in Angola shows that, even with UN presence, at least cessation of hostilities and political will of all parties are required. Both in the early as well as the mid-1990s peace accords collapsed in Angola mainly due to lack of political commitment on both sides. Real demobilization was never completed. In Sierra Leone, the rebels of the Revolutionary United Front (RUF) failed to dismantle their war machine and frequently violated the ceasefire with impurity.[18]

The demobilization process was seriously disrupted by the outbreak of renewed fighting in April 2000.

Right from the beginning of the demobilization phase, it is also necessary to have an authority with an effective police force able to protect the ex-combatants and their dependants. Once they return to the areas where they want to (re)settle, internal security problems, including lack of material, physical and legal security, have often threatened ex-combatants and others, especially in areas with continuing political unrest. In northern Uganda, for example, demobilized soldiers were confronted with the difficult situation of limited protection by the state, while there were on the other hand few peaceful economic opportunities for reintegration and considerable risks and pressures to be absorbed, by force or incentives, into rebel forces. Similarly in Angola: even if former fighters of the National Union for the Total Independence of Angola (Unita) had tried to return to civilian life, they would have been subject to pressure from their former officers, while lacking any form of protection by the state. At the same time, there would have been few opportunities for peaceful economic reintegration. It has been in such regions that demobilized soldiers have been drawn back into the military build-up or direct fighting.

Tensions, disputes and minor conflicts are inevitable in difficult socio-economic situations. This applies especially to post-war situations. However, it is the lack of mechanisms to resolve such disputes peacefully that can lead to the escalation of conflict and the outbreak of violence.[19] Communities often have their own internal instruments for managing or resolving conflict, without having to resort to the formal mechanisms of the state. As a result of war and destabilization, however, these communities are often split or scattered, and these mechanisms weakened or destroyed as a result.

The confidence and security perceptions of citizens including ex-combatants is also affected by how past and ongoing human rights violations of members of the armed forces are handled. However, this is not a simple matter, and often creates substantial dilemmas. It is generally felt that soldiers and ex-combatants who violated human rights should be appropriately punished. But harsh punishments might increase tensions, for example, between ex-soldiers and the rest of society. In addition, some groups might believe that the violations they perpetrated during the war are treated differently to those of others. African nations have dealt with this dilemma in several ways. It is still too early to generalize about the impact of human rights violations by the military on the peacebuilding processes. These issues are still being worked out, for example, with regard to the position of ex-soldiers and liberation fighters in South Africa. The amnesty clause in the Truth and Reconciliation Commission is believed to have prevented political instability, and even bloodshed. But the decision not to give a general amnesty for all human rights violations under apartheid might also prove important in this respect. The long-term impact of past violations by the apartheid regime's armed forces or the liberation movements will ultimately depend on broader processes of national reconciliation. Sierra Leone also faces major dilemmas in the establishment of a system to try the (military) perpetrators of the mass atrocities that occurred during the war.

Economic Opportunities and Competition for Natural Resources

Opportunities for ex-combatants to establish new livelihoods have a crucial bearing on the threat of conflict. Even if the exact potential sources of conflict cannot be pinpointed, it should be noted that most intra-state conflicts are caused by weak states, poor governance, and by poverty, deprivation and inequality. One potential source of disputes is access to arable land, or the reclaiming of property in general. Many conflicts are rooted in a struggle for resources, while environmental stress and degradation aggravate these problems. In Zimbabwe, the continuous struggle for land has been further complicated by violently expressed demands by ex-combatants for more equitable redistribution of land.[20]

The official termination of some of the armed conflicts in Africa brought high expectations. After so much suffering, a peaceful new life with ample economic opportunities was usually anticipated. Expectations were especially high in cases where oppressive regimes were pushed out, as in Eritrea, Namibia, South Africa and Zimbabwe. In the short term, when soldiers returned to their villages, they needed to feel a sense of concrete achievement. But, as in the case of the ex-People's Liberation Army of Namibia (PLAN) fighters the expectations of being able to set up sustainable livelihoods were often not met, causing frustration.

The post-war reconstruction efforts in the countries concerned usually included policies to stabilize and readjust the economy. Tightened macro-economic policies generally led to fewer public sector jobs and increased urban unemployment during the adjustment period. In addition, certain income-generating opportunities that existed as a result of the war disappeared. As a result of peace, economic opportunities in the rural areas are generally improving, but at a slow rate. Large numbers of young people without job opportunities can be seen as a time-bomb that threatens the peacebuilding process in countries such as Liberia, Mozambique, Sierra Leone and South Africa. Those with military skills and no stable livelihood can all too easily be mobilized for political purposes. This has happened over the years, for example, in Liberia and Sierra Leone. Paradoxically, the security threat posed by demobilized soldiers is mostly felt in urban centres. However, the long-term threat around which ex-combatants could potentially be remobilized, comes in most cases from remaining disparities between urban and rural areas.

Although probably not prompted simply by poverty, significant numbers of ex-soldiers of the former South African Defence Force (SADF) and some other African armies have found their way into mercenary companies. In many countries, large numbers of ex-combatants have joined the private domestic security sector. In these cases, the demilitarization of the state through demobilization fed the militarization of society.

Availability of Weapons

A connection often exists between demobilizations and the potential for conflict, as a result of easier access to small arms and light weapons. Although in some countries, the disarmament of the demobilized was carefully conducted and strictly controlled, in other cases, large numbers of weapons remained in the hands of ex-combatants, or ended up in the hands of others. For example, inadequate disarmament of combatants in Mozambique during the UN Operations in Mozambique (UNOMOZ) has significantly increased the number of uncontrolled weapons circulating in Southern Africa. Small arms are easy to smuggle across the long and porous African borders. In Angola, disarmament was also poorly conducted, which made the return to war all the more easy. Less than half of Unita's fighters surrendered functional weapons when entering demobilization camps, and many turned in no weapons at all.[21] Considerable numbers of weapons are also believed to have 'leaked' from government forces during and after several demobilizations in Africa.

Easy access to these weapons increases the risk of people resorting to violence in the case of disputes. These weapons also facilitate violence in banditry and robbery, for example, in Mozambique and South Africa. Uncontrolled access to weapons could also facilitate armed conflict on a larger scale. Some of the weapons currently used by Unita soldiers in Angola are believed to have been in the region for a decade or more.

Social and Cultural Norms and Psychological Impact

In the complex process of reintegration, conflicts might result from social and cultural differences that have developed between civilians and fighters during the war. Even if ex-combatants do find employment, their military norms and lack of certain life-skills might create difficulties. In addition, it has been shown that ex-combatants tend to identify themselves as such for a considerable period after they have been demobilized. This has been particularly noticeable in Eritrea, Mozambique (combatants from the liberation struggle), Namibia and Zimbabwe, especially when ex-combatants face difficulties with reintegration or perceive that they have not been sufficiently supported or rewarded. This issue appears to be central to many of the conflicts in which ex-combatants are involved.

Female ex-fighters, as well as other women in war-affected communities, face specific problems once peace is achieved. They have usually acquired new roles as a result of the war, but men or the wider community often refuse to accept these roles in peacetime. In Eritrea for example, where about one-third of the fighters of the Eritrean People's Liberation Front (EPLF) were women, they were after the war expected by men to return to their traditional roles. A high divorce rate has been observed. In the sample of a survey conducted in Eritrea in 1997, 27 per cent of the female ex-fighters were divorced or separated; 4 per cent were widows.[22] These women very often had to raise children by themselves. Lack of childcare facilities was one of the impediments for economic reintegration of female ex-fighters in Eritrea. In Uganda, wives from returning soldiers, who came from other regions, were frequently not accepted by his family and community. This led to enormous stress, economic hardship and often separation.

Yet another cause of potential future conflict lies in post-war trauma that is often not dealt with adequately. In the cases reviewed, many people have been victims or perpetrators of horrendous violence. This has left deep emotional and psychological scars among ex-combatants and others, damage that is reflected in depression, apathy or rage. Post-war trauma, especially in combination with alcohol or drug addiction, can disturb public life and affect the capacity for non-violent resolution of conflict. Although this is hard to substantiate, persisting anger and fear are potentially root causes of future violent conflicts. Initial problems could be crime, suicide, and drug and alcohol abuse. But these could affect broader national peacebuilding processes in the longer term. On the positive side, however, it is important to note that many ex-combatants (in rural Mozambique and Uganda, for example) underwent cleansing rituals in order to be accepted back into their communities.[23] These acceptance rituals have a positive impact not only on the community, but also on the state of mind of ex-combatants themselves.

With regard to the threats indicated above, special attention needs to be given to former child soldiers (especially to girl ex-soldiers, who face multiple problems after demobilization). At demobilization, these young ex-combatants often lack parental care and access to education. Many of the child soldiers in Mozambique, Rwanda, Sierra Leone and Uganda were orphans. Many former child soldiers have been seriously traumatized by the brutal experiences they have undergone, which usually have a profound impact on their social and emotional development. If reintegration of these former child soldiers fails, it could lead to new 'cycles of violence',[24] as they could easily be recruited into new armed opposition groups.

Appropriateness of Reintegration Assistance

Reintegration assistance has the potential to contribute to peacebuilding. It has indeed helped to 'buy time', and for large numbers of ex-combatants, it has contributed to their establishing new livelihoods. Assistance in the process of resettlement and reintegration has been provided by governments, local and international NGOs, bilateral and multilateral agencies. The Namibian experience shows that the government initially neglected the need for reintegration support. Only after tensions led to disturbances did it respond hastily with assistance initiatives.

Since the early 1990s, several of the main international development agencies have overcome legal constraints or initial reluctance to be involved in development activities that somehow relate to the military, or the security sector in general. Governments and some donor agencies seem to have grasped that the long-term implications are likely to be serious if ex-combatants cannot find new livelihoods and reintegrate into communities. However, this section will also show that the way in which reintegration support is actually provided poses several risks of future conflict.

Reintegration assistance can actually obstruct peacebuilding, and lead to tensions and conflict, if there are perceived to be unjustified inequalities in the assistance that different groups receive. The provision of aid should be guided by needs, equity and a degree of political pragmatism. In the case of demobilization, resettlement and reintegration support, policy makers usually face the dilemma of whether or not to treat ex-soldiers as a special target group, especially if there are many more people in need and some of the ex-combatants are alleged to have committed atrocities during the war.

It has been argued, however, that some direct support for the reintegration of ex-soldiers and guerrillas is justified for at least the following reasons:[25]

- Demobilized soldiers and fighters require support from a humanitarian point of view. Upon demobilization, they are out of a job and often far from their homes. Therefore, they require at least the provision of basic needs for some time, as well as assistance with resettlement.
- In some cases, it can be argued that demobilized combatants have sacrificed several years of their life to liberate their country and to improve the development prospects of their compatriots (for example, EPLF in Eritrea and PLAN in Namibia). In other cases, some of the demobilized might have been recruited under pressure (such as the Derg army in Ethiopia and fighters of the Mozambican National Resistance – Renamo).
- With a little assistance, ex-combatants could make a significant contribution to development in their community and their country as a whole. Utilizing some of their skills might bring new economic activities and employment opportunities.[26]
- Last, but in some cases most important, lack of attention to the risks involved in demobilization and reintegration could jeopardize peacebuilding. Without support, demobilized soldiers and guerrilla fighters might become frustrated and threaten the peace and development process by becoming active in crime or violent political opposition.

Any support given to ex-combatants therefore has to strike a balance between dealing with their specific needs and not creating discontent among the other members of their often impoverished communities. In Zimbabwe, for example, rural people resented the benefits given to ex-combatants, whom they believed had suffered less than they had.[27] Among analysts, a consensus has developed that special aid for ex-combatants and their dependants is required during the immediate demobilization and resettlement phase, but that support for reintegration should be aimed as much as possible at the entire community, and be part of general rehabilitation efforts. Area-based programmes are therefore seen as an appropriate approach.

There have been obvious exceptions to the above principles regarding targeting. In Mozambique, for example, Renamo leaders received lavish 'demobilization packages' to keep them satisfied, at least during the critical stages of dismantling Renamo's military structures. Providing early clarity about assistance is also important. In several cases, ex-combatants have demonstrated their potential for violence in order to put pressure on donors to commit more resources for reintegration programmes. Political awareness and astuteness among aid workers could make it easier to anticipate problems and conflict, and prevent assistance from being manipulated.[28]

The question of the use of (foreign) military to help in the delivery of demobilization and resettlement assistance needs to be raised. Because of the logistical skills and equipment available, it is sometimes tempting to use the military for the delivery of assistance in difficult situations, such as that faced by the UNOMOZ in Mozambique. One advantage is that military units can be mobilized quickly. However, there are serious doubts as to whether using the military is cheaper than civilian government agencies or NGOs that can do the same job. Soldiers have the tendency to militarize the social environment, and this generally does not contribute to self-reliance, sustainability and peacebuilding. Military organizations are often interested in 'winning hearts and minds', for instance by building bridges and health-care facilities. But they often still need to learn the basic principles of development and cooperation; for example, letting go of a 'top-down' approach, including women in the process, and showing the required cultural sensitivity. This is not always successful. There are thus many grounds for keeping the delivery of assistance as demilitarized as possible. According to Ball and Campbell: 'There is widespread agreement among those with experience in planning and implementing demobilization and reintegration activities that civilian organizations should take the lead.'[29]

Timing can be critical in resettlement and reintegration assistance. During demobilization efforts in Angola and in Sierra Leone frustration and upheaval among the ex-combatants occurred at the encampment and discharge stage, because the provision of basic needs (such as water, sanitation, shelter and food) was insufficient. Many similar problems flared up in Mozambique as well, largely due to the urge to get the demobilization process over with quickly. These experiences show that if the prospects for the ex-combatants are not clear, and the period of encampment is stretched too much, violence and rebellion are likely to undermine the demobilization and resettlement process and potentially, the overall peace process.

The benefits of peace therefore need to be made visible as swiftly as possible. A UN Security Council Mission to Sierra Leone in October 2000[30] saw quick-impact projects as vital to build confidence. Also the 2000 Brahimi Report on UN peace operations emphasized the positive role that such projects can play in the peacebuilding process.[31] Such assistance projects could for example be in the form of labour-intensive public works, the construction of health centres or the provision of agricultural inputs, tools and building material.

It is also worth noting that if the reintegration support relies heavily on external funding, the terminating or scaling down of this aid can lead to the collapse of the reintegration services causing frustration and unrest. Similar lessons concerning sustainability have been learned by those involved in general humanitarian and development assistance. For example, assistance through quick-impact projects is indeed very important and helps people to cope with difficult initial periods re-establishing a livelihood. But experience in development cooperation indicates that processes started with this type of aid are often not sustainable. Assistance may create unrealistic expectations, and the actual termination of assistance is often inadequately anticipated. In Zimbabwe, veterans began expressing frustration when they stopped receiving demobilization money.

Given the above concerns it is important to plan the phasing out of external assistance. However, these risks are not universal. For example, in Mozambique, there were fears of an outbreak of unrest after ex-combatants received their final payment in early 1997. However, very little of the anticipated unrest occurred, which seems to confirm the finding that in Mozambique families and communities had actually provided the most important reintegration support, and continue to do so.[32]

Conclusions

This essay has identified and analysed links between demobilization and reintegration in African countries on the one hand, and peacebuilding processes and potential sources of conflict on the other. It should first of all be noted that in the post-war situations in which demobilizations were initiated, many complex and inter-linked socio-economic processes were taking place simultaneously. Most of these have political implications. The demobilization and reintegration process is thus only one of the factors that could either disrupt or support peacebuilding. This means that it could be part of a set of factors causing conflict, or it could occur in a situation alongside several existing sources of structural violence.

Demobilization and reintegration have in most cases and in various ways contributed to human development and peace processes in the region. Nevertheless, this essay has identified several aspects of demobilization, resettlement and reintegration that have had a direct negative impact on the potential for violent conflict, and on peacebuilding processes in general.

The essay has shown that demobilizations in Africa have led to a series of different short-term conflicts mostly at the local level. In several of the demobilization exercises disturbances have occurred during the encampment phase. These were mostly triggered by impatience, uncertainty, long stays or bad living conditions in the assembly camps. Fortunately, most of these conflicts have been resolved through negotiation, the immediate provision of material resources and other confidence-building measures. In countries with limited resources, conflict at this stage shows the need for early involvement (and financial commitment) of external donors in planning processes, and the importance of reliable data for such planning. External donors are increasingly aware of this, and have already improved their responsiveness.

In the medium term, several other problems have arisen. But in the light of the concerns held at the outset of most demobilization exercises, these have not been as grave as expected. Policy interventions and support programmes usually with external finance have generally had a positive impact by helping the ex-combatants to integrate into civilian life.

In some countries, such as Angola and Sierra Leone, ex-combatants did turn to violent political opposition against governments. In these cases, however, this was mainly due to the persistent unwillingness of the leaderships to resolve their differences in non-violent ways. At this level, the commitment of the respective leaders to peace is possibly the central and largely independent factor. It is debatable whether the current fighting in parts of Liberia is linked to the demobilization in 1996–97. But it is believed that significant numbers of those demobilized are involved in fighting in the region. There are no clear indications that the effects of the demobilizations in the 1990s in Eritrea and Ethiopia caused in any way the war that broke out between the two countries in 1998. But in both countries the dramatic remobilization did draw substantially on combatants demobilized in the early and mid-1990s.

Although in most of the countries concerned there have been cases where demobilized combatants have turned to banditry, the experience indicates that the initial fears of crime by ex-combatants have generally been exaggerated. Badly managed disarmament associated with some of the demobilizations has indeed increased the number of uncontrolled weapons, and thereby facilitated the use of violence. But in most countries it is still disputed whether significant numbers of robbers and bandits are actually ex-combatants.

The downsizing of national armies in the region has led to a growing number of mercenaries for hire, particularly in Southern Africa. However, the actual number is not known, and it is hard to assess the impact of the 'supply side' on the activities of mercenary firms in the region. The current efforts in South Africa to ban these practices seem promising, but mercenary firms and their networks are hard to root out.

Problems related to (perceived) inequalities and unjustified rewards might become more significant in the long-term. Expectations on the part of the ex-combatants were generally high in terms of the benefits of peace. However, lack of appropriate rewards continues to be a source of tension long after the demobilization, as shown in Zimbabwe. In such cases, ex-combatants tend to identify (and organize) themselves as such for long periods after demobilization. Inequalities in pensions for different armies have caused tensions, for example in Mozambique and Zimbabwe. If ex-combatants are subjected to confusing delaying tactics, as has occurred in Namibia, problems are pushed into the future, and the resulting outbreaks of dissatisfaction could be seriously disruptive. Mismanagement of funds intended for ex-combatants has added to the frustration of ex-liberation fighters in Namibia and Zimbabwe. The problems of ex-combatants have in some countries also acted as catalysts that bring to the fore protests from other groups in society on more general political and socio-economic issues.

Looking ahead into the long term, this essay has also identified further risks of conflict. In most cases where women made up a large part of the fighting forces, they received very little extra attention at demobilization. The specific problems that these female ex-fighters face might have affected the social fabric in these countries. In addition, post-war trauma and drug addiction of ex-combatants, which are already serious social problems in the short term, might in the medium to long term trigger new cycles of violent conflict and undermine peacebuilding processes. The plight of former child soldiers in particular needs to be addressed. Serious thinking about the future role of the demobilized combatants and their potential contribution to peacebuilding in Africa has started rather late. In most countries, there is scope for efforts to change the ways people perceive ex-combatants.

With regard to the role of assistance to demobilization, resettlement and reintegration, the essay concludes that such support has helped to 'buy time' and has contributed to establishing new livelihoods for large numbers of ex-combatants. The assistance has been provided by governments, local and international NGOs, bilateral and multilateral agencies, that all seem to have grasped that the long-term implications are likely to be serious if ex-combatants fail to reintegrate into civilian life. The above analysis has provided several lessons in order to reduce the risks that demobilization 'done badly' would contribute to future conflict. The most important policy directions to be considered are: to ensure a solid political and institutional base for the demobilization and reintegration (assistance), to link reintegration policy with the general economic policy framework, to sufficiently consider the psychological effects of the war, to ensure control of the weapons of those to be demobilized, to be fully aware of (perceived) inequalities in the assistance that different groups receive, and to be sensitive to the proper timing to phase out the assistance.

ACKNOWLEDGEMENTS

This essay is part of ongoing work at the Bonn International Center for Conversion (BICC) to assess the impact of demobilization and reintegration support. It draws heavily on research that the author conducted within a collaborative research project on 'Demilitarization and Peace-building in Southern Africa', coordinated by BICC and the Centre for Conflict Resolution (CCR), Cape Town. Funding for the research by the International Development Research Centre (IDRC), Ottawa, Canada, is gratefully acknowledged. An earlier version of the essay was presented at the International Studies Association (ISA) Conference in Chicago, 20–24 Feb. 2001.

NOTES

1. United Nations, 'The Causes of Conflict and the Promotion of Peace and Sustainable Development in Africa'. Report of the UN Secretary-General, A/52/871 – S/1998/3/318, New York: United Nations, 1998, p.14.
2. United Nations, 'The Role of United Nations Peacekeeping in Disarmament, Demobilization and Reintegration'. Report of the Secretary General to the Security Council, S/2000/101, 11 Feb., New York: United Nations, 2000.
3. United Nations, 'Report of the Panel on United Nations Peace Operations'. A/55/3055–S/2000/809, New York: United Nations, 2000.
4. United Nations, 'Report of the Panel on United Nations Peace Operations'. A/55/3055–S/2000/809, New York: United Nations, 2000.
5. The term 'combatant' is used here to refer to both government soldiers and members of an armed opposition group.
6. Bonn International Center for Conversion (BICC), *Conversion Survey 1996; Global Disarmament, Demilitarization and Demobilization*, Oxford: Oxford University Press, 1996.
7. Kees Kingma (ed.), *Demobilization in Sub-Saharan Africa: The Development and Security Impacts*, Basingstoke: Macmillan, 2000.
8. Kees Kingma and Natalie Pauwels, 'Demobilization and Reintegration in the "Downsizing Decade"', in Natalie Pauwels (ed.), *War Force to Work Force: Global Perspectives on Demobilization and Reintegration*, Baden-Baden: NOMOS, 2000, p.13.
9. Nat J. Colletta, Markus Kostner and Ingo Wiederhofer, *The Transition from War to Peace in Sub-Saharan Africa*, Directions in Development Series, Washington, DC: World Bank, 1996; Nat J. Colletta, Markus Kostner and Ingo Wiederhofer, *Case*

Studies in War-to-Peace Transition: The Demobilization and Reintegration of Ex-Combatants in Ethiopia, Namibia and Uganda, World Bank Discussion Paper no. 331, Africa Technical Department Series, Washington, DC: World Bank, 1996; Nicole Ball, 'The International Development Community's Response to Demobilization', in Kiflemariam Gebrewold (ed.), Converting Defense Resources to Human Development, Proceedings of an International Conference, 9–11 Nov. 1997, Report 12, Bonn: BICC, 1998, pp.21–7; Kees Kingma (ed.), (n.7 above); and World Bank, Demobilization and Reintegration of Military Personnel in Africa: The Evidence from Seven Country Case Studies, Africa Regional Series Discussion Paper IDP-130, Washington, DC, Oct. 1993.
10. Eva-Maria Bruchhaus and Amanuel Mehreteab, 'Leaving the Warm House: The Impact of Demobilization in Eritrea', in Kees Kingma (ed.), (n.7 above), p.113.
11. Planning for renewed demobilization and reintegration support started in both countries after the peace agreement signed in December 2000.
12. Boutros Boutros-Ghali, An Agenda for Peace: Preventive Diplomacy, Peacemaking and Peace-keeping, Report of the Secretary-General, New York: United Nations, 1992, p.11.
13. For example, Giles Carbonnier, 'Conflict, Postwar Rebuilding and the Economy: A Critical Review of the Literature'. Occasional Paper No. 2, Geneva: UNRISD, War-torn Societies Project, 1998; Henning Haugerudbraaten, 'Peacebuilding: Six Dimensions and Two Concepts', African Security Review, Vol.7, No.6, 1998, pp.17–26; John Paul Lederach, Building Peace: Sustainable Reconciliation in Divided Societies, Washington, DC: United States Institute of Peace Press, 1997; Roland Paris, 'Peacebuilding and the Limits of Liberal Internationalism', International Security, Vol.22, No.2, pp.54–89.
14. Haugerudbraaten (n.13 above), pp.17–26.
15. For example, Ken Booth, 'A Security Regime in Southern Africa: Theoretical Considerations', Southern African Perspectives, No.30, Centre for Southern African Studies, University of Western Cape, 1994; and Barry Buzan, Ole Wæver and Jaap de Wilde, Security: a new framework for analysis, Boulder and London: Lynne Rienner, 1998.
16. For an overview of demobilization and reintegration experiences in Africa and elaboration of the specific cases, see: Kees Kingma, 'Demobilization and Reintegration Experiences in Africa', in Pauwels (ed.), (n.8 above), pp.301–28.
17. Laurie Nathan, 'Good Governance, Security and Disarmament: The Challenge of Demilitarisation in Africa', African Journal of Political Science, Vol.3, No.2, 1998, pp.69–79.
18. Francis Kai-Kai, 'Disarmament, Demobilization and Reintegration in Post-War Sierra Leone', in Anatole Ayissi and Robin-Edward Poulton (eds), Bound to Cooperate: Conflict, Peace and People in Sierra Leone, Geneva: UN Institute for Disarmament Research, 2000, pp.113–28.
19. See, for example, Adebayo Adedeji (ed.), Comprehending and Mastering African Conflicts, London and New York: Zed Books, in association with the African Centre for Development and Strategic Studies, 1999; and the European Centre for Conflict Prevention, People Building Peace: 35 Inspiring Stories from Around the World, Utrecht: European Centre for Conflict Prevention, in cooperation with the International Fellowship of Reconciliation and the Coexistence Initiative of State of the World Forum, 1999.
20. T. Knox Chitiyo, 'Land Violence and Compensation: Reconceptualising Zimbabwe's Land and War Veterans' Debate', Occasional Paper, Track Two, Vol.9, No.1, 2000.
21. Nicole Ball and Kathleen F. Campbell, Complex Crisis and Complex Peace: Humanitarian coordination in Angola, Report prepared for the United Nations Office for the Coordination of Humanitarian Affairs, 1998, accessed at www.reliefweb.int/ocha_ol/pub/angola/index.html.
22. Bruchhaus and Mehreteab (n.10. above), pp.95–131.
23. Iraê Baptista Lundin, Martinho Chachiua, António Gaspar, Habiba Guebuza and Guilherme Mbilana, 'Reducing Costs through an Expensive Exercise: The Impact of Demobilization in Mozambique', in Kees Kingma (ed.), (n.7 above), pp.173–212;

Alcinda Honwana, 'The Collective Body; Challenging Western Concepts of Trauma Healing', *Track Two*, July 1999, 1999, pp.30–35.
24. For example, Malvern Lumsden, 'Breaking the Cycle of Violence'. *Journal of Peace Research*, Vol.34, No.4, 1997, pp.377–83; Michael Wessels, 'Children, Armed Conflict and Peace', *Journal of Peace Research*, Vol.35, No.5, 1998, pp.635–46.
25. Kingma (ed.), (n.7 above), p.226.
26. Irmgard Nübler, 'Human Resources Development and Utilization in Demobilization and Reintegration Programmes', in Kees Kingma (ed.), (n. 7 above), pp.45–77.
27. Norma Kriger, *Zimbabwe's Guerrilla War: Peasant Voices*, Cambridge: Cambridge University Press, 1992.
28. Mary Anderson, *Do No Harm: How Aid Can Support Peace or War*, Boulder and London: Lynne Rienner, 1999.
29. Nicole Ball and Kathleen F. Campbell, *Complex crisis and complex peace: Humanitarian coordination in Angola*, Report prepared for the United Nations Office for the Coordination of Humanitarian Affairs, 1998, accessed at www.reliefweb.int/ocha_ol/pub/angola/index.html.
30. UN document: S/2000/992.
31. United Nations, 'Report of the Panel on United Nations Peace Operations'. A/55/3055–S/2000/809, New York: United Nations, 2000.
32. Lundin, et al., (n.23 above), pp.173–212.

Building Peace after Mass Crimes

BÉATRICE POULIGNY

The study of mass crimes, and their social and political consequences, constitute a largely underdeveloped concern of the literature on peacebuilding. The individual and collective traumas engendered by such criminal practices are rarely taken into account during peace processes. This neglect has considerable political and social consequences for both the societies in question and the individuals that comprise them. Among scholars themselves, the topic has been considered within general analyses of the political situation of countries in which massacres have taken place. Rarely however has 'massacre' been considered as a research subject in its own right, and even less so in a comparative perspective. This deficit appears even less understandable in the light of the fact that the widespread practice of massacre throughout the twentieth century has characterized the strategies of certain actors, particularly in the context of war. The annihilation of civilian populations may in fact be central to their logic of action and have an important impact on post-war situations. The denotation of these crimes as 'mass crimes' stresses the fact that they imply more than simply the killing of great numbers of people. Mass killings are usually preceded or followed by other atrocities such as mutilation, rape, the destruction of villages and the deportation of people. The ensemble of such acts, in addition to the actual massacres, is termed 'mass crime'.

How may peacebuilding proceed in the aftermath of mass crime? In order to attempt to answer this question, analysts and practitioners alike must face two challenges. First, they should try to understand, in one way or another, how the carrying out of mass crime may have come about. In most cases, a large percentage of crime is committed in the immediate domestic or communal environment. Ideology or political manipulation are not sufficient to 'explain' the breakdown of social regulatory processes. Second, capacities for peace that already exist within the society concerned should be identified. Indeed, for the rules of the social and political game to function or, in other words, for all actors to find interest in participating in the collective game of cooperation and peace rather than confrontation, such resources cannot be ignored. Peacebuilding must draw upon local resources and methods that, in almost all cases, have been constructed over time, while at the same time borrowing in various ways from the outside. Even those societies that, for various reasons, are generally presented as particularly belligerent and capable of concealing the self-destructive forces that threw them into extraordinary violence, have at their disposal social modes of regulation and resources able to serve as a basis for reconstruction. It is only after having identified these somewhat more precisely that it may be possible to consider the role of external intervention in whatever form it may take. In proceeding in this two-pronged direction (in the second and third parts respectively of this essay), one must be ready to cut to the core of highly paradoxical situations for which I shall, in the first part, advance several methodological propositions.

Thinking the 'Unthinkable': A Mechanism for Analysis and Intervention

Faced with mass criminality, political decision makers, military actors, humanitarian workers, psychiatrists and researchers have to overcome certain psychological and moral obstacles. They have to try to account for the intermingling of the rationalities and irrationalities that led to the crime or, in other words, to think the 'unthinkable'. Such a process entails taking one's distance from a number of the presuppositions that have in fact shaped studies of international security for over a decade. No longer open to interpretation through the prism of the confrontation between East and West, nor through the single-minded framework of rationalism, conflicts too often tended to be characterized as irrational, in line with the regrettable habit of seeing all that which the pre-existing frameworks cannot (or can no longer) explain as non-existent or inexplicable. In this context, the theme of 'barbarism' (in its variable formulations) returned with force,[1] particularly due to the effect of the rise in the importance of human rights. Thus, the categorization of someone as a 'barbarian' generally serves not to designate this most specific part of human beings, present in each of us, but rather the behaviour of the 'other'. It most often, even unconsciously, responds to a need to ensure distance, as a means of reassuring ourselves that *we* are not this way. This position, in particular, is unable to admit that both rationality and madness are the two faces of extreme violence and that each cannot imagine itself without the other.[2] Indeed, mass crime partly entails the irrational, the insane, partly the imaginary, but it also echoes tenacious fears and hatreds. It reflects individual and collective rationales. Above all, it relates to human stories. This explains the twofold effort that, it appears to me, is necessary for both researchers and practitioners to make in dealing with these types of situations: to pass from 'object' to 'subject' and to embark on a comprehensive sociology.[3]

From the 'Object' to the 'Subject' of Research

The negation of humanity that holds mass crime within it, the negation of that which binds human beings together, this 'other wordly' expulsion,[4] deeply affects each individual. In order to grasp it, it is again necessary to embark on the process of trying to 'understand', in the primary sense of the word. To this end, one must enter the other's subjectivity, in an attempt to decentre oneself in order, as we are invited to do by the philosopher Paul Ricoeur, to try to 'understand the other'. Such a step is not an easy one to take. How can one make sense of the other's psyche when the latter is a torturer? In the words of Raymond Aron, how to split oneself without becoming lost? Understanding the logic of massacres and the nature of the interactions that they put into play does not entail either banalizing or excusing them. Understanding is not a synonym for absolving.[5] Similarly, being interested in individuals who participate in the massacre of their compatriots, including their old neighbours or members of their families, is not to excuse but to admit that, in this descent into violence, they are not always 'insane', as was notably highlighted by Roland Marchal with regard to several African situations.[6]

This relates to a second problem of the humanitarian approach governing the majority of interventions into situations following mass crime. Frameworks of analysis as well as intervention are largely based upon the figure of the civil, passive victim, conceived of as a catch-all, as undifferentiated. Thus, it is necessary to consider the other as someone who is capable of being something other than a victim, someone capable of affirming themselves – at least in part – as an authentic actor, of rethinking their situation and commenting on it.[7] Psychiatrists emphasize, in this regard, the possibly dehumanizing elements of a humanitarian approach: the 'humanitarian object' largely appears as a foreign object, separated from the normal world where human life has a price.[8] Within the field of psychological intervention, the notion of mass crime most often goes in the direction of a dehumanizing way of thinking that reduces the other to a symptom rather than a story. In the spring of 1995, the refugees of northern Kivu were no more than points on a satellite picture for the diplomats who, in New York, discussed the opportunity of carrying out a humanitarian operation. For several humanitarian agencies that intervene in post-massacre situations, the very description of the traumatic troubles undergone by the populations whom they assist aims at externalizing the trauma and objectifying it rather than taking it for what it is, beyond words, gestures or impossible narratives.[9] During my previous field research, the fact that survivors had never had the opportunity to recount their stories – an activity considered by Hannah Arendt as specifically human[10] – and to have their experiences acknowledged was a leitmotif of the interviews I conducted. Listening to others putting their stories into words is to reintroduce them to their own humanity, to that in them which is unique. For Bernard Doray, a psychiatrist with experience in intervening in such contexts, faced with the effects of such a profoundly dehumanizing enterprise, therapy must first recreate the bases for a 'recognition in humanity'. For the psychiatrist, this consists of dealing with the brutal confrontation between monstrous acts and the human figure of those responsible for them.[11] But this cannot be achieved in a flat, global, moralizing and binary way which merely evokes the battle between good and evil. Even if the victim is unable to recognize the humanity of those who caused them immense suffering, it is necessary for the therapist to establish a personal representation of the torturer because if it is not possible to humanize this figure, the victim too is dehumanized and the traumatic fragment of their story is removed from the human exchange. By doing this, the cleavage of the traumatic representation – already organized by the psyche – is intensified.

This process of subjectivation[12] applies to all, both practitioners and researchers. It has consequences for the relationship to the field and the research materials. Above all, making those questioned/assisted no longer mere 'objects' but also the 'subjects' of the research or of aid entails an engagement in the dynamic of participation and partnership. This also concerns the manner in which members of a given community are to be involved in this work and the development of a widespread cooperation with researchers and local students or other partners such as local associations. We also need to pose the question as to the effect of the results of the research within the societies concerned (particularly through tools for training or community work, seminars, involvement in organizations for the development of aid programmes). At a minimum, it is necessary to ask what benefit local people may reap from the research. For the practitioner, the question could be posed in the following terms: how does one help people to reflect upon their own practices, identify their own resources and empower them in order to heal themselves and attempt rebuilding ties with others?[13] In addition, this work of subjectivation poses specific questions of method.

The Terms of a Comprehensive Sociology

For analysts, 'thinking the unthinkable' means that, at a certain stage of the research, they abandon their objectivized role and locates themselves as closely as possible to the point of view of local actors. Their objective will certainly not be to retrace exactly what has happened, as this is impossible, but to take seriously the way in which the individuals and groups concerned have understood and subjectively and empirically explained these events. This involves at least four things.

First, restoring the victim's (but also sometimes the perpetrator's) humanity primarily involves listening to their story as a person, attempting to reconstitute their personal trajectory in itself and in the history of the different groups to which they belong. This approach takes on particular importance for certain groups of people such as children: child soldiers, orphaned or abandoned children, child victims of rape and numerous cruelties. It is necessary to reconstitute the place in which they live, their trajectories and their environment. This may, in particular, be achieved through an interviewing process in which the researcher needs to display patience and extreme caution. The way in which questions are posed may greatly influence the results of the investigation. The same can be said of one's social position as a researcher or practitioner and, above all, the position as outsider. Both are positions of power. In many contexts, children are not accustomed to talking directly to adults, especially in a formal manner, and in some cases, questions shall remain forever unanswered. When working with children affected by war (including child soldiers), more can often be learned by just playing with them.[14] Last but not least, whether or not the researcher speaks the local language or needs to employ an interpreter is a decisive factor. Jean Hathzfeld's work in Rwanda is a beautiful and most moving example of such an effort of listening and reconstituting narratives.[15]

Second, the analyst must account for the daily life and the concrete reality experienced by the social groups concerned. This entails not only going beyond appearances, the 'common-sense' views that generally inform our approach to such situations, but also beyond what internationalists generally term the 'events'. One must (re)learn to observe the non-event, in other words that which does not occur or which appears too 'banal', 'the terrible, unutterable, unthinkable banality of evil' which Hannah Arendt spoke of with regard to Adolph Eichman,[16] or better, 'the ordinary' described by Christopher Browning.[17] From this perspective, the analyst may rehabilitate certain aspects generally considered to be 'anecdotal'. For instance, the fact that the inhabitants of working class neighbourhoods of the capital declare that they are finally able to once again sleep at night would constitute an important indicator, signalling the ability to begin to go beyond the level of minimum survival (staying alive) and speak of 'rebuilding'. These types of signals should be confirmed by other indicators.

Third, and in the same spirit, analysts must try to increase their reference points in order to make sense of the behaviours observed in the fullest subjectivity. In particular, they should include the perceptions and the institutional and social processes that shape the worlds in which the individuals and groups evolve. It is in this framework that the researcher should become particularly interested in the stories told about what happened, in the myths that fashion them, the themes that organize them, the narrative codes used, the events which structure them and in the channels that allow for their transmission. They will have to improve their imagination, in addition to traditional interviewing techniques, so as to gain access to other forms of oral or graphic expression, to the rituals that lead to the telling of such narratives,[18] to the accounts reconstituted by displaced persons and refugees,[19] to those led by actors external to the group (journalists, international organizations, humanitarian actors, research missions and international tribunals[20]). The researcher will be concerned with the entangling of individual and collective memories, in the way in which they come to rewrite more distant memory – including that of long-term history, as in the case in the Balkans or the Great Lakes – in the strategies of instrumentalization and appropriation put in place by politicians and by the state authorities that search in this imaginary world for what Castoriadis has called 'the necessary compliment to their order'.[21] For this reason, the analyst will be interested in non-narratives, in impossible or confiscated narratives (what Paul Ricoeur has called 'hindered memory', 'manipulated memory', 'obliged memory'[22]), in the authorized public narratives of the past that either give sense to individual memories or mutilate them.[23] In Cambodia, particularly among the young (the under thirties, the great majority of the population, have no memory of the period of the Khmer Rouge), the memory of genocide appears totally absent from their terms of reference, as if lost in a collective amnesia that leads the majority of commentators to remark that the Cambodians 'want to forget'. Nonetheless, if researchers take the time to carry out non-directive interviews over a period sufficiently long to allow for the establishment of a relationship of confidence with the people concerned, if they show interest in the victims' writings and in their various tools of expression, they will discover the omnipresence of this history. This is true precisely because it is impossible for them to tell their stories in consideration of it because this history was transmitted to them through the understanding that their parents had themselves to construct in order to survive in the light of such a past.

In comprehending what happens to members of societies in which mass crimes have been committed, the gap between 'facts' and 'paranoia', 'proof' and 'rumour' is often tiny. All these levels of knowledge and imagination refer to dreams. What is known is understood in vast zones of the unknown or even of the imagined. It is for this reason that, in the narratives one attempts to reconstruct, the historical structures of fear and enmity for example must be studied in themselves and not simply discredited as paranoia or extremism. Similarly, rumours may teach a lot, not in terms of the direct information they convey but of what they reveal about what is in the process of being played out within a given social group. To a large extent, like the legends studied by Marie-Louise von Franz, rumours constitute people's dreams and tell the community what goes on below the collective consciousness.[24] All of these elements and tools of analysis, largely foreign to students of peacebuilding, allows them to get a little closer to the changes taking place at the heart of social groups that have suffered the trauma of mass crime, at the crossroads of individual and collective histories. These elements can be decisive if one wishes to understand what happens in the 'post'-mass crime context, if one wishes at least to take seriously what is said by those concerned, beyond 'impossible' narratives, and especially beyond appearances.

Fourth, this cannot be achieved, it appears to me, without work in trans-disciplinary teams that assist in the reintegration of these various dimensions of post-crime trauma. Each perspective, on its own, is insufficient for capturing these multiple links while, from the point of view of the trauma, these links are made naturally between those based on psychiatry, politics, sociology, anthropology or on law, in a historical perspective.[25] It is extremely difficult for one researcher to simultaneously work in two disciplines, let alone more than this. By allowing for the meeting of researchers from different disciplines, each one maintaining their own language and together advancing towards the understanding of a single social fact, one can hope to penetrate the complexity of the situations under investigation.

Understanding What Mass Crime Reveals about a Political, Social and Communal Crisis

This analysis should assist in placing mass crime in its context. If one wishes to help a society to 'build peace' following such dramatic situations, it is first necessary to try to understand how it could have allowed such an act to have been committed. This approach naturally supposes the immediate rejection of the notion of a singular explanation, be it ideological or culturalist (that is, seeing certain people as particularly belligerent or violent). A twofold line of questioning should assist in this process of comprehension. First, one should make an effort to investigate what mass crime tells us about the threefold crisis of political relations (with the state), the social (relations with the community and the immediate environment, such as the neighbourhood) and the domestic (familial and inter-generational relations). The elements playing a role around each of these relations and in the links between them should be examined. Second and more specifically, time should be spent looking at the violence committed in the immediate environment, including that within the family. In most contemporary wars where mass crime has been committed, crime within the community makes up a large proportion. Indeed, so-called 'intimate' crime, both individually and collectively, leaves particularly deep marks, weakening the regulatory foundations of the society.

Mass Crime, a Symptom of the Deep Transformation of the Political, Social and Communal Modes of Regulation

The carrying out of mass crime within a society points to a profound crisis of its various modes of regulation and thus to significant changes under way. In addition to perceptions, institutions – understood in their anthropological sense[26] – are directly related to the outbreak of extreme violence. Indeed, the latter often coincides with the deep transformations undergone by these institutions. Understanding them is thus indispensable for whoever hopes to help a post-conflict society to rebuild itself.

At the political level, the perpetration of mass crime may be located within the process of state building, the seizing of power, riches and territory and of collective mobilization. In this aim, it is well known the extent to which political manipulation, aimed at exacerbating the mutual fear between communities, can have heavy consequences. However, in an analytical perspective, the choice between the perspective of a 'war of all against all' and the 'pure manipulation of peaceful populations' is a false one. The two always coexist; capable both of the build-up of violence and of deliberate political manipulation. Researchers who have looked at such situations generally believe that, for mass crime to exist, it is necessary for several elements to coincide. The political level, albeit significant, is never the only important factor.[27] It contributes, in particular, to the construction of new social identities.

In this regard, the forms taken by ethnic divisions in the society are generally no more than one element of a wider problem, as they belong to other conflicts such as those between the generations, between men and women, between social groups, and between urban and rural dwellers. These different divisions recur within the dynamics of conflict in places where mass crime has been committed, in situations as varied as Cambodia, Bosnia, Rwanda and Algeria. A good illustration of such can be found in the example of the role played by 'cadets', often young men or even teenagers. They generally make up a high proportion of those carrying out mass crime. The paramilitary networks or the simple fighter groups to which they belong during wartime endow them with status and economic resources to which they had no access within the traditional social structure. In particular, war throws existing hierarchies into question, creating new ones with their own values and codes. This distortion of social regulation has to be coped with during the period of reconstruction.

For the majority of the members of a given society, things are generally much more ambiguous: lost in the torment, they do nothing out of the ordinary in any sense and thus can equally be generous and cowardly or non-committal and complicit opponents. In Rwanda, as in many other places, some made use of this period to resolve personal problems, revenge and vendettas. The explosion of horror only came about at a later stage. The testimonies collected also include stories of mutual protection or services returned, however limited. There are numerous examples from the Bosnian case of individual self-help or even cases of more collective resistance, the most well-known of which comes from the town of Tuzla, where intercommunal relations were relatively preserved. There were cases of agreements made between villages. For example, at the end of the war only one mosque remained standing in the Serbian Republic, in a Muslim village in the depths of a valley. To access this valley, it was necessary to pass through a Serb village whose inhabitants were always opposed to the passing through of paramilitaries. The Serbs, in a manner of speaking, 'paid back' a 50-year-old debt to the Muslim village that had itself protected them during the Second World War. All such behaviour enters into what the writer Primo Levi called the 'grey zone' that generally envelops the majority of the members of a society in times of conflict.[28] To the key question of 'when, why and how does the acceptance of, and respect for the Other, become transformed into the demonization of the Other?',[29] there can only be partial, ambiguous answers. The role played by communal solidarity is, in this sense, extremely revealing.

In reality, communal relations may indeed play a role of dissuasion, regulation or, on the contrary, precipitate the irrational descent into violence by way of the settling of old scores or the denunciation of others. The case of *komsiluk* or 'neighbourliness' in Bosnia is a revealing one. *Komsiluk* covers a variety of practices between neighbours or those living in nearby villages, belonging to different communities. This ranges from everyday self-help (agricultural jobs, house building, financial loans) to the association with religious festivals and family ceremonies (baptisms or circumcisions, marriages). Before the war, this practice was located at the core of intercommunal relations and ensured their peaceful nature[30] to the point that the word 'neighbour' was often used instead of 'citizen' or 'mister'. However, it consisted of an ambivalent system. It was a system of the permanent reassurance of peaceful relations between communities, at the level of the street, neighbourhood or village but was linked with quite conflictual relations at the political and institutional levels, in the struggle over the allocation of scarce resources such as land or public employment. Non-democratic states (the Ottoman Empire, followed by the Socialist Federation of Yugoslavia) had ensured the political status quo between communities. Nevertheless, each time this balance is put into question, the *komsiluk* is threatened. Moreover, the *komsiluk* implies respect for the private and familial sphere that neighbours from a different community do not infringe. Therefore, in traditional Bosnian homes the arrangement of the rooms is important. There is one room for receiving guests who are not allowed to enter the other rooms. When the *komsiluk* is overthrown, all such intimate and familial boundaries are violated by means of the destruction of houses, the rape of women, the strangling of men in front of their families and so on. Such crimes are often committed overtly, by people who have known each other for many years and who penetrate the family sphere, previously unreachable during the times of neighbourly relations. Many conflicts relate to these modifications of the relations between private and public spheres. They are the illustration of an extreme case of 'intimate crime'.

'Intimate Crime': When Crime is Committed by Another 'Self'

The proportion of crimes committed at the heart of the community, or even within single families, is often higher than is imagined. Frequently, perpetrators come from the same areas as those they assassinate or mutilate. In Cambodia, family relations were sometimes the reason for killing and at other times, the reason for protecting. François Ponchaud, the last foreigner to have left the country after the coming to power of the Khmer Rouge, evokes the numerous testimonies of the cases of children charged with spying on their parents or even with killing them.[31] In Liberia, Sierra Leone or the Democratic Republic of Congo, child soldiers played an active part in the extortion that took place in their own villages, including among their own families. In the time following war and its crimes – known alternatively as peacetime, the time of reconstruction or of healing – the traumatic consequences of such practices must be accounted for in themselves. Indeed, if there is to be 'reconciliation', it is first to be made with oneself as an individual, with one's body, one's spirit but also with one's history.

Mass crime belongs to a world made up of all the dimensions that it comes to profoundly disturb and reshape. Understanding the conditions in which peace may be built in a given society is to attempt to render intelligible these numerous transformations and that to which they lead in order to evaluate the basis upon which society may reconstruct itself.

Identifying Local Resources for Peacebuilding

Any 'culture' – a 'system of meanings commonly shared by the individual members of a single collectivity', to follow Clifford Geertz[32] – is characterized by a high level of heterogeneity. It consists of ensembles that, although allowing actors to conceive of themselves and of their actions, are not necessarily coherent. Moreover, in times of war they undergo profound changes. Identifying the norms and values but also the institutions that, within a social group, may constitute the basis of reconstruction is to locate that which changes and continuously reinvents itself within a threefold dialectic: the insider–outsider dialectic, that of emotion and rationality, and the dialectic of tradition and innovation.[33] In other words, one must attempt to understand that which takes place within the group itself and in its exchange with outsiders, the emotional and the apparently rational and that which relates to the past or looks to the future. This implies that it is possible to adopt a positive approach to post-conflict situations and to consider that they may also produce new codes of peaceful regulation. Empirical data are seriously lacking on the way this process is actually occurring. This is crucial in order to identify what the role of an outsider might be to contribute to its success. I will advance some proposals to contribute to this understanding and to a better training of international and regional organizations as well as NGO staff who intervene in situations following mass crime.

Post-War Situations as Productive of New Social Fabric and Values

For better or worse, it is never possible historically to completely relate to a previous situation. In the aftermath of a conflict, researchers often look for so-called 'traditions' that, in fact, are no longer practised. Nonetheless, this does not mean that there is nothing left and that societies exist in situations of total anomie. It is thus necessary to be able to identify, at the political, social and communal levels, what has been created by war and mass criminal practices. Thus, both representations as well as the expectations from the state will no longer be the same, in particular when the latter had legitimated, supported or even armed the perpetrators of massacres. The notion of the control of the legitimate use of violence by the state is usually profoundly affected, a fact which carries consequences for the possibility of building or reforming a police force. The representations of the collective 'self' are also deeply affected. Questions such as 'who are the people?', 'what is the state?' or 'what will happen to us as a people?' should be answered in new ways.[34] Such self-representation and also the ways of exercising citizenship undergo change with consequences both for the perspective of the political system and for its participation in the electoral process among other things. This redefinition of the 'us' also involves a redefinition of the 'them', of a rewriting of its relation to the world, to the immediate environment, to this 'community of people' that literally abandoned us, this powerless and versatile 'international community' that today intends to come to help towards reconstruction.

In post-war situations, the necessity of 'restoring the social bond' is also often evoked. Although this is a laudable concern, such a formula runs the risk of biasing our vision of things. First, the social bond cannot be merely reduced to the inter-ethnic one (between communities). It is also the bond between generations and social groups. Moreover, war may not be reduced to a process of destruction. It is transformative, also producing new forms of relations and social identities that should be taken into account in the post-war period. The politics of reconstruction in Bosnia-Herzegovina integrates well one of these new social identities, that of the refugee. However, they reduce the experience of the refugee to one of the passage from ethnically mixed to homogeneous milieux while it is much more complex. Furthermore, such politics of reconstruction create an almost total deadlock for new post-war identities, those of the fighter or ex-fighter. This subject appears to be almost taboo in that it does not belong to the pre-established categories of thought according to which Bosnians were seen as victims, not as fighters. This neglect has benefited the nationalist parties who have made room for this category of the population, channelling their demands to their own advantage. Similarly, where neighbourly bonds have been broken, new forms of solidarity have also appeared and new bonds created, for example during the displacement of people and in the refugee camps, as witnessed in both Kosovo and Rwanda.

The transformation of the form and content of kinship and family solidarity or the questioning of patriarchal authority are primary factors in post-genocidal Rwanda or in the Sierra Leone of today. Following what has been observed in other African societies, the status of children in particular is undergoing profound change. Having become new, sometimes military or economic, actors they no longer observe certain 'traditional' rules. The position of elders and religious leaders – those traditionally occupying the position of broker – has also changed drastically. In some cases, parallel structures have arisen to replace the 'traditional' ones.

In establishing the methods of understanding the transformation of the societies under consideration, observation obliges one to go beyond appearances. As the anthropologist Georges Balandier reminds us, such an enterprise necessitates in particular the giving up of 'a way of thinking that attaches order to stability, to a design that rejects the irrational and the imaginary in the aim of, at all costs, achieving a society of reason'.[35] Classical approaches to conflict, as much in their retention of the sometimes incorrect friend–enemy dichotomy as in their concern with the re-establishment of, albeit forced, order may in fact bear significant risks. In most cases, the stake of the conflict is primarily to re-establish the conditions of a social contract and of a common life in the community, in its various dimensions. Historians and sociologists have reminded us that such processes rarely enjoy blissful harmony and are rather the products of continuous bargaining and of concrete struggle. Nor can they result uniquely from a 'dogmatic voluntarism', to use an expression introduced by Georges Balandier.[36]

This last comment should lead us to questioning the various definitions of peace. For the diplomat, peace is undoubtedly the absence of war or, more precisely, the safe and stable environment defined more often by the international forces at the time than by the actual situation on the ground. Hobbes defined peace as the absence of violent death, a situation that the inhabitants of Cambodia, Rwanda, Bosnia, Kosovo or Guatemala would no doubt like to see in their countries today. It is also possible to define peace more substantively as the time when society may reconstruct itself upon foundations in which cooperation, where possible, is preferable to confrontation, in the interaction between its various components. Each society, whatever the traumas of war experienced, may reach such a level of peace. Once again, it is necessary for outsiders intending to assist such societies to equip themselves with the means to locate and support these local foundations of lasting peace.

Avenues for Further Investigation and Training for Field Staff

Reflecting on what the role of an outsider should be in such contexts remains very complex. The mandates of UN operations or of NGO programmes often seem ill-prepared when confronted with situations of post-mass crime. In my view, further intensive field investigations are crucial in order to understand the processes described here and their limits, as they appear in particular socio-political contexts. Indeed, the challenge of peacebuilding in a situation of post-mass crime is to ensure that the choices made by both individual actors and collectivities would give preference to the values and norms that prioritize peaceful conflict resolution and cooperation rather than confrontation. As Georg Simmel – one of the founders of the Interactionist school[37] – observed, in any interactive situation, any actor, whether individual or collective, wants to win. There are many different ways of winning: by cooperation or, on the contrary, by confrontation, using peaceful means or violent ones. One of the methods that may be used to encourage actors to prioritize non-confrontation would be to convince them to value not only their belonging to the group but also the sustaining of interaction with others with the idea that both may prove to be of use in the future. This would involve the construction or reactivation of mediation, connecting together the different components of a given society. It is precisely at this point that outsiders may certainly play an important intermediary role, as an 'aid to communicate'.[38] However, the outline of this function may only be made more precise if we know more about the sites, rules and rituals constructed by a society in the prevention of internal conflict.

Further investigations should comprise three important components. First, they should concern the means used by societies to ensure survival, at levels beyond that of the individual – the ways in which the 'community' becomes redefined and reinvested in suburban and rural areas, as well as in camps of refugees and displaced persons. The objective would be to understand the means through which such networks are organized, who are the local actors playing a role of intermediary, and which values are stressed. The evolution of different codes regarding conflicts, friendship, neighbourliness, as well as new values and solidarities developed in refugee camps would be important to study more closely. Specific investigations should be undertaken on the evolutions occurring within the family sphere, with contributions from anthropologists and psychoanalysts. Second, the observation should also involve an examination of the rituals through which the different ruptures experienced by the society are reinterpreted, the rules are reasserted and the links between the individuals recreated, particularly within the symbolic order. Exchanges between villages, organization of collective works, celebrations, but also rituals of healing should be particularly observed in that perspective. Third, investigations should be made on the means through which exchanges and bargaining now occur between groups and interests, both at the social and political levels. This should include an analysis of the way people identify themselves *vis-à-vis* the society and the state. The analysis of political discourse and communication channels appearing at such occasions would be important. This work, which should be undertaken in close relationship with practitioners, should inform us more precisely about the role outside agencies may play in such contexts. Distinctions could then be made according to the category of agency (intergovernmental, governmental).

For the time being, any staff sent to the field should be conscious of what happens in periods following mass crime, beyond appearances of disorder, chaos and extreme physical and mental survival. Indeed, outsiders should never forget that, whoever they are, they represent the outside world which abandoned, neglected, denied local populations while they were under attack. They should also never forget that peacebuilding has never been a linear process. Therefore, the roads to peace are much less like highways, as it may be hoped, than like bumpy and potholed roads, sometimes barely marked, which are the general rule in the countries concerned. It is these roads that outsiders who want to contribute to peacebuilding must be ready to take, both physically and symbolically. The analysis proposed in this essay should give them a certain number of keys in that perspective. This should be included in specific training before deployment in the field. Indeed, such experiences are particularly stressful and difficult, including from a psychological point of view. Whatever the political pressures to send people quickly, pre-briefings should never be neglected. It is crucial that field staff understand the international and local context in which they will have to work, and are psychologically prepared to face and manage what will probably be a trauma. Facing the horror of extreme violence, it may be difficult for anyone to grasp situations in their complexity, even more to adopt a 'comprehensive' approach or go beyond the usual dichotomy between victims and killers. Any staff member needs to work on this and on the different reactions they may have before arriving in the field. This is a never-ending process. In the field, the staff should get specific support in order to be able to manage, day after day, the human, intersubjective dimension of the job. Group discussions and psychological support teams should be available for this. Psychoanalysts should also be closely associated with the communication process inside each team and between the teams. Specific work should also be done in order to develop a real politics of communication with local populations. These suggestions should help improve the current practices.

Conclusion

More than in any other post-conflict situation, peacebuilding following mass crime calls for a fundamental reform of the way in which both analysts and practitioners most often envisage such situations. First, the situations must be considered in their different socio-political, historical and human dimensions, by means of a transdisciplinary approach. Second, the behaviour of actors must be considered by their subjectivity, within their own frames of reference, shaped by perceptions as well as institutional and social processes, at both local and international levels. Third, they should be analysed at the crossroads of individual and collective histories, in the interaction between individuals and groups, and agencies and structures. This involves the adoption of a methodology that permits one to get as close as possible to the trauma experienced by the populations concerned. This approach may help to highlight interests, strategies, events, places, actors and institutions usually underestimated by outsiders. It may show that what happens in everyday life may be as relevant for the evolution of the actual situation as the debates of the UN Security Council or an International Criminal Tribunal. It may underline the various interactions between two orders generally considered distinct. The process of reconstituting the narratives of massacres in refugee camps, through exchanges with the diaspora, the international and local media, the reports of international organizations and humanitarian actors, the hearings at the International Criminal Tribunal, and the official discourse of the state authorities reveal such processes of interaction.

This effort must permit the understanding of what was at stake in mass crime, for society, the groups and individuals of which it is composed and what is fundamentally transformed in the political, social and communal matrices of the countries examined. It is then that one may identify what, even in the apparent 'chaos', can be reconstructed in the post-war period and upon which it is possible for peace to be built.

Analysts have a particular responsibility in this effort because they must assist in the consideration of these themes in all their complexity. This also requires that they rethink the question of the status of their work, the question of who they address. These types of situation invite researchers to question the value they place on their own humanity and on that of others. Too many academic, diplomatic or bureaucratic discussions take place as if the subject was not of this world, as if those in question were not women and men like us. If the notion of human security is one day to have a concrete meaning, it should integrate such consciousness raising.

ACKNOWLEDGEMENTS

This essay draws upon the work of a transdisciplinary research group created in early 2001, made up of researchers and practitioners from different disciplines (political science, sociology, history, philosophy, anthropology, law, psychoanalysis etc.). See '"Making Peace": From Mass Crime to *Peacebuilding*', thematic website, Center for International Studies and Research (CERI – Sciences Po, Paris) accessed at www.ceri-sciences-po.org.

NOTES

1. Among other revealing studies in this approach, see J. Davis (ed.), *Security Issues in the Post-Cold War World*, Aldershot, UK and Brookfield, MA: Edward Elgar, 1996; J.C. Rufin, *L'empire et les nouveaux barbares*, Paris: Lattès, 1991; a volume emerging from a colloquium organized by the United States Institute of Peace: A.C. Crocker, F.O. Hampson and P. Aall (eds.), *Managing Global Chaos: Sources and Responses to International Conflict*, Washington DC: US Institute of Peace Press, 1994.
2. Jacques Sémelin, 'Rationalités de la violence extrême', *Critique Internationale*, No.6, Winter 2000, p.124.
3. I developed this methodological and ethical reflection in a paper presented at the 4th Pan-European International Relations Conference in Canterbury, Sept. 2001, entitled 'How to analyse situations of post-mass crimes from an International Political Sociology viewpoint?', accessed at www.ceri-sciences-po.org/cherlist/pouligny.
4. Regarding totalitarian violence, Hannah Arendt has evoked this 'experience of not

belonging to the world at all, which is among the most radical and desperate experiences of man'. Hannah Arendt, *The Origins of Totalitarianism*, New York and London: Harcourt Brace Jovanovich, 1979 (sixth edn), p.475.

5. This position, with all the ethical claims that it presupposes, has been very well analysed by Christopher R. Browning, *Ordinary Men: Reserve Police Battalion 101 and the Final Solution in Poland*, London: HarperCollins, 1992.
6. Roland Marchal, 'Atomisation des fins et radicalisme des moyens: De quelques conflits africains', *Critique Internationale*, No.6, winter 2000, pp.159–75.
7. Conversations with Roberto Beneduce, psychiatrist and anthropologist (University of Turin).
8. Report of the research group '"Making Peace": From Mass Crime to *Peacebuilding*', section on Ethics, 6 March 2001.
9. Ibid.
10. Hannah Arendt, *La Condition de l'homme moderne*, rééd., Paris: Calmann-Lévy, 1994, p.110.
11. As was so well pointed out by Christopher Browning, in the final analysis, the Shoah was possible because, at the most basic level, individual human beings put other human beings to death in large numbers and over a long period of time. See Browning (n.5 above).
12. This term refers to the importance of approaching the 'other' as an authentic subject, with their own history, rationality and psyche.
13. I refer to the seminar organized in March 1999 by the Initiative on Conflict Resolution and Ethnicity (INCORE), which results from a collaboration between the United Nations University and the University of Ulster: 'Researching Violent Societies: Methodological and Ethical Challenges', accessed at www.incore.ulst.ac.uk/home/research/complete/rvs-methods.html.
14. Here, I partly refer to exchanges I had during the workshop 'Filling Knowledge Gaps: A Research Agenda on the Impact of Armed Conflict on Children', co-organized by the Office of the Special Representative of the UN Secretary-General for Children and Armed Conflict, the Social Science Research Council and the Italian National Childhood and Adolescence Documentation and Analysis Centre, Florence, 2–4 July 2001.
15. Jean Hathzfeld, *Dans le nu de la vie: Récits des marais rwandais*, Paris: Seuil, 2000.
16. Hannah Arendt, *Eichmann à Jérusalem: Rapport sur la banalité du mal*, Paris: Gallimard, 1991, p.408.
17. Using the testimonies (gathered in the framework of legal proceedings in Hamburg), of 210 ex-members of the 101st battalion of the German reserve police during the Second World War in Poland, the historian Christopher Browning allows them to describe in their own words their participation in the 'final solution' – what they did, what they thought and how they rationalized their murderous behaviour. Browning (n.5 above).
18. In Mozambique, mediums and healers (the *mambos* at the head of *feiticeiros* and *curandeiros*) have allowed for the peaceful reintegration of child soldiers into their communities of origin through the use of purification rituals involving the whole of the community. The reference to the notions of *pollution/purification* allowed for what happened to be termed 'abnormal' and 'unacceptable' and to redefine the rules of coexistence. In Cambodia, *kruu* and *ruup* have also played a decisive role in the process of reintegration of displaced persons and refugees. They have particularly allowed for the recreation of links, within the symbolic order, and the reinterpretation of the various ruptures experienced by the society. On Mozambique, see in particular the work of Alcinda Honwana including, 'Children of War: Local Understandings of War and War Trauma in Mozambique and Angola', in Simon Chesterman (ed.), *Civilians in War*, New York: Lynne Rienner, 2001. For Cambodia, see Maurice Eisenbruch, 'Mental Health and the Cambodian Traditional Healer for Refugees who are Resettled, were Repatriated or Internally Displaced, and for those who Stayed at Home',

Collegium Antropologicum, Vol.18, No.2, Dec. 1994, pp.219-30; 'The Ritual Space of Patients and Traditional Healers in Cambodia', *BEFEO*, Vol.79, No.2, 1992, pp.283-316.

19. An interesting example of the analysis of these constructions may be found in the work of Liisa Malkki. She concentrates in particular on how the circumstances of exile transform the meaning of history and belonging and, in particular, how a refugee camp became a site of memory in which experiences, memories, nightmares and rumours of violence converged in the making and remaking of moral categories, of good and evil. See Liisa Malkki, *Purity and Exile: Violence, Memory, and National Cosmology among Hutu Refugees in Tanzania*, Chicago: University of Chicago Press, 1995. A complementary interesting reflection can be found on the case of Armenia in Janine Altounian, *La survivance: Traduire le trauma collectif*, Paris: Dunod, Coll. 'Inconscient et culture', 2000.

20. Regarding the role of legal proceedings in this process of collective memory and the numerous contradictions that this may provoke, see Mark Osiel, *Mass Atrocity, Collective Memory and the Law*, New Brunswick, NJ: Transaction, 1997.

21. Cornelius Castoriadis, *L'Institution imaginaire de la société*, Paris: Le Seuil, 1975, p.179.

22. Paul Ricoeur, *La mémoire, l'histoire, l'oubli*, Paris: Seuil, 2000. See also his previous work more specifically dealing with the link between memory and history, Paul Ricoeur, *Temps et récit*, Paris: Seuil, Vol.3, 1983-1985.

23. I refer to the work of Maurice Halbwachs, *La mémoire collective*, Paris: Albin Michel, 1997, new revised and improved edition, and that of Marie-Claire Lavabre, 'Usages et mésusages de la notion de mémoire', *Critique Internationale*, No.7, Apr. 2000, pp.48-57. The psychiatrist René Kaës has emphasized that the 'erasing of collective murder and State violence undermines the engendering of narcissist foundations; it takes over, in order to destroy it, memory and transmission. That which has been erased as not having taken place has no place in which to inscribe itself, to be thought and to relate the lesson of individual histories with that of collective history'. René Kaës, *Violence d'Etat et psychanalyse*, Paris: Dunod, 1989, p.xv.

24. Marie-Louise von Franz, *L'Interprétation des contes de fées*, Paris: La Fontaine de Pierre, 1980, pp.51-61; Marie-Louise von Franz and Emma Jung, *La Légende du Graal*, Paris: Albin Michel, coll. Sciences et symboles, 1988. I refer also to the work by Frantz Fanon on the subject of the function of stabilization and the exorcism of mythical and hallucinatory structures among the colonized. Frantz Fanon, *Les damnés de la terre*, Paris: Maspero, 1961, pp.42-3; see also G. Althabe, *Oppression et libération dans l'imaginaire*, Paris, 1982.

25. A concrete example of this type of link, in a post-dictatorial situation, can be found in J.-C. Stagnaro, 'Les masques de Thanatos: effets cliniques et psychosociaux à court et long terme du terrorisme d'Etat en Argentine', *L'information psychiatrique*, Vol.76, No.3, 2000, pp.259-63.

26. Shmuel Eisenstadt has defined the institution as a 'mode of organisation of the mechanisms of exchange between the individual and the social group', which may relate to so-called 'primary' institutions such as the family or community.

27. Report of the research group, '"Making Peace": From Mass Crime to *Peacebuilding*', 'Social link, the processes of acting out of mass crime and reconstruction', 20 June 2001, accessed at www.ceri-sciences-po.org

28. Primo Levi evoked this 'grey zone' to explore the spectrum of behaviour of the victims of the concentration camps. He also suggested that this zone included the killers, without nonetheless considering that there to be a symmetrical relationship between perpetrators and victims. Primo Levi, *Naufragés et rescapés*, Paris: Gallimard, 1989.

29. Denis-Constant Martin, 'Identity, Culture, Pride and Conflict', in Simon Bekker and Rachel Prinsloo (eds), *Identity? Theory, Politics, History*, Pretoria: Human Sciences Research Council, 1999, p.197.

30. The *komsiluk* is not, nonetheless, synonymous with 'mixing' between communities. It

refers to two people from two different communities, living in two different houses, while a mixed marriage refers to two people from different communities living in one house.
31. See François Ponchaud, *Cambodge, année zéro*, Paris, 1977 and personal communications.
32. This system allows the actors to put themselves in the social game and give a particular meaning to the action and the social institutions in the collectivity concerned. The culture so defined does not create permanent identities but organizes the behaviour of the different actors (including those who take power). See Clifford Geertz, 'The Politics of Meanings', in *The Interpretation of Cultures*, New York: Basic Books, 1973, p.89.
33. On this threefold dialectic, see Denis-Constant Martin, 'La découverture des cultures politiques. Esquisse d'une approche comparatiste à partir des expériences africaines', *Les Cahiers du CERI*, No.2, 1992, p.13; also Georges Balandier, *Sens et puissance: Les dynamiques sociales*, Paris: PUF, 1971.
34. I refer here to the work carried out by Liisa Malkki among Hutu refugees in Montreal. 'Dystopia and Subjectivity in the Social Imagination of the Future', Colloquium on 'La guerre entre le local et le global: Sociétés, Etats, Systèmes', CERI, 29–30 May 2000, pp.31–2 (see CERI website: www.ceri-sciences-po.org).
35. Georges Balandier, *Le désordre. Eloge du mouvement*, Paris: Fayard, 1988, p.247.
36. According to Georges Balandier, it is necessary to renounce this 'dogmatic voluntarism that pretends to ignore that although men produce social forms, they do not do so either absolutely freely (they are confronted by limitations) or arbitrarily (neither decree nor constraint are sufficient)'. Ibid.
37. See for instance Georg Simmel, 'The Sociology of Sociability', *American Journal of Sociology*, Vol.55, No.3, Nov. 1949, pp.254–61.
38. According to the definition given by F.G. Bailey, *Les règles du jeu politique*, Paris: PUF, 1971, p.186.

Notes on Contributors

Edward Newman is an Academic Associate in the Peace and Governance Programme at the United Nations University. He is a founding executive editor of the journal *International Relations of the Asia Pacific*. Recent publications include *The United Nations and Human Security: Beyond Peacekeeping* (co-edited, Palgrave, 2001), *The UN Secretary-General from the Cold War to the New Era: A Global Peace and Security Mandate?* (Macmillan, 1998), *The Changing Nature of Democracy* (co-edited, UNU Press, 1998), and *New Millennium, New Perspectives: The United Nations, Security and Governance* (co-edited, UNU Press, 2000).

Albrecht Schnabel is an Academic Officer in the Peace and Governance Programme of the United Nations University. He currently serves as President of the International Association of Peacekeeping Training Centres. Recent publications include *Southeast European Security: Threats, Responses, Challenges* (edited, Nova Science, 2002), *Kosovo and the Challenge of Humanitarian Intervention: Selective Indignation, Collective Action, and International Citizenship* (co-edited, UNU Press, 2000) and *United Nations Peacekeeping Operations: Ad Hoc Missions, Permanent Engagement* (co-edited, UNU Press, 2001).

Sorpong Peou is an Associate Professor of Political Science/ International Relations on the Graduate Programme of Sophia University in Tokyo. He has written on peacekeeping and peacebuilding, as well as security in East Asia and in other regions. His major publications include *Conflict Neutralization in the Cambodia War: From Battlefield to Ballotbox* (Oxford University Press, 1997) and *Intervention and Change in Cambodia: Toward Democracy?* (St. Martin's Press, Institute of Southeast Asian Studies and Silkworm, 2000).

Jean-Marie Guéhenno is Under-Secretary-General of the United Nations Department of Peacekeeping Operations. During his career in the Ministry of Foreign Affairs of France (1979–95) he served as head of cultural affairs at the French Embassy in the United States (1982–86) and Ambassador to the Western European Union (1993–95). He was educated at the Ecole Normale Supérieure in Paris, and has been chairman of the Institut des Hautes Etudes de défense nationale since 1998. He has published numerous articles on international affairs and is the author of *The End of the Nation-State* (1993).

Vesna Bojicić-Dzelilović is Research Fellow at the Centre for the Study of Global Governance, London School of Economics and Political Science. Her recent publications include 'War and Reconstruction in Bosnia-Herzegovina' in *Scramble for the Balkans*, edited by C.U. Schierup (Macmillan, 1998).

Jean Daudelin is Principal Researcher, Conflict and Human Security, at the North–South Institute, in Ottawa, and Adjunct Research Professor at the Norman Paterson School of International Affairs, Carleton University. He has published on human security, political violence, ethnic and religious movements, Latin American and continental integration, as well as Canadian foreign policy.

Lee J.M. Seymour is a Research Associate at the North–South Institute in Canada with a fellowship from the Canadian Department of National Defence's Security and Defence Forum, focusing on humanitarian intervention and human security issues. He is currently studying towards a doctorate in political science at Northwestern University. His general research interests include the political economy of violence, with a regional focus on sub-Saharan Africa, and Canadian foreign policy.

Benjamin Reilly is a Research Fellow in the National Centre for Development Studies at the Australian National University, Canberra. He was previously a Senior Programme Officer at the International Institute for Democracy and Electoral Assistance (IDEA) in Stockholm. His books include *Democracy in Divided Societies: Electoral Engineering for Conflict Management* (Cambridge University Press, 2001), *Electoral Systems and Conflict in Divided Societies* (National Research Council, 1999), *Democracy and Deep Rooted Conflict: Options for Negotiators* (International IDEA, 1998), and *The International IDEA Handbook of Electoral System Design* (International IDEA, 1997).

Sally Morphet was educated in the Middle East, the United States and the United Kingdom. She worked as a Research Analyst in the UK Foreign and Commonwealth Office specializing on Indo-China and on general international and UN issues. She now works on a freelance basis, and was appointed a Visiting Professor at the University of Kent in January 2001. She has published articles and chapters in books on human rights, the environment and NGOs, the non-aligned movement, peacekeeping and the Security Council.

B.S. Chimni is Professor of International Law at the School of International Studies, Jawaharlal Nehru University, New Delhi. He was a Fulbright Visiting Scholar at the Harvard Law School (1995–96) and Law Fellow, Centre for Refugee Studies, University of York, Canada (1993). He was a member of the Academic Advisory Committee of the Office of the United Nations High Commissioner for Refugees, 1997–2000. His most recent publication is a *Reader on International Refugee Law* (2000).

Kees Kingma is a Dutch economist, working as Project Leader for Demobilization and Peace-building at the Bonn International Centre for Conversion (BICC). He has published and lectured widely on various development and demilitarization issues and conducted advisory and other consultancy work for several multilateral, governmental and non-governmental organizations. He edited and coordinated the research for *Demobilization in Sub-Saharan Africa: The Development and Security Impacts* (Macmillan, 2000).

Béatrice Pouligny is a Research Fellow at the Center for International Studies and Research (CERI/Sciences-Po), in Paris. She has just finished a book, *Les défis de la paix: Interventions onusiennes et populations locales*, Paris: Karthala/ Recherches Internationales (forthcoming, with an English version in 2003).

Abstracts

Introduction: Recovering from Civil Conflict *by Edward Newman and Albrecht Schnabel*

Conflict-torn societies are characterized by the traumatic impoverishment of economic, political and social relations between groups and individuals. Previously existing divisions within society are exacerbated, and new divisions are created. Violently divided societies are cursed by institutional breakdown: weak or non-existent political institutions; weak or non-existent civil society institutions; and limited government legitimacy and authority. Once violence ceases, it becomes extremely difficult to re-create a sense of identity and belonging among communities that have experienced political, economic and socio-cultural breakdown. While it may be possible to impose a sense of order from outside, the sense of community has to grow from within. The tasks of rebuilding physical infrastructure are no less daunting.

Post-Conflict Peacebuilding and Second-Generation Preventive Action *by Albrecht Schnabel*

In response to the human suffering and regional instability caused by internal conflicts, the United Nations, regional and subregional organizations, as well as groups of concerned states, seem to be increasingly willing and able to launch interventions into states that cannot and will not provide for the security of all of their citizens, or that tolerate or instigate gross human rights violations. However, the jurisdiction and capacity of international organizations to prevent internal conflicts, successfully manage and end them once they have broken out, and prevent their re-emergence through sustainable post-conflict peacebuilding, are still weak. The contribution argues that peacebuilding is only sustainable if it embraces core principles of conflict prevention; that preventive action is more feasible (although more complex) in the post-conflict environment; and that lessons from post-conflict preventive action must inform and encourage pre-conflict prevention.

'Transitional Justice': The Impact of Transnational Norms and the UN *by Edward Newman*

A perennial challenge in post-conflict societies is how to balance claims for justice, truth and accountability with the need for peace and stability. Increasingly in recent years, international norms are impinging upon this process with the growing consensus that some form of justice and accountability are integral to peace and stability. This essay explores the modalities of dealing with past abuses of human rights, and considers whether the growing prominence of international law, international tribunals and courts that have a humanitarian remit is changing the balance of transition in favour of accountability and justice. The essay concludes that dealing with past abuses of human rights is as much about politics and trade-offs as it is about justice and accountability, especially in post-conflict and transitional situations. Whilst the input of international norms and institutions may increase the prospects of justice, transitional societies must embrace other values – such as peace, stability, development – that are not necessarily co-terminal. Moreover, the process will inevitably be conditioned by the predilections of powerful political actors outside the societies in question.

The UN, Peacekeeping, and Collective Human Security: From *An Agenda for Peace* to the Brahimi Report *by Sorpong Peou*

UN peace operations should be seen as part of a broader theoretical framework based on the novel concept of collective human security. The concept has developed as an integral part of positive peace and security, most notably from *An Agenda for Peace* to the Brahimi Report, and this essay expands upon this vision as a part of the idealist faith in the potential for human emancipation. The concept of collective human security embedded in recent UN thinking differs from that of national security: the former focuses on the individual, as opposed to the latter whose emphasis is placed on the state, as the referent point for security. At the same time, the UN vision for human security should be viewed in collective terms: it not only stresses the need to meet basic human needs and to promote distributive justice and political participation but also points out that human security can be achieved through collective action. Collective human security has challenged the traditional concept of national security, but the UN will need to think more seriously about how to overcome the existing hurdles, also acknowledged in the Brahimi Report.

On the Challenges and Achievements of Reforming UN Peace Operations *by Jean-Marie Guéhenno*

Against the background of the tumultuous evolution of peacekeeping since the end of the Second World War, the essay discusses the key challenges of post-Cold War peace operations, some of their greatest failures as well as accomplishments. It considers Kofi Annan's effort to turn around the doomed fate of UN peacekeeping through self-reflection, soul searching and practical and feasible recommendations. The result was the Brahimi Report which, if implemented, will allow the UN to equip itself not only to avert failures, but to ensure success in the future. This concerns not only traditional, but also complex and post-conflict peace missions. While UN peace operations cannot be risk free, the risks and gambles associated with involvement in ongoing conflicts or exceedingly fragile security environments can be better managed if missions match the needs on the ground, if resources match those mandates, and if peace operations are deployed in a more judicious and deliberate manner.

World Bank, NGOs and the Private Sector in Post-War Reconstruction by Vesna Bojicić-Dzelilović

Addressing violent conflict is increasingly becoming an integral part in the agenda of many international organizations, including those traditionally involved in development assistance. Their approach and operational practices, however, continue to be based on the postulates of a neo-liberal economic paradigm, which lacks the conceptual tools for understanding conflict as a specific social construct. This analysis looks at recent experience of the World Bank, NGOs and the private sector in assisting the rehabilitation of war-torn societies. It argues that the engagement of these three social actors in reconstruction in the aftermath of new types of conflict characteristic of the contemporary era has failed to penetrate to the root causes of conflict. It suggests that a new approach to understanding the nature of contemporary violence is needed as a precondition for formulating a response that can adequately correspond to the needs of the conflict-affected population.

Peace Operations Finance and the Political Economy of a Way Out by Jean Daudelin and Lee J.M. Seymour

Two conspicuous features of the contemporary global security *problématique* need to be explicitly connected. Diplomatic, humanitarian, developmental and military responses to conflict are hampered by a basic lack of resources. Yet, paradoxically, these underfunded interventions are increasingly directed at conflicts that thrive on resource abundance. In other words, while the global peace regime is constrained by resource shortfalls, rapacious competition over commodity rents perpetuates local conflict and frustrates peacemaking efforts. The essay shows how using local resources promises to expand the scale and scope of activities otherwise inhibited by the international system's inability to provide adequate financing for peace operations and related activities. It shows how control over local resources by external political intermediaries is often a necessary step towards decisively establishing an environment of security and stability, the conditions for confidence building, and eventually, a centre of gravity around which a new authority structure can coalesce. It argues that external control of key sectors of conflict-affected economies is crucial in the interim period between external intervention and the rehabilitation of administrative structures. By managing the reconstruction of local economies, interveners can help consolidate an environment of security and stability supported by sustainable development patterns. Finally, the essay outlines in practical terms the specific mechanisms that would allow peace operations to 'live off the land'.

Post-Conflict Elections: Constraints and Dangers by Benjamin Reilly

Elections have become an integral element of many UN peacekeeping missions over the past decade. Elections provide an inescapable means for jump-starting a new, post-conflict political order; for stimulating the development of democratic politics; for choosing representatives; for forming governments; and for conferring legitimacy upon the new political order. They also provide a clear signal that legitimate domestic authority has been returned – and hence that the role of the international community may be coming to an end. Despite this, there has been a considerable variation in the relative success of elections in meeting the broader goals of democratization from case to case. In any UN mission, the holding of elections forces critical political choices to be made. Should post-conflict elections be held as early as possible, so as to fast-track the process of establishing a new regime? Who runs the elections? Are the political parties contesting the election narrow, personalized, sectarian or ethnically-exclusive entities, using the political process to pursue their wartime objectives? Elections are part of the broader process of democratization, but ill-timed, badly-designed or poorly-run elections can actually undermine the broader process of democratization.

Current International Civil Administration: The Need for Political Legitimacy by *Sally Morphet*

This contribution examines the three current international transitional civil administrations in Bosnia, the Federal Republic of Yugoslavia and East Timor, as well as the former UN Transitional Administration in Eastern Slavonia, Baranja and Western Sirmium (UNTAES) in Croatia. The findings suggest that transitional civil administrations are more likely to achieve political legitimacy, nationally and internationally, if peacebuilding work is based on international legal standards and norms. The essay argues that the contribution of civil administration to peacebuilding needs to be considered in terms of wider contextual factors. It discusses the legal and practical problems raised by governmental disregard of certain international legal norms within former Yugoslavia, the particular problems regional actors encounter in dealing with civil administration in their region and the rest of the world community, and the usefulness of thinking about the past experience of civil administration in preparing future exit strategies.

Refugees and Post-Conflict Reconstruction: A Critical Perspective by *B.S. Chimni*

This contribution argues that there is an absence of a systematic theoretical and legal framework that allows reconstruction, reintegration and peacebuilding to be derived from a critical and integral understanding of the problems that characterize 'post-conflict' societies or of refugees who return to them. The result is an array of measures that have rarely been arrived at in consultation with refugees and returnees, which are often working at cross-purposes with each other, and have been assembled in the matrix of a neo-liberal vision which, among other things, does not focus on the international causes of internal conflicts and excludes the possibility of building a participatory 'post-conflict' state. The essay suggests that the basic problem with current policies relating to return and reintegration of refugees to 'post-conflict' societies is the poverty of epistemology deployed to identify suitable measures that will go to promote 'sustainable return'. On this basis, the essay concludes with concrete policy suggestions.

Demobilization, Reintegration and Peacebuilding in Africa by Kees Kingma

This contribution considers the extent to which demobilizations and the reintegration of ex-combatants into civilian life in Africa have had an impact on peacebuilding. Demobilization and reintegration assistance have in most cases contributed to human development and peace processes. General lessons on their implementation are presented. However, the essay identifies aspects of demobilization, resettlement and reintegration that can have a negative impact upon peacebuilding. In the short term, demobilization has led to different conflicts mostly at the local level. Problems related to inequalities and rewards of post-conflict situations become more significant in the long term. Long-term risks of conflict are largely related to the psychosocial impact of war.

Building Peace after Mass Crimes by Béatrice Pouligny

This essay explores the meaning of 'peacebuilding' in situations in which mass crimes have been committed. It underlines the specific difficulties that these situations pose to both analysts and practitioners. It also makes a number of methodological proposals regarding the study of the impact that mass crimes have on rebuilding social and political relations in war-torn societies. Further to this, the essay emphasizes the importance of a better understanding of these processes, as they emerge in particular socio-political situations, in order to highlight the most effective programmes of assistance following mass crime. In order to attempt to address this sensitive issue, analysts and practitioners alike must face two challenges. First, they should try to understand, in one way or another, how the carrying out of mass crime may have come about. Second, capacities for peace already existing within the society concerned should be identified. Indeed, for the rules of the social and political game to function or, in other words, for all actors to become interested in joining in the collective 'game', such resources cannot be ignored. Peacebuilding must include local methods that, in almost all cases, have already been constructed over time, while at the same time borrowing in various ways from the outside.

Index

Accountability (for crimes) 4, 31–48, 113
Africa, conflicts in 9–10, 25, 62–3, 102–7
Agenda for Peace 51–5, 59, 63, 108, 185
Albanians 151–2
ANC 136
Angola 104, 110, 118, 120, 156
Annan, Kofi 14, 16, 38, 57, 71–2
Arendt, Hannah 35, 204, 205–6
ASEAN 9, 63
Axworthy, Lloyd 14

Balandier, Georges 213
Balkans 62
Bildt, Carl 147–9
Bosnia 122, 132, 133, 147–50
Boutros-Ghali, Boutros 12–13, 108–9
Brahimi Report 14, 51, 55–60, 61–3, 65, 72–6, 79, 100, 101, 105
Burundi 123

Cambodia 45–7, 64–5, 69, 125–6, 156
Carnegie Commission 14
Child soldiers 43
Civic culture 1
Civil administration 5, 6
    capacity building 143–4
    Congo 140
    consultation 143
Civil conflict 7, 8–11, 19
Civil society 1, 94
Civilian victims of war 10, 83
CIS 71
Cold War 8
Collective human security 51, 55, 60–65, 66
Complex emergencies
Confidence building 1
Conflict prevention 4, 7–26, 55–6
Consolidation of democracy 32, 37
Croatia 145–7
Culture of violence 2

Dayton Agreement 147
De Mello, Sergio 121, 143
Demobilization 6, 77, 87
    Angola 184, 195
    children 192, 198
    definition and process of 182–5
    Ethiopia 183
    Mozambique 194–5

    Namibia 183, 192–3
    NGOs 195, 198
    recurrence of conflict 187–96
    Rwanda 183
    Sierra Leone 190, 195
    timing 183–95
    women 192, 198
Democratic peace 65
Democratic Republic of the Congo (DRC) 78, 100–104
Democratization 1, 5, 33, 74, 88
De Soto, Alvaro 157
Disarmament 77, 87, 170–71, 181
Donors, international 90–91
Dos Santos, Eduardo 120
DPA (UN Department of Political Affairs) 59
DPKO (UN Department of Peacekeeping Operations) 59, 74–5

Elections
    Angola 118, 120
    Cambodia 118, 123, 125–6, 130–31
    East Timor 121, 124, 125
    electoral mechanics 124–32
    Haiti 118, 125
    Indonesia 122, 125–6
    Kosovo 121, 122, 130
    political parties 122
    post-conflict societies 118–19
    power sharing 133–7
    proportional representation 127–30
    timing 119–124
    winner takes all 133
Early warning of conflict 12
East Timor 19, 62, 71, 75, 77–8, 108, 112, 114, 121, 124, 140, 141–4, 151, 153, 157–8
Eastern Slavonia 140, 145
ECOMOG (Economic Community Military Observer Group) 103, 105–7
Economy of war 99, 101–7
ECOWAS (Economic Community of West African States) 71
ECPS (Executive Committee on Peace and Security) 58
EISAS (Executive Information and Strategic Analysis Secretariat) 58, 63
Elections 5, 56, 69
El Salvador 156

Eritrea 192
Ethnic cleansing 3, 16
European Union (EU) 9, 22
Exit strategies (for international organizations) 157–8

Forgiveness 35
Fretelin (Revolutionary Front for an Independent East Timor) 144

G8 149
Germany 157
Good governance 11, 90, 108

Haiti 118, 125
High Representative, Office of (Bosnia) 147–50
Holbrooke, Richard 100
Human rights 32–7, 47, 59, 69, 74
Human security 4, 51, 52, 56, 59, 66
Huntington, Samuel 40

Identity 1
IDRC (International Development Research Centre) 14
Indonesia 122, 125–6
INTERFET (International Force in East Timor) 142–3
Internally Displaced Persons (IDPs) 3
International Court of Justice 153
International criminal tribunals 32, 38, 40, 42–3, 54, 58
International financial institutions 166–7 (see World Bank and International Monetary Fund)
International Monetary Fund 86

Justice 4, 8, 31–48, 54

Kabila, Laurent 103
Karadzic, Radovan 111
KFOR 7, 21, 63
Khmer Rouge 46–7, 206, 211
KLA (Kosovo Liberation Army) 65
Kosovo 19, 64, 65, 71, 75, 100, 110, 112–13, 130, 140–41, 150–53, 158–9

Landmines 170
Latin America 33, 36, 40, 65
League of Nations 157

Macro-economic stabilization 92
Mass crimes 6
 banality of evil 206
 Bosnia 209–10, 212
 Cambodia 206
 children 205
 intimate crime 210–11
 Liberia 211
 NGOs 214
 neglected subject of study 201
 peacebuilding 201, 211–16
 study of, and methodology 202–5
Milosović, Slobodan 38, 141, 145, 151, 152
Minority protection 3
MONUA (United Nations Mission of Observers in Angola) 105
MONUC (United Nations Mission in the Democratic Republic of the Congo) 61, 78
Mozambique 194–5
Multidimensional peacekeeping operations 69, 74
Multinational corporations 111

Namibia 192–3
NATO 8, 22, 39, 64–5, 71–2, 100, 152, 155
Negative peace 64
Netherlands 144
NGOs 81–96, 195, 198, 214
Nigeria 135–6

OAS (Organization of American States) 9
OAU (Organization of African Union) 9, 10, 102
Ogata, Sadako 170
OSCE (Organization for Security and Cooperation in Europe) 22, 121, 136, 147

Papua New Guinea 137
Peacebuilding (see post-conflict peacebuilding)
Peacekeeping 1–6, 51–66
 future of 78–80
Peace maintenance 103–4, 107–8, 114
Peace operations 51–2, 55, 61, 64, 69, 70, 74, 99
 financing 99–114
Pluralism, political 90
Political parties 133–7
Political will, of international community 12, 17, 66
Positive peace 52–3, 59, 63, 64
Post-conflict peacebuilding
 capacity building 143–4
 definition and concept 141, 166–7, 185–7
 democracy 186
 disarmament 181

identity 155
international assistance 91, 95
justice 141
local resources 211–12
massacre, history of
role of private financial sector, 89
Post-conflict societies 4, 7–26
  administering 114
  assistance 4, 23
  difficulty of conceptualizing 164–6
  environment 21, 24
  financial institutions 166–7
  private sector 4
  rebuilding 4, 5, 19
  reconstruction 5, 82–6, 91–5
  transition 31
  World Bank 86
Post-war generation 3
Power sharing 133–7
Preventive diplomacy 12
Protectorate 7, 26, 104

Quick impact projects 74

Rambouillet 152
Rapid deployment capacity 73
Reconciliation 1, 19, 36, 41
Refugees 2, 3, 6, 19
  gender 169–79
  problems of return 163–4, 168
  sustainable return 167–8
  UNHCR 171–3
Resource wars 99, 101–7, 114
Risk assessment 15
RUF (Revolutionary United Front) 76, 105–6
Rwanda 43, 72, 100

Safe Area 72
Sanctions 111
Sankoh, Foday 44, 106
Savimbi, Jonas 120
Secession 155
Self-determination 152
Sen, Hun 46, 123
Serbs 145, 146, 151–5
Sierra Leone 76–7, 104–6
Societies
  at risk of conflict 19, 20, 24
  divided 1
  post-conflict 5
  transitional 36, 41
  traumatized 83
  war-torn 1, 3, 10, 18, 81, 85, 89, 92, 95

South Africa 189
Srebrenica 70, 72
Standby peacekeeping force 57

Taylor, Charles 44
Terrorism 16, 53
Transitional justice 31–48
Truth and Reconciliation Commission 39, 42–4
Tudjman, Franjo 145

Uganda 188–9
UN Charter 152
  Article 53 155
  Chapter VII 154
UNAMSIL (United Nations Mission in Sierra Leone) 61, 77, 106
UNAVEM II (United Nations Verification Mission in Angola II) 104
UNAVEM III (United Nations Verification Mission in Angola III) 110
UNDP (United Nations Development Programme) 171
UNFICYP (United Nations Force in Cyprus) 69
UNHCR (United Nations High Commissioner for Refugees) 145, 151, 164–7, 171–3
UNITA (National Union for the Total Independence of Angola) 104–5, 120
Universal Declaration of Human Rights 36
UNMIK (United Nations Interim Administration Mission in Kosovo) 7, 19, 22, 24, 110, 141, 150–53
UNTAES (United Nations Transitional Administration in Eastern Slavonia, Baranja and Western Sirium) 145–7
UNTAET (United Nations Transitional Administration in East Timor) 7, 19, 24, 77, 108–9, 114, 141–4 (see also East Timor)
UNTSO (United Nations Truce Supervision Organization) 69

War economy 83
Warsaw Pact 8
West Irian 144, 156
World Bank 21–2, 81–96, 108, 110, 167, 172

Yugoslavia, former 147–54, 157–9